ROBIN PHILIPSON

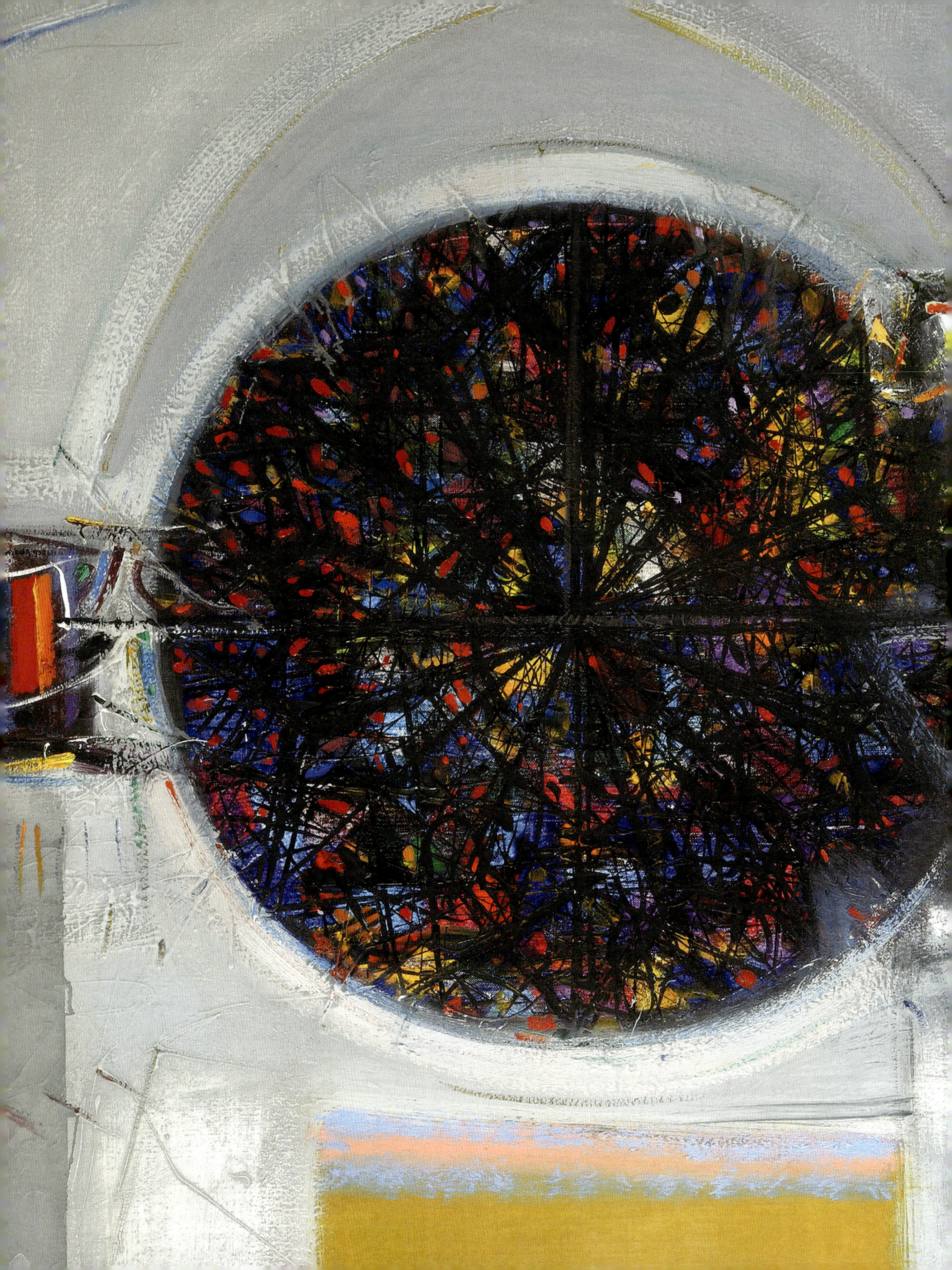

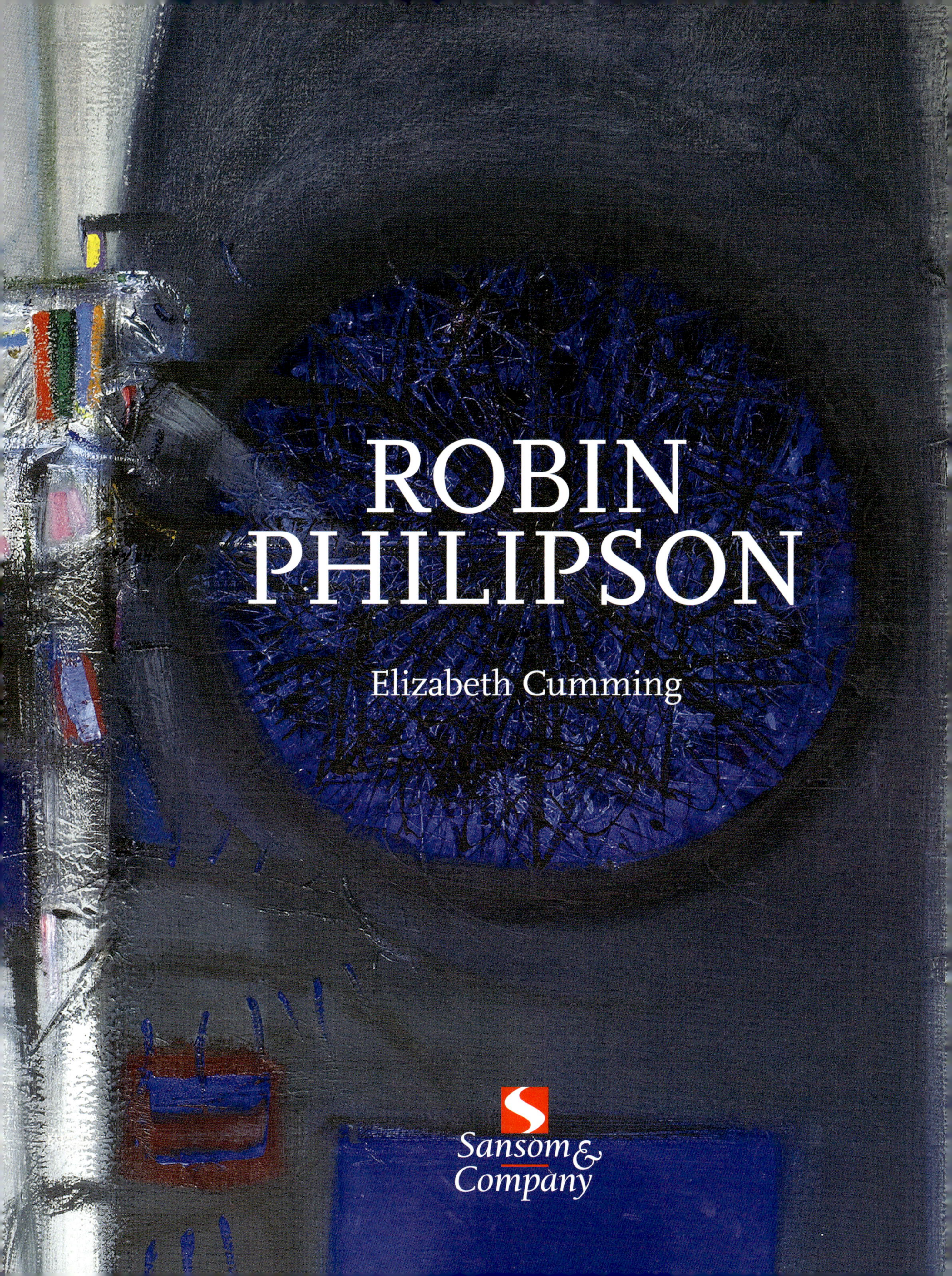

ROBIN PHILIPSON

Elizabeth Cumming

Sansom & Company

First published in 2018 by Sansom and Company,
a publishing imprint of Redcliffe Press Ltd.
81G Pembroke Road, Bristol BS8 3EA
www.sansomandcompany.co.uk / info@sansomandcompany.co.uk

ISBN 978-1-908326-93-5

British Library Cataloguing-in-Publication Data
A catalogue record for this book is available from the British Library.

Design and typesetting by E&P Design

Printed and bound in the Czech Republic via Akcent Media

FSC www.fsc.org
MIX
Paper from responsible sources
FSC® C014138

Title page: *Cool Interior: A Remembrance*
*c.*1968 / oil on canvas / 90 x 120 cm
University of Stirling

CONTENTS

INTRODUCTION

In the summer of 1992 the poet George Bruce wrote a short piece on his late friend, the painter Sir Robin Philipson, for the catalogue of a memorial exhibition of his work in Haddington, East Lothian during the Edinburgh Festival. This had been planned to be a retrospective to mark the silver anniversary of the Lamp of Lothian Collegiate Trust in a special way, but with the painter's death that May its purpose had changed. Bruce told of his many visits to his studio, of encounters with paintings still wet on the easel, and of experiencing 'the explosive energy of fighting cocks and dogs, not comfortably domesticated, but powerfully alive, savage, even frightening in their primal strength (for example, fig. 0.2). Sometimes the savagery of the animals was paralleled by the cruelty of men and the pathetic bodies of odalisques'.[1]

Today Robin (as he is called throughout this book) is remembered primarily for the expressionist power of such paintings or the voluptuous yet fragile beauty of his late paintings of poppies (fig. 0.1). Whatever the subject, every one had been a technical challenge and to a degree experimental. He would be the first to confess that his painting never came easily and was the fruit of almost endless working and reworking in the studio. His palette and subjects may have changed over the years but his art remained connected with the real world and exposed the traumas and joys of experience. His earliest representational oils from the early 1950s, somewhat neglected in recent times, had already explored the sensations of the countryside through extraordinary colour and texture. Over the following years his art was a reflection on what life delivered to him and to the world.

Robin was very much his own man. He had a huge respect for the work of the Old Masters, studying their art at every possible opportunity. His series of multi-panelled large-scale oils from the 1960s formalised his response to this. As the illustrations here show, colour was always a principal tool in Robin's art, and it evolved through his career: he was one of Scotland's major colourists. It was this as much as technical experiment which drove all his work, whether easel painting, printmaking or his involvement in textile enterprises, here explored for the first time.

For the last quarter century of Robin's life he was acknowledged as a major figure in Scottish art, with his work regularly seen in Scotland and London. The way he tackled big subjects was appreciated by the students he taught over

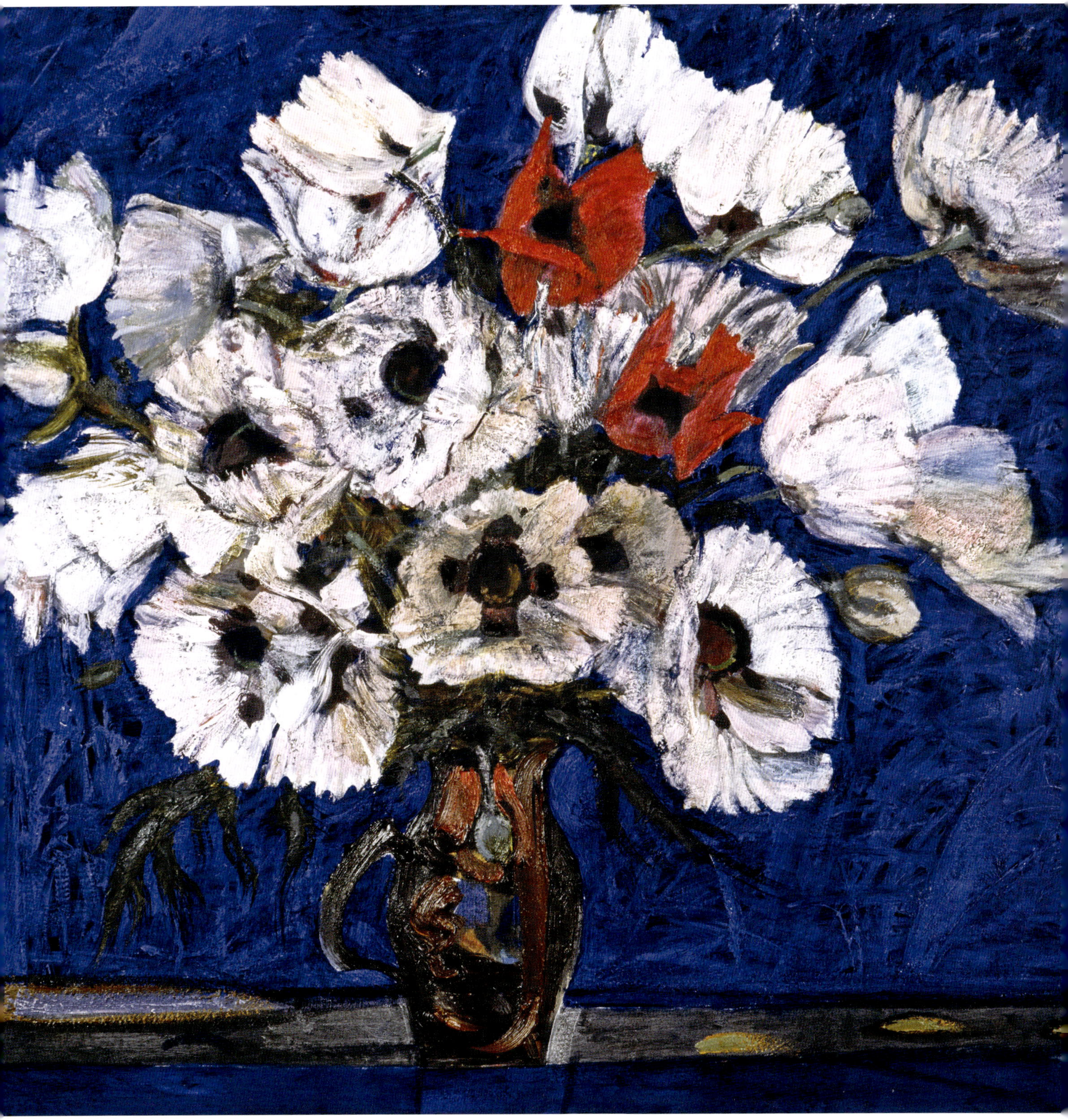

FIG. 0.1
Poppies
*c.*1987 / oil on canvas / 90 x 90 cm
private collection · photo: Antonia Reeve

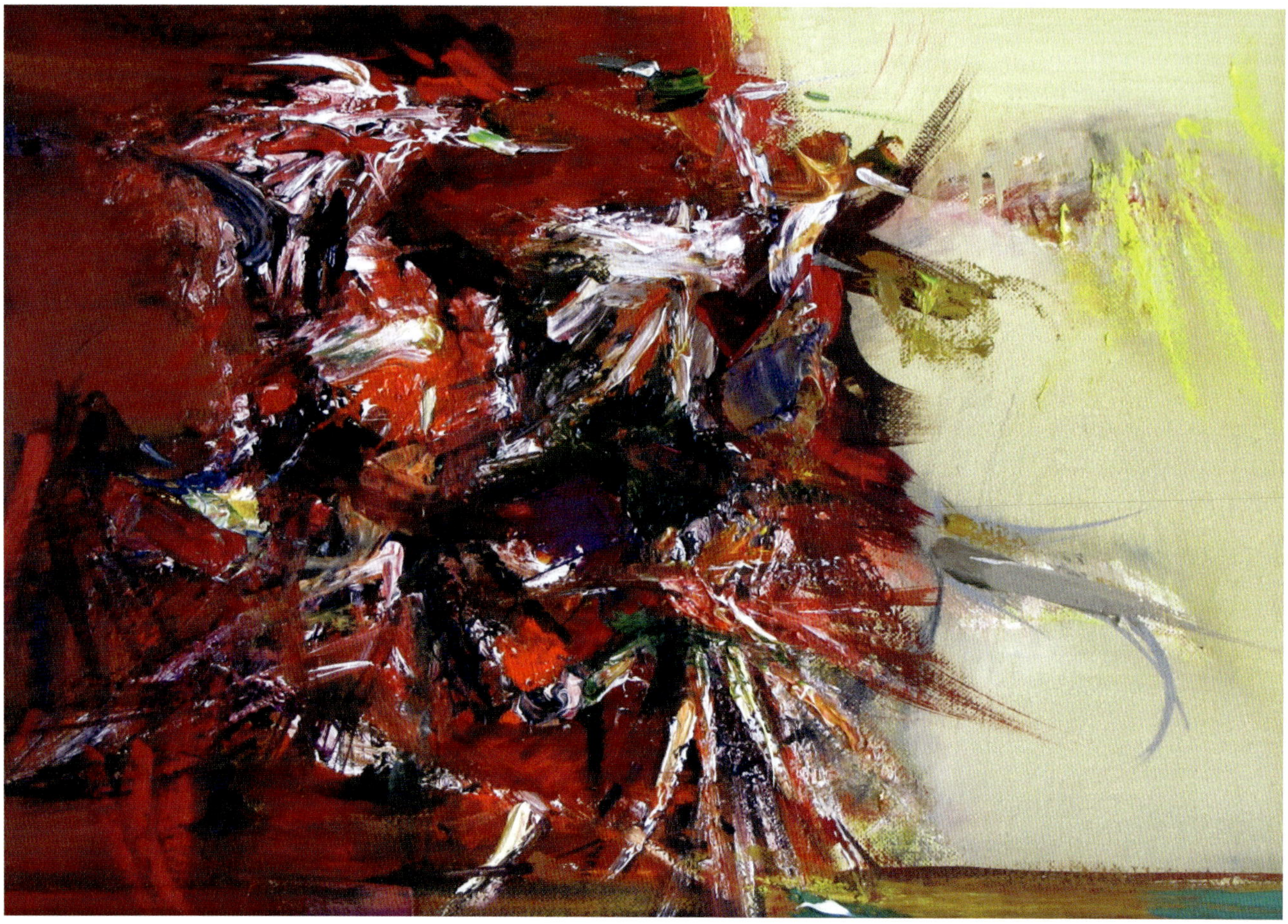

FIG. 0.2
Cockfight in Red and Yellow
*c.*1968 / oil on canvas / 25 x 36 cm
private collection • courtesy of the Scottish Gallery

a long art school career. He steered the School of Drawing and Painting of his alma mater, Edinburgh College of Art, through a period of intense modernisation. In fact, it was the ambition and success of his own painting which a number of his students have said was the main reason they applied to Edinburgh. His studies of 'the human condition' struck them with force and his importance extended far beyond the walls of exhibitions. To study in an art school where such art was being created in a studio along the corridor was thrilling.

George Bruce contrasted the dynamic of Robin's art with his personality. The friend he knew was thoughtful, courteous, generous and 'understanding of others very different from himself'.[2] He cut an elegant, dapper figure – his father was always well turned out, and early on Robin developed a lifelong habit of wearing a neat bowtie. This was the man the world saw. As his students got to know him they found him to be humane and understanding. As a teacher he could be strict but was always an artist who wanted the best possible opportunities for his students – the solid, traditional education similar to the one that he himself had enjoyed but also with access to contemporary ideas. Both staff and students had a degree of space and independence to get on with their work in their own way. Students have told of how Robin, doubtless pressurised by daytime committees and paperwork, would walk round the studios of an evening for a one-to-one chat. He was firm but kind, and, as another of his friends, Jack Firth, has recorded, was known to have slipped a five-pound note surreptitiously into a student's pocket. He was definitely on the side of the artists of tomorrow. He was fun, had a rich sense of the ridiculous and also enjoyed a party, these coming together in the students' annual 'revel' parties before Christmas – one year he dressed as a Morningside matron.

Robin and his painting were also right at the heart of Scottish art society for some forty years. In his late fifties he became President of the Royal Scottish Academy, serving it keenly and well for a full decade. He was showered with honorary degrees and was knighted for his services to art. As this book shows, he also served on an extraordinary number of cultural committees from the Royal Fine Art Commission to the British Council and gave of what little spare time he had to charitable causes. As curator of the Edinburgh City Art Centre in the early 1980s, I tentatively asked if he might find time to help judge an exhibition of amateur art called 'Artists Unlimited' and he agreed without a moment's hesitation.

Most biographers have a bookshelf of diaries or a nice cache of personal letters on which to base their book, but with Robin this has not been the case. However, and in addition to help from the family, several institutional archives have provided invaluable information to correct facts and offer much that is new. The principal one is, of course, the archive of the Edinburgh College of Art, now part of the University of Edinburgh Collections. There are also papers with the Royal Scottish Academy and the National Galleries of Scotland as well as those of the printers Harley Brothers on deposit with the University of Glasgow's Hunterian Art Gallery and several others scattered across the country. All are acknowledged elsewhere in the book. With many new discoveries, this account of Robin's life is longer and fuller than any that have previously been told. It will surely not be the last word but my hope is that it will provide a greater understanding of the man and his art.

1 THE MAKING OF AN ARTIST

Despite his reputation as a leading Scottish painter of the twentieth century, Robin Philipson was in fact a Cumbrian. He was born Robert James Philipson in Walk Mill House, a fine farmhouse in the picturesque landscape of Broughton Mills on 17 December 1916, the final day of the Battle of Verdun. He arrived shortly after his twin sister Phyllis Margaret (1916–2018). They were the first children of James Philipson (1891–1982) and his wife Agnes (née Postlethwaite, 1883–1978), the widow of Edward Barrow, a local farmer with whom she had had three children – Frank, Elizabeth (known as Betty) and Mary. Walk Mill House is situated upstream from Broughton-in-Furness, and its farmland had been bought by Agnes's first husband. James Philipson would tell the children of how his family were related to the Philipsons who had owned Calgarth Hall at Windermere from the fifteenth to the early eighteenth centuries and of how they had once been prosperous local landowners but had long since fallen on hard times.[1] The boy was named after both his paternal great-grandfather and father, but always known as Robin, the name of choice of his mother. The twins were inseparable for the first few years, going around everywhere hand-in-hand [fig. 1.2], and they would remain close. They would be followed by a sister, Audrey, and a brother, John.

Walk Mill House [fig. 1.3] had its own garden and small orchard. Robin would remember the simple, rural atmosphere of his early childhood home with much affection. His Philipson ancestry included craftsmen and this may partly account for his lifelong fascination with materials and workmanship. His great-grandfather, a shopkeeper by trade and the son of a blacksmith, was also a basketmaker and a gardener. Gardening in fact was in the genes, with several generations of the Philipson family said to have worked on the remarkable topiary gardens at Levens Hall, south of Kendal. Robin's mother came from a farming family but her paternal grandfather was a master tailor – a very different occupation from the slate quarrying and farming by which most locals earned their living.

Robin's father was employed as a station clerk by the London, Midland and Scottish Railway Company, on the Coniston branch line. When the children were young he was moved to Whitehaven and the family settled there at 40 The Gardens. Phyllis and Robin first attended the Irish Street School before starting at Whitehaven County Secondary School in September 1928.[2] Robin later recalled the futility of the old-fashioned art lessons at the senior school, where he was expected to draw a bucket with a perfect ellipse top and bottom. Sundays also were hard

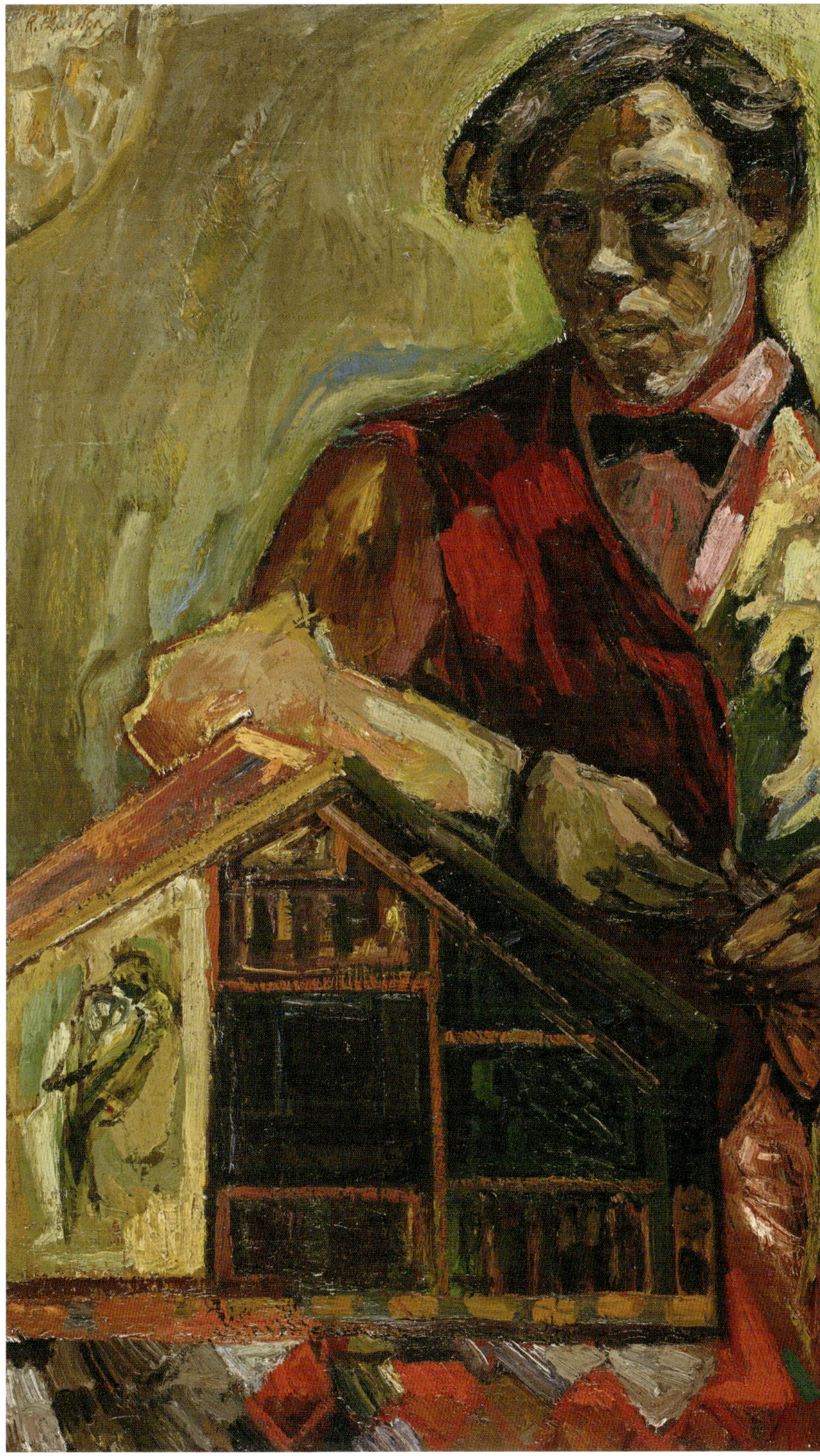

FIG. 1.1
Self-portrait
*c.*1946–47 / oil on canvas / 90 x 51.5 cm
private collection • photo: Antonia Reeve

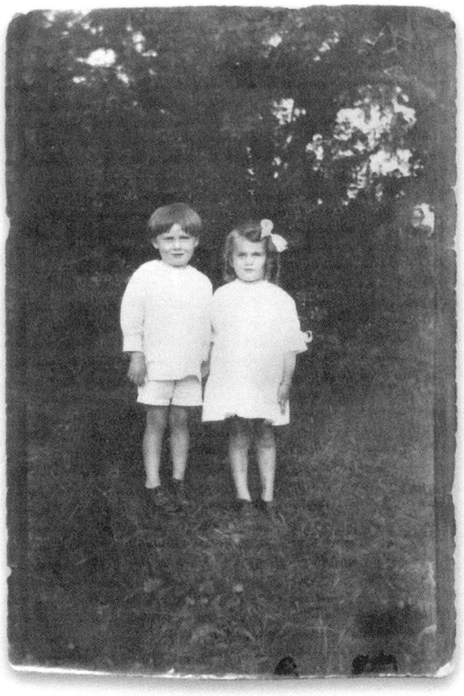

FIG. 1.2
Robin and Phyllis, *c.*1920
private collection

work: musically inclined, he sang in the local church choir, taking part in services all day and having to wear a stiff collar 'that nearly cut my throat'.[3]

When their father was moved by the railway company to the little town of Maryport, in 1929 or 1930, the children remained Whitehaven pupils until Christmas 1932, when the whole family moved again – this time into Scotland, to Gretna, where home was at 76 Annan Road, a modest, detached late Arts and Crafts house. It was decided that for schooling the twins should be sent to Dumfries Academy, where they started on 9 January 1933 when newly sixteen years old.[4] As this was too far to travel on a daily basis, the children boarded on weekdays in Dumfries, only coming home on Friday afternoons. Robin stayed in the Park House boys' hostel. Although a bursary student, he seems not to have been particularly academic; he repeated two of his Whitehaven years in Dumfries and had more than one attempt at English in the Scottish Leaving Certificate. However, he did have poetry published in the school magazine and was especially encouraged in art. The art master, Jock Ramsay, was also secretary of the school cricket club. This was the one sport Robin enjoyed, and he served in the Dumfries Academy Cricket Club First XI in his final year, 1935–36. It was a sport which he would continue to follow, if not play, in adulthood.

Living away from home on weekdays brought a degree of self-reliance and independence, although by his own confession joining the school at age sixteen made Robin feel a relative outsider.[5] He did make some school friends, however, and these included the future ceramicist Tom Lochhead (1917–2005). Robin applied to study at both Glasgow School of Art and Edinburgh College of Art. When he first saw the College building in Lauriston Place he had been struck by the atmosphere of the place, the classical, finely proportioned Edwardian building with its large sculpture court and generous, well-lit studios.[6] Both he and Tom Lochhead were accepted by Edinburgh, where they started in the autumn of 1936, initially sharing student digs at Marchmont, a district within pleasant walking distance of the College across the Meadows. Then the boys moved to a caravan they built from the chassis of an old farm tractor. They double-skinned it for warmth, though exactly with what sort of material is unknown. Parked in the Bonaly district by Colinton, south-west of the city, this offered free if cramped accommodation and easy access by tramcar to the College. Much of the day, and evenings, were spent in the College, and living was frugal with the simplest of meals (chips, peas and so forth) taken in the College canteen. Despite such cramped conditions, they remained in the caravan until the start of their fourth and final year, when for comfort they returned to digs and a Marchmont landlady.

In the mid-1930s Edinburgh College of Art had been open for less than thirty years, and it still retained its core Arts and Crafts values mixed with the strict academicism of the painting and sculpture classes previously taught by the

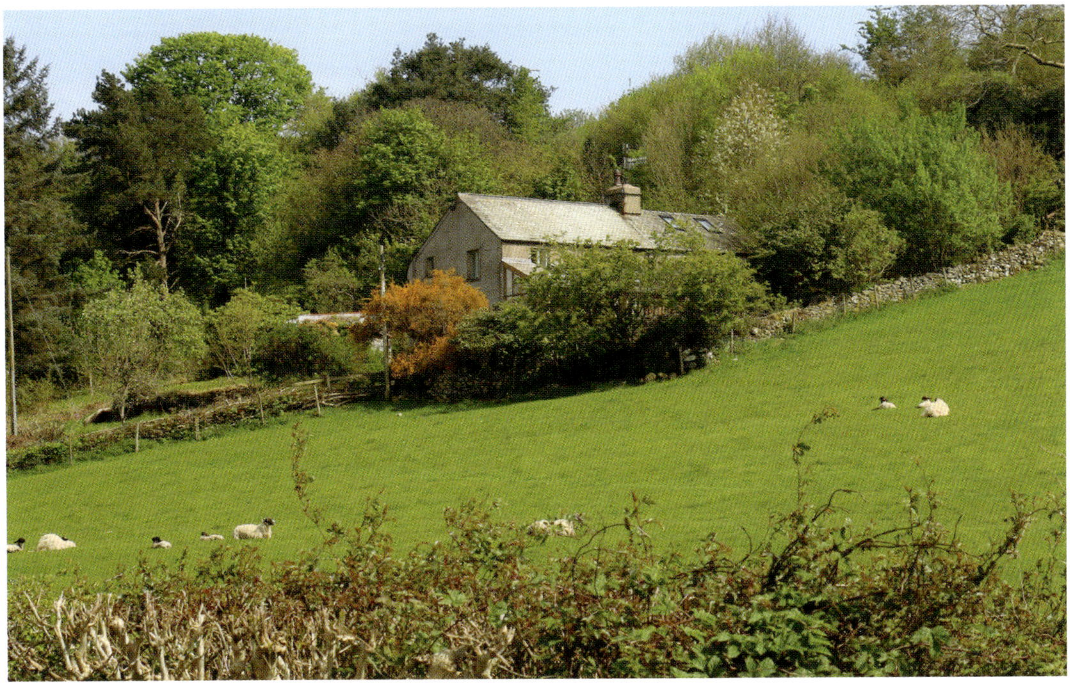

FIG. 1.3
Walk Mill House in Broughton Mills, Cumbria, 2017
private collection • photo: Bob Sharp

Royal Scottish Academy. The curriculum for students of drawing and painting was rooted in ideas transferred from the various schools it had replaced in the late 1900s – the School of Art and classes of the Royal Scottish Academy, the School of Applied Art, and the trade classes of the Heriot-Watt College. The aim under successive principals Frank Morley Fletcher, Gerald Moira and Hubert Wellington, the last from 1932, was to graft a degree of modernity on to solid, tried-and-tested methods of teaching which involved close study of various forms. Painting was grounded in preliminary classes devoted to draughtsmanship. In 1933 the 'Colourist' S.J. Peploe had been invited to teach still life, and would have taught Robin the rudiments of classical still-life painting had he not been forced to retire through ill-health. William Gillies (1898–1973, known to Robin as Bill and to some others as Willie) took over his teaching, including still-life [fig. 1.4] and life painting.

The College prospectuses and Robin's student records offer us a picture of what was taught and learnt. A full-time Diploma in Drawing and Painting (known within the College as 'D&P'), in Sculpture or in Design and Crafts took four full years, with the first two occupied by a wide variety of classes, as was then common across Scottish higher education. Only in years three and four did students specialise in their preferred discipline. So in his first year Robin took elementary drawing in D&P; foliage, ornament and details from the antique in Sculpture; geometry, perspective and history in Architecture; and plant form, lettering and formal writing in Design and Crafts. These were subjects in which he obtained passes, but he also tried his hand at other crafts including jewellery, fashioning a silver ring for Phyllis's twenty-first birthday and also a pendant, again with a stone setting. In his second year he dropped Sculpture, keeping on drawing in Architecture and pattern design and historic ornament in Design and Crafts. The greatest emphasis was on the skill

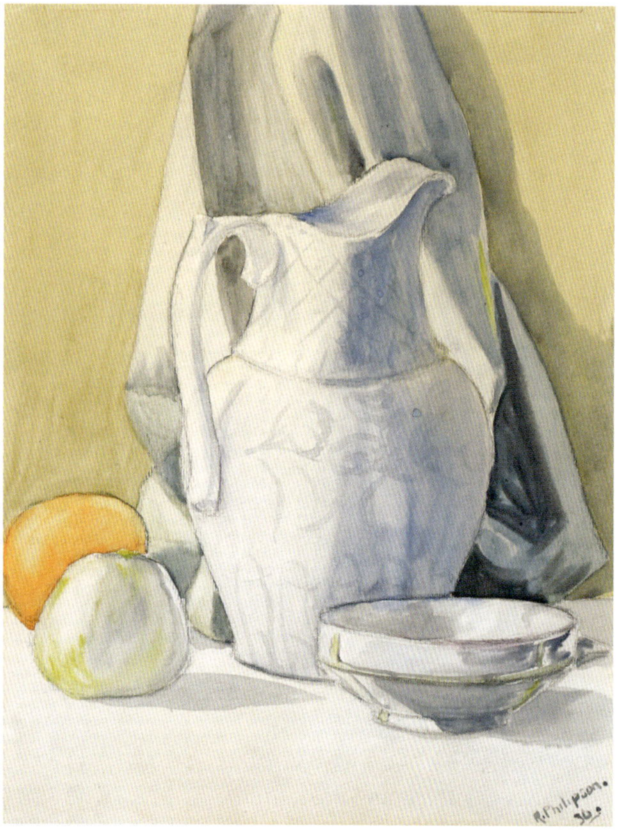

FIG. 1.4
Still life
1936 / pencil and watercolour on paper / 36 x 27.2 cm
private collection • photo: Bob Sharp

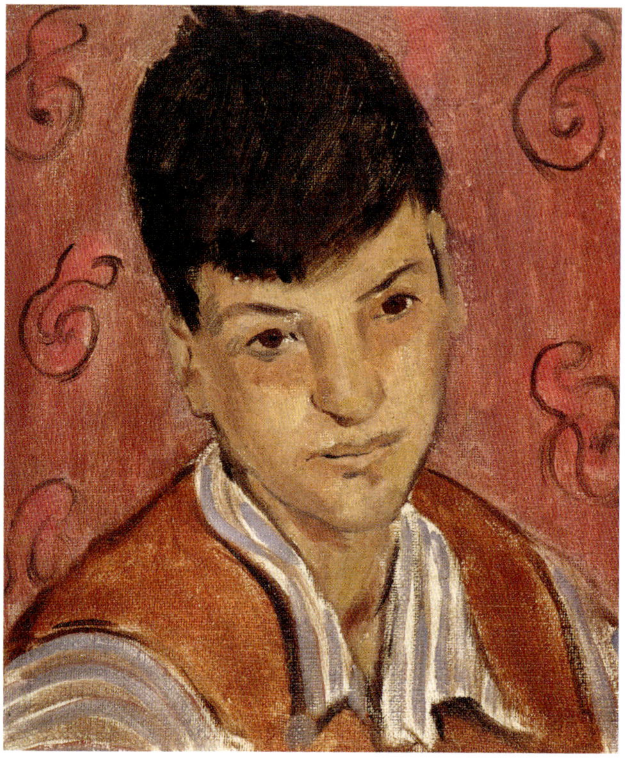

FIG. 1.5
Portrait of Jimmy
1939 / oil on canvas / 30.5 x 25.7 cm
private collection • photo: Antonia Reeve

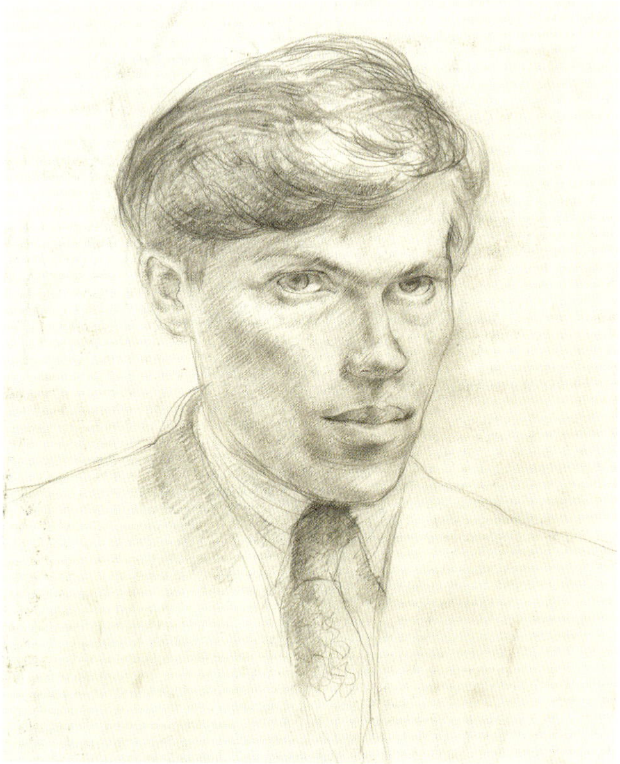

FIG. 1.6
Self-portrait
*c.*1940 / pencil on paper / 37.8 x 27.8 cm
private collection • courtesy of the Scottish Gallery

of drawing, which in D&P included anatomy work, plus drawing from life and from 'the antique', using the fine collection of nineteenth-century classical casts in the Sculpture Court and nearby corridors. Still-life painting was added in this second year, but perhaps as important was a course in colour theory which illustrated a range of potential forms of expression. As a small child Robin, who was always keen on drawing, had been attracted to colour in even the smallest thing: his sweet of choice was a Fruit Gum, with its magic colours when held up to the light. Colour would remain key to his life and work.[7]

The staff in D&P were of all ages. The School was led by David Alison (1882–1955), a portrait painter with a United Kingdom-wide clientele. Robin remembered how, in his later years, Alison would apply the most beautiful colour during teaching – painting vermilions and ochres and cobalt blues 'on top of the black and green torsos that I was struggling like hell with' – and how he inspired a student to go beyond playing safe, to see how colours might work against each other; but equally Alison taught largely by imposing his own ideas on a student.[8] Other long-serving teachers included artists such as Henry Lintott (1877–1965), whose classical approach to subject matter and interest in historical media, particularly tempera, contrasted with that of the younger ones such as William MacTaggart (1903–1981). Still life was then taught by four very different artists: MacTaggart, Adam Bruce Thomson (1885–1976), Bill Gillies and John Maxwell (1905–1962) – the last two specially encouraging regarding a student's individual ideas. Within drawing, the teachers had their distinctive approaches. Of the older generation, David Foggie (1878–1948), who took advanced life drawing, was a master of the fine line and this is reflected in Robin's delicate early pencil portrait studies, such as an early self-portrait [fig. 1.6]. Penelope Beaton (1886–1963) taught the students 'the significance of shapes'.[9] But there were many other teachers at the College with different agendas, all of which impacted on a student's way of working. Few of Robin's paintings from these years have survived, but a still life from his first year shows sensitivity for colour. Another, carried out swiftly in the summer of 1939 (at the end of his third year), shows him to be a natural painter. A study of Jimmy Gardner, a lad from Glasgow boarding in Gretna as a wartime evacuee, it has the simplicity and directness encouraged by Gillies and the delicately nuanced colour values of a Maxwell painting [fig. 1.5].

Robin also recalled how Robert H. Westwater (1905–1962), a painter now remembered for his portrait of the poet Hugh MacDiarmid, could make painting look almost easy. He led classes in composition, life drawing and the history of technique. Principal Gerald Moira had begun to involve students and new graduates in the decoration of many different city buildings, including churches and schools. Thanks to the then-current principal Hubert Wellington's equal passion for public art and children's education, Edinburgh schools and colleges were continuing to be embellished by College artists.[10] Some of these decorations were being executed while Robin was in his first year: he would have been well aware of them and probably attended a class in mural decoration.

Beyond studio practice, a mandatory course in the history and technique of painting was given by Dr Thomas Elder Dickson (1899–1978). Nicknamed 'the Dome' by his students, he was an academic who would still be quoting reams of Berenson

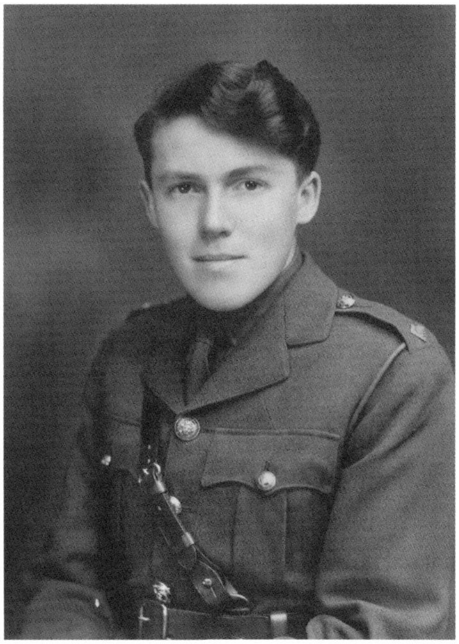

FIG. 1.7
In army uniform, 1941
private collection • photo: Tassell of Carlisle

to students in the early 1960s.[11] Although Robin found this side of an art education interesting, if daunting, he was more drawn to the trade classes with their no-nonsense approach to materials. Charlie Howison, the head of the housepainters' and decorators' evening classes, was willing to spend time with keen students to teach the essentials of sound professional techniques, how to prime a canvas and so on. At this early stage Robin was already firmly committed to studying the craft of painting, and this would dominate his career. But alongside these classes, other disciplines were also available, and they included printmaking. Classes ranged from etching, led by Bruce Thomson, to lithography, at this time taught (as was life drawing) by Donald Moodie (1892–1963). In the post-war years Moodie would switch from teaching printmaking to anatomy studies, always an important subject at Edinburgh and of them all the most purely academic.

For his fourth and final year in Drawing and Painting Robin was awarded an Andrew Grant Scholarship, which covered his College fees and some maintenance costs. War had broken out at the start of the academic year, but the College authorities decided to keep the place open and functioning. Staffing and especially student numbers were reduced, resulting in a more open, collegiate relationship between staff and students. Robin was able to complete his course and received his Diploma in Drawing and Painting in June 1940. Almost immediately he was conscripted into the King's Own Scottish Borderers, carrying out early training at Berwick-on-Tweed. He received his commission soon after, and as a second lieutenant from 1941 he would serve in India, attached to the Royal Indian Army Service Corps [fig. 1.7]. This involved a great deal of travel, moving with his troops across a substantial area from the North-West Frontier to Bangalore. Service with his Gurkha men in Burma near the Kohima front followed. He drove supplies to wherever they were needed – and was involved in at least one major motor accident when the vehicle left the road.

The startling contrasts between the beautiful landscapes bathed in the extraordinary colours of day and evening and the savage war atrocities he witnessed would remain with Robin for many years. They were described in letters home to his parents and to Phyllis, then stationed as a welfare officer in Italy. The wanton destruction of the countryside, of that 'fragile loveliness' he described to his first biographer Maurice Lindsay (1918–2009), seems to have had a worse effect on him than any fear of fighting.[12] But during these years the Gretna family, now living at 21 Victory Avenue, suffered personal tragedy when John, the youngest of the four children, died of tubercular meningitis in 1943 while training at an army camp in Elgin. He was only nineteen years old, the age his elder brother had been when leaving home for Edinburgh's art world. Like Robin, John had had leanings towards becoming an artist, the second in the family, and after the war might well have followed Robin to Edinburgh. The family was deeply saddened by the unexpected loss of a much-loved son and brother.

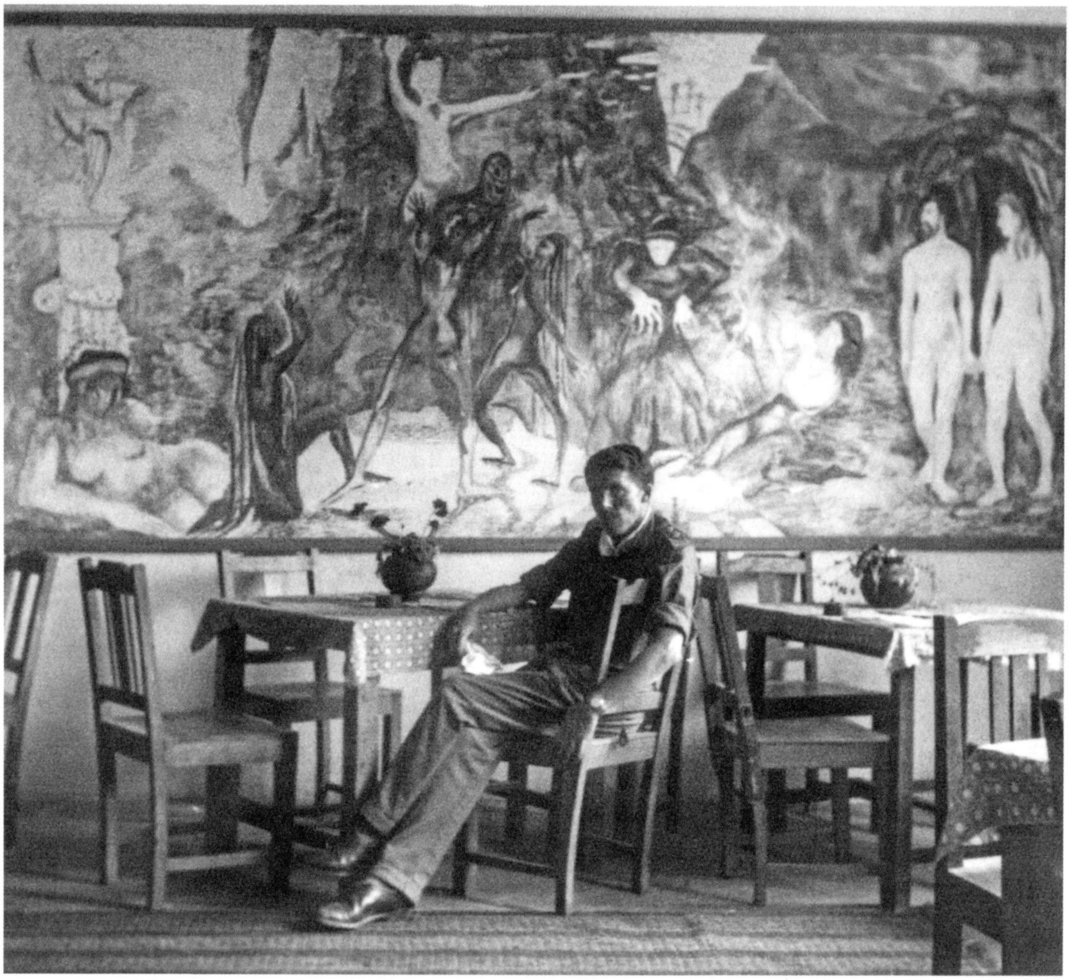

FIG. 1.8
Relaxing in the men's rest room in eastern Bengal, 1945
private collection

Robin's years in India, in Burma, and in 1945 as a captain in Singapore, were not wholly devoid of art. He had art materials sent out, writing home of how the life he encountered called out to be painted, 'thrilling material for a brush and palette knife'. He sketched and drew when he could, and painted portraits of some of his fellow servicemen. His superiors recognised the artist in their midst and he was allowed to conduct an army art school in eastern Bengal. The classes he led were in both art and craft – painting in oil and watercolour, plus poster design, scene painting and construction for amateur theatricals, leatherwork, weaving and book-binding, the last three subjects not part of his official College studies but ones he had tried out in evening classes. Already the attraction of a wide range of materials and their potential usage and expression was feeding his approach to art. He remembered Hubert Wellington's encouragement of mural art as a social activity and was soon involving his men in painting not only theatrical scenery but also in working with him on a mural. Only one archive photograph has survived of this large figurative panel made specifically for the rest room, where his men could read or write letters home [fig. 1.8].

In 1946 Robin returned to Edinburgh, lodging first at 56 Manor Place. At this stage he was considering a career as a school art master, and applied successfully to the

Ministry of Labour's Edinburgh office for a further education and training award. He embarked on the one-year Course in Practical Training at Moray House College of Education in the city, renting Torphin Cottage on the outskirts of Colinton, the residential area he had come to know well as a student. By all accounts the students with war service, such as Robin and Alan Davie (1920–2014), found the ways of the course excruciatingly dull and instead 'had a ball' of a time. A confident self-portrait in loud colours and quick, broad brushwork dates from this year [fig. 1.1]. In his final report he was considered 'exceptionally promising' but school teaching was not to be his vocation. He had picked up again with some of his former College tutors, especially Gillies and Maxwell, and, persuaded by them, on 19 February 1947 he completed an application for the post of 'assistant' (as a College tutor was then called) in D&P. Although not immediately taken on as a teacher, that October he became a member of the College of Art staff, and was initially employed for one term as a library assistant before teaching full-time in D&P from early 1948.

Of course the College was now a different place. Although on the surface the College curriculum had altered little in the 1940s, there had been a significant turnover in key College staff which continued in the post-war years. A number of the painters who had taught him had gone, as had the former heads of all three Schools. The principal since 1942 was Robert Lyon, a painter from Newcastle today primarily remembered for his extramural work with a group of Northumbrian coalminers (the Ashington 'pitmen painters'). Like many institutions at the time, he was keen to strengthen and modernise its practice while maintaining traditional values rooted in an empirical approach to the making of art. Above all, Lyon and his Board of Governors sought to provide the students with a balance of different ways of thinking about art and design, and D&P teaching staff were recruited from across Britain – breaking the habit of hiring recent College graduates in that subject. Bill Gillies had recently been promoted to head of Drawing and Painting. Among the other painters now being taken on in these years were Allan Carr (born 1914), Derek Clarke (1912–2014) and Leonard Rosoman (1913–2012). Of the three only Clarke, who like Carr had trained at the traditionalist Slade School of Fine Art, would remain a colleague throughout Robin's College career. Rosoman, from Camberwell School of Art, was appointed specifically to teach mural painting, still an important subject, and virtually the only interdisciplinary one. He was tempted north by what he called 'an irresistible offer which included a specially built studio'.[13] The college prospectus commented that 'there is a large studio for the teaching of mural painting. This class forms a vital link between the various Schools, particularly Drawing and Painting, Design and Crafts, and Architecture, and operates under the supervision of a specialist master.'[14] During his Edinburgh years Rosoman would continue this tradition.[15] His students included David McClure (1926–1998), who would work on decorations for the reconstructed King's Room at Falkland Palace in 1957 and in 1971 on a mural in the staff common room at the University of St Andrews. Robin took over Rosoman's class on the latter's return to London in 1954 and would later paint two public murals of his own – although both would be panels painted in the studio. Robin was involved in teaching on both the College diploma and on the new Fine Art degree, a joint one offered by Edinburgh University and the College. In particular, he taught anatomy in the late afternoon on Tuesdays and Thursdays, and still life to the fourth- and fifth-year students on Fridays, teaching them how to set up their still-life subjects piece by piece.

The new staff who became friends in these early years of College teaching were Robert Henderson Blyth (1919–1970), James Cumming (1922–1991) and Sax Shaw (1916–2000). Other former students from the late 1940s were joining the College staff as part-time assistants – John Houston (1930–2008) in 1955, for example, and, later on, David Michie (1928–2015) and also William Baillie (1923–2011). A Glaswegian, Bobby Henderson Blyth was three years Robin's junior and a man who, as Robin would recall, always took a cup-half-full view of life; yet his war experiences had also been life-changing. In his time with the 157 Ambulance Unit in Hamburg he too had witnessed the human devastation of war. He joined the College in 1946, moving to Aberdeen in 1954 to take up a post at Gray's School of Art. James Cumming, six years Robin's junior, had first studied at the College from 1939 to 1941. After serving in the Royal Air Force Volunteer Reserve, he completed his diploma studies and, like Robin, had been awarded an Andrew Grant scholarship. In 1950 he joined the D&P staff.

Sax Shaw turned out to be Robin's closest College friend from this time. He had studied painting in Huddersfield and the Edinburgh College of Art but his time in Scotland had been interrupted. After the war he completed his College studies and was awarded an Andrew Grant travel bursary. This took him to Paris, where, on visiting the Gobelins workshop, a dyer reportedly said to him, 'hold the wool in your hands and then think with your heart'.[16] On his return to Edinburgh he had taken up weaving and was employed from 1949 by the College initially as a 'colour master' to teach drawing and stained glass within the School of Architecture. He was soon painting a mural at Torphin Cottage, at this point still rented by Robin for weekend entertaining: during the week he lodged with a landlady, Mrs Cole, at 41 Scotland Street. The Torphin artwork apparently occupied a whole wall and totally dominated the interior. Although Sax is best known for his stained glass and for teaching that subject to a whole generation of College students, he also wove tapestry in his home studio and became director of weaving at the Dovecot Studios from 1954 to 1958. Robin himself never had the inclination to work in glass but was intrigued by it as a medium, as he was by a weaver's skill in interpreting a design. Indeed, in the early 1960s he would be tempted to accept an invitation from the Dovecot to design for tapestry – an ambition only to be realised in retirement following thirty-five full years of teaching at Edinburgh College of Art.

2 PAINTER, PRINTMAKER, DESIGNER

In the post-war years Robin Philipson the academic artist would be informed by both his College training and available museum art. His experience of the War was naturally much to mind, and a classical painting from 1946 of the meeting of a soldier and a villager was executed vigorously in thick oil paint. A portrait – the sitter remains unknown – was accepted by the Royal Scottish Academy (RSA) for their annual exhibition in 1947, and the first post-war visit to northern France that summer resulted in one or two further freely painted oils and watercolours shown the following year. *A Family Dispute* [fig. 2.2] is a particularly animated figural composition. The shallow perspective suspending the individual figures evens the picture plane and concentrates the telling of a narrative. It was a style of composition which combined well with the raw plasticity of his materials.

The move towards becoming part of the professional art world was underway, and in 1948 Robin was elected a painter member of the Society of Scottish Artists (SSA). This was and remains one of several important exhibiting societies apart from the RSA itself: at the time the other principal societies were the Royal Glasgow Institute of the Fine Arts (RGI), with whom Robin exhibited from 1949 and would become a member (much later, in 1980), and the Royal Scottish Society of Painters in Watercolour (RSW) which, although also based in Glasgow, presents its annual shows at the Royal Scottish Academy. These exhibitions, rather than commercial dealerships, were where young artists could advertise their work: for all generations they were the heart of the art market and, not least, locations where artists could socialise. Edinburgh was then expanding its post-war city culture with the establishment in 1947 of the Edinburgh International Festival, aimed at fostering international harmony through the arts: in the course of the first twenty plus years some key art exhibitions were presented in the RSA building on Princes Street – Degas in 1952, Renoir in 1953 and Cézanne in 1954. Much later, when Robin was secretary of the RSA, he would be deeply involved in the detail of exhibition planning.

Apart from the RSA, plus the relatively more open exhibitions of the SSA and RSW, the Scottish Arts Club in Rutland Square provided another local social hub for meeting and a changing display of paintings. The city's art culture was also served by its school art teachers, whose own art could be seen across these exhibitions. The Edinburgh Education Authority (EEA) was then responsible for maintaining and upgrading standards in education in state schools in the city,

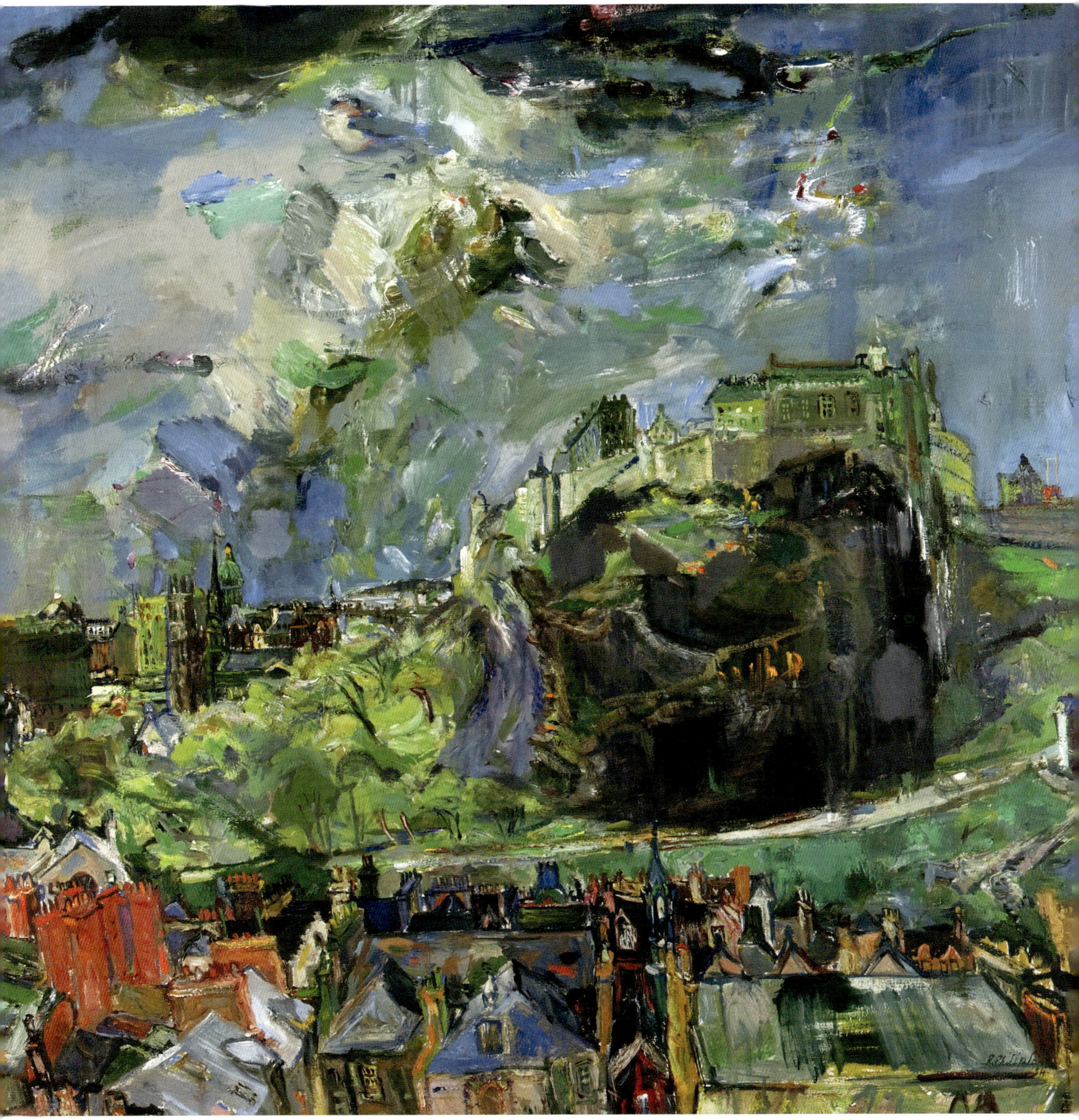

FIG. 2.1
View from My Studio Window
1954 / oil on canvas / 99.7 x 101.6 cm
image courtesy of the Hunterian, University of Glasgow, 2018

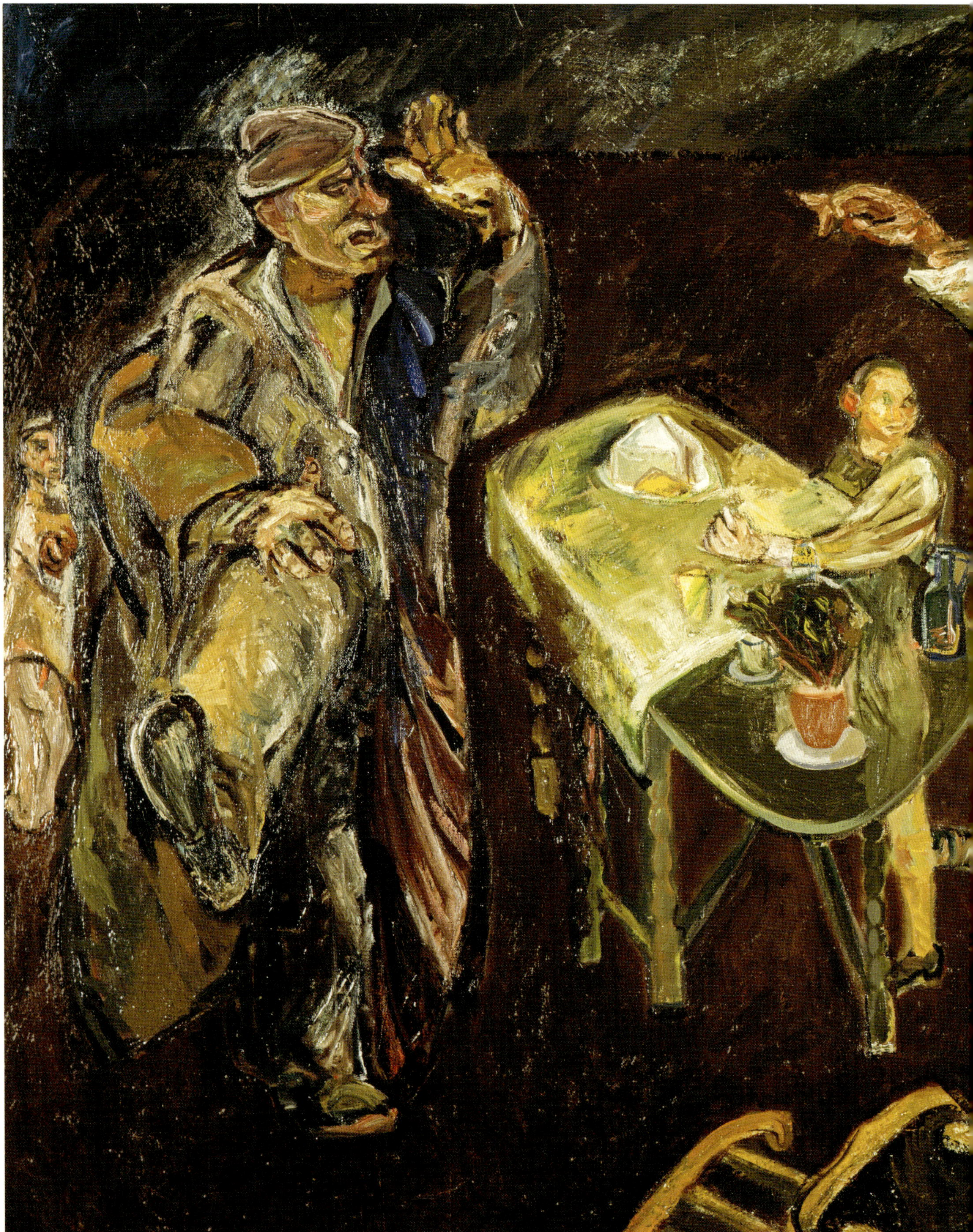

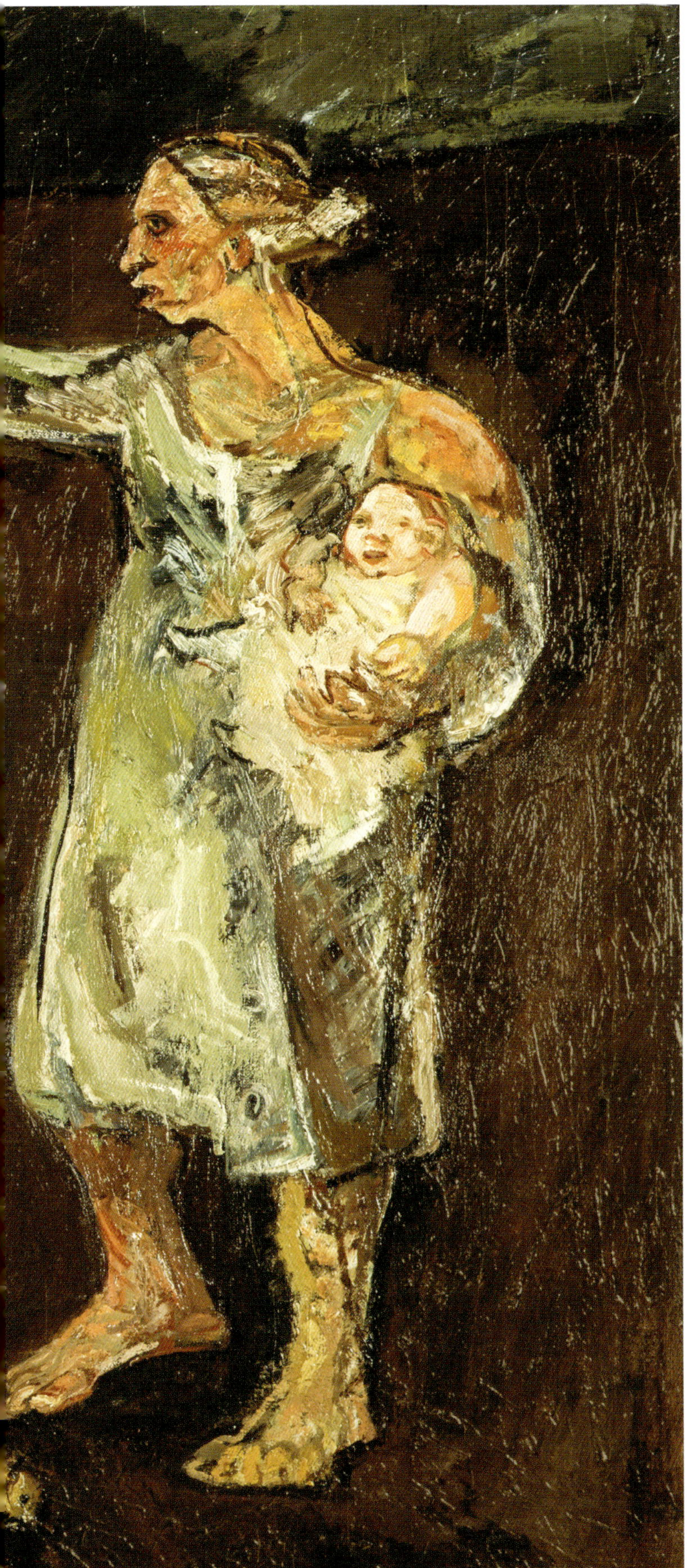

FIG. 2.2
A Family Dispute
*c.*1948 / oil on canvas / 101.5 x 127 cm
National Galleries of Scotland • photo: Antonia Reeve

with a team of subject advisers who included George Wright Hall (1895–1974), the first director of Edinburgh's City Art Centre from 1971, and Jack Firth (1917–2010), a friend of Robin's. The EEA also employed recent art graduates as school supply or advisory teachers. One such in the mid-1940s was Brenda Ellis Mark (1922–1960), a young painter who had moved from Hull to Edinburgh as a girl. She had been educated at St George's School for Girls, one of Edinburgh's many independent schools, and taken her diploma in D&P at the College of Art, graduating aged twenty in 1942. Brenda had tutored in art and 'handicraft' at Moray House College of Education, where she had gained her teacher's certificate in 1944, before working for the EEA, and would conclude her teaching career at St Denis's School for Girls in Edinburgh. Robin painted two portraits of her: *Brenda: Winter Portrait*, shown at the RSA in 1948, and *Brenda: Summer Portrait*, exhibited the same year at the SSA. By now clearly they were a couple: they were married on 4 April 1949 in the Roxburghe Hotel on Charlotte Square.

The Philipsons first took a flat at 87 West Bow in Edinburgh's historic Old Town at the foot of Victoria Street [fig. 2.3]. They had been tipped off about its availability by a College colleague, Kathleen Horsman (1911–1998). Katie Horsman had joined the College in 1943 having previously taught at Liverpool School of Art. In Edinburgh, she taught ceramics plus some classes in sculpture and already had a flat in the West Bow block where the Philipsons would live. Despite being cramped for space, their flat was ideally located as it was a short walk through the Grassmarket to the College of Art, along the Cowgate to Moray House, or down the Mound to Princes

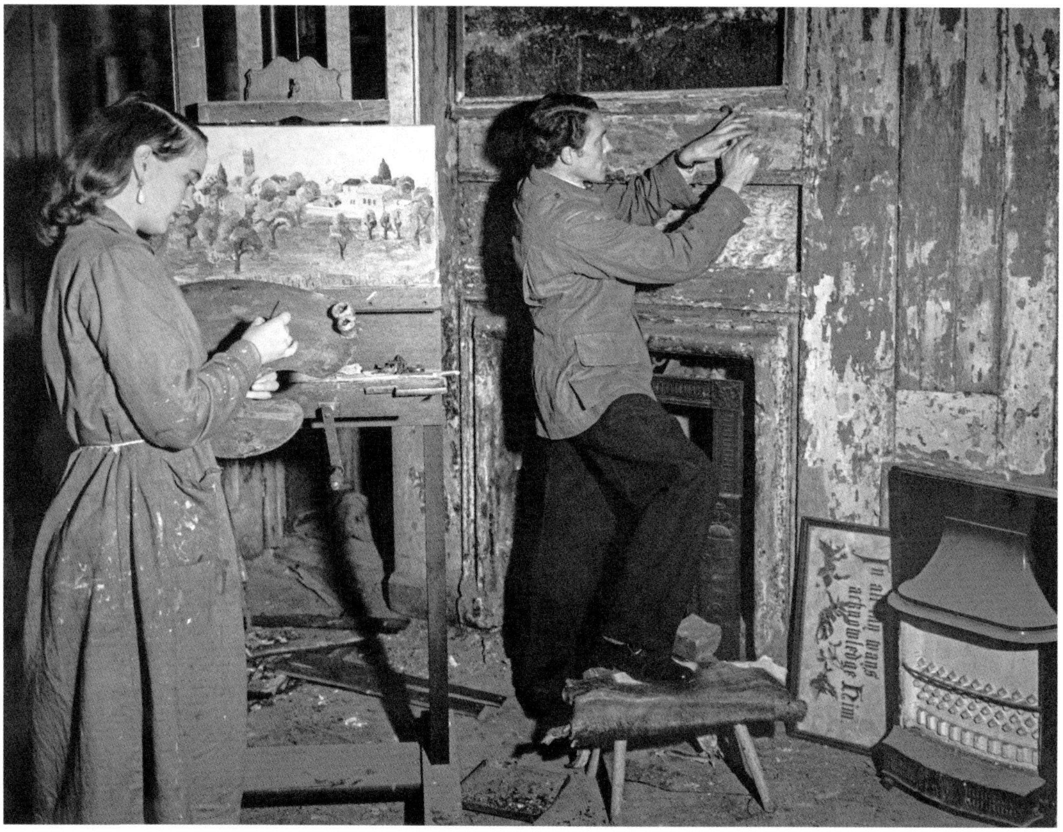

FIG. 2.3
Brenda and Robin at home in 87 West Bow, *c.*1951
private collection

Street. How their Saturdays were spent was recorded by Robin in 1983 and offers a neat picture of their social circle as well as the hours given to painting:

> *After breakfast we'd put on what we called our weekend attire and go out. We used to retire to Princes Street, which was very much the thing then. On the way, we'd probably browse at Bauermeister's Bookshop* [in North Bank Street] *which was always a great temptation, but then we'd go for coffee at Sinclair's, which was a famous place at that time. This was a must for our small circle of friends, mostly artists. There were painters like John Maxwell, Willie Wilson, Bobby Blyth, Anne Redpath, Sax Shaw, Nora O'Brien, Gloria and Suds Sutherland and James Cowie with his funny wee specs.*
>
> *After that we'd all go to a pub in Rose Street where we'd meet up with Maurice Lindsay, Sydney Goodsir Smith and Charles Pulsford ... After a pub lunch we were in good shape for the afternoon, but it was probably about 4 p.m. And then Saturday evenings were special. We didn't have a rota system but we'd spend those evenings in the houses of friends and took turns to provide dinner. And that was the weekend because on Sundays we worked from very early in the morning until late at night.*[1]

Robin particularly relished the weekend company of Cowie, 'who would talk about literature all the time but his wife would keep interrupting about buying food for lunch which brought us both back to earth'. He teased Robin and Brenda pleasantly: 'when we broke up to go to lunch James Cowie would give Brenda a peck on the cheek and say to me "Don't forget there is only one painter in your household and you are not it."'[2]

The couple remained in West Bow for nearly five years, moving in 1954 to a larger, top-floor flat at 6 St Vincent Street, north of Howe Street on the fringe of the New Town. New Town living was not new to Robin, who had first lodged with Mrs Cole in Scotland Street during the desperately cold winter of 1947. Then a district considered slightly bohemian, Scotland Street had been nearer the homes of the painters William MacTaggart at 4 Drummond Place, Redpath at 7 London Street and Nigel McIsaac at 4 Dundonald Street; the writers Sydney Goodsir Smith and Sir Compton Mackenzie lived nearby. The main attraction of St Vincent Street, however, was its space: here at last they could each have a dedicated home studio, with Robin's a larger space while Brenda's studio also served as a cosy sewing room.[3]

By the mid-1950s they were something of a local celebrity young couple and featured as the subject of a 1955 newspaper article 'At Home with the Philipsons, Artists'. This documented their way of life, with even a mention of recent treatment of dry rot through their home. The flat's handsome entrance hall, like that of some others in the New Town, doubled up as the dining space for weekend entertaining, and the flat was furnished with a good number of pot plants as a substitute for a garden. The importance Robin gave to his own art as opposed to teaching was underlined by the fact that he was keen to spend three days a week in term time in his home studio, teaching at the College for up to two days plus taking evening classes most days. The classes he taught were life drawing (drawing from the nude), portrait painting and, from 1954, life painting (painting from the nude) – the last being a class which he alone taught.[4] This concentration of teaching freed up quiet

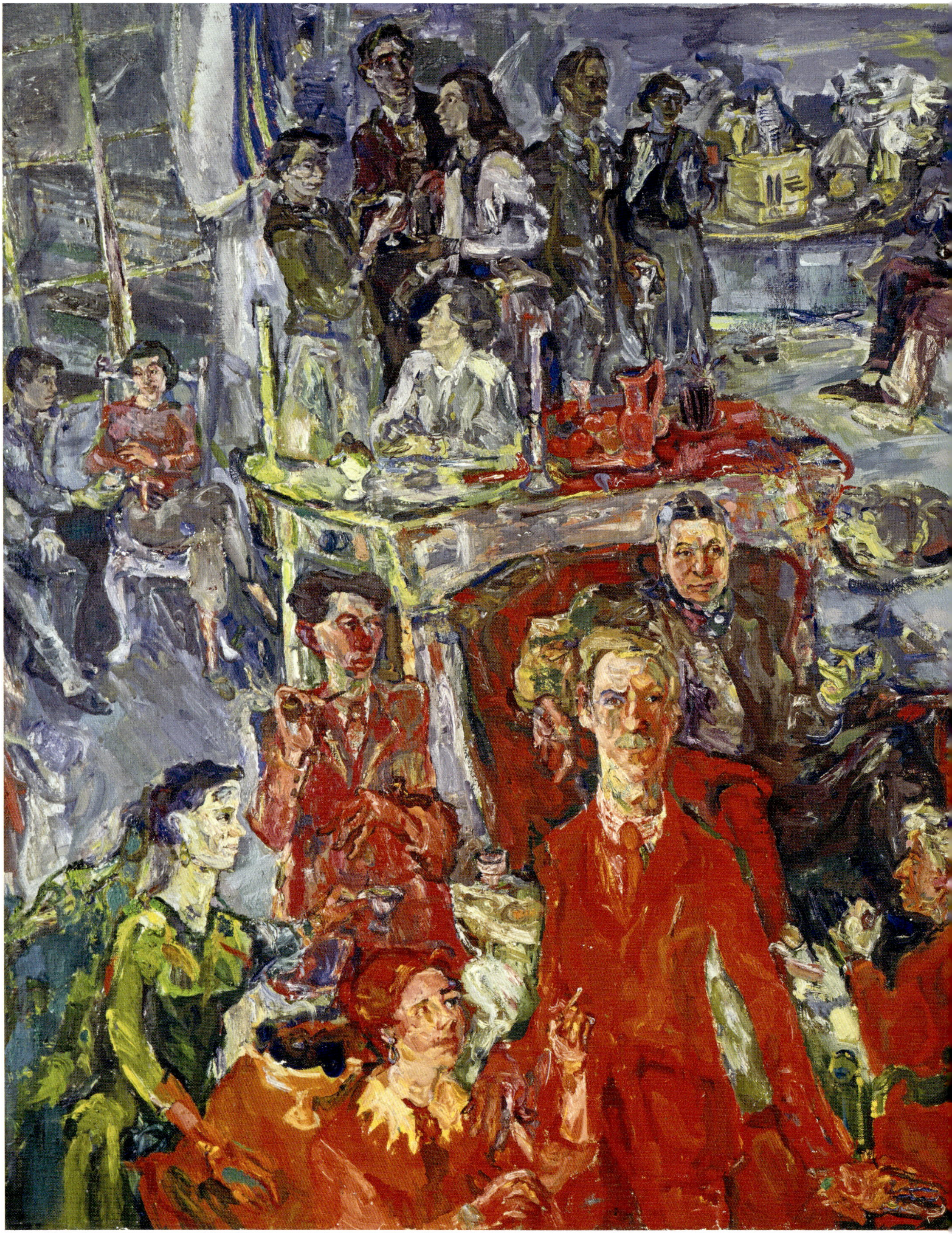

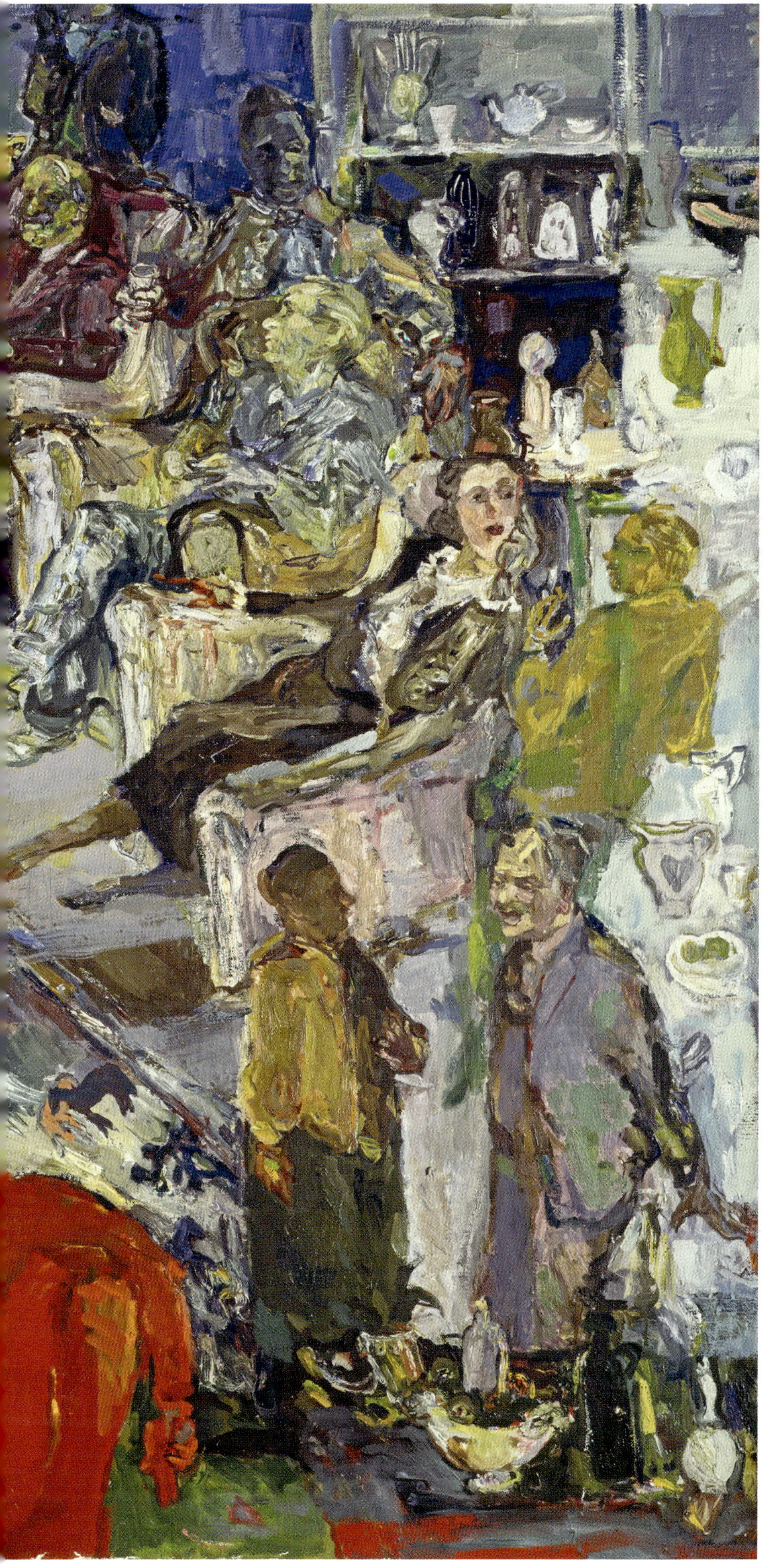

FIG. 2.4
Gathering at 7 London Street
*c.*1954 / oil on canvas / 137.7 x 183.2 cm
private collection
on loan to the National Galleries of Scotland
photo: Antonia Reeve

times in daylight for his own painting, while Brenda fitted her painting into the evenings and Sundays. A lively young couple, the Philipsons quickly became a valued part of the local art scene, and in *Gathering at 7 London Street* [fig. 2.4] Robin celebrated their arrival by recording a party at Anne Redpath's home. The arrangement of colour and animated figures dotted across the canvas and choice of palette reflects the optimism and buzz of urban culture at mid-decade.

The paintings produced by the couple were very different. Robin, encouraged by Gillies, had initially used a quiet palette with thick paint blocked in with longish strokes. He retained a penchant for traditional subject matter, for still life and figure studies plus a few landscapes. He was, and remained, also a fine water-colourist. However, during the early 1950s colour and texture began to be explored in his oils through layers of energised, thick impasto surfaced with thin colour glazes. His vibrancy of colour was undoubtedly in part due to his College education and local cultural awareness – and to his happiness with Brenda – but to this was added a new dimension which explored the potential of structure and surface. A few years earlier, in 1947 or 1948, Robin had had the brass neck to telephone the painter Oskar Kokoschka from the Tate Gallery to invite himself to the Austrian's London home. On his return to Edinburgh he had regularly visited the National Gallery of Scotland store on the Mound to study Kokoschka's use of materials in his painting *Zrání (High Summer)* of 1938–40.[5] This provided a useful and indeed inspirational technical resource, with its mix of thin oil and many 'intricate layers of cruder painting with fine glazes'. As Robin recalled, Kokoschka's ability to 'create resonances of colour and animation of the surfaces of the picture plane' resulted in a 'dynamism ... created in the forms themselves ... [which] appealed to me ... this enabled me to create the kind of vitality and compressed energy that I was looking for.'[6] At this point the working of materials dominated his thinking: it spoke loudly for process and value, for a degree of meaning, in art.

The impact of such work, to be joined from the early 1950s by study of the paintings of the École de Paris and especially Chaïm Soutine, would last into the early 1960s. By focusing on the physical properties of paint, Robin reached a new approach independent of his College training. Underpainting, consisting of square blocks of disparate colours smoothed out over the canvas, was followed by a working up of the surface here and there to build up an overall sense of energy. By this time Soutine's work, and a degree of awareness of the new expressionist art being made in the United States, had also filled his mind with fresh possibilities, and, interestingly, the family archive includes a cutting of an illustrated magazine article on Soutine's art from around this time. Robin's new ways did not go un-noticed: he secured the Keith Prize in 1951 for a third portrait of Brenda, *Brenda: Spring Portrait* (a painting adapting Soutine's favoured pose of clasped hands) [figs 2.7, 2.8], and was elected an Associate member of the Academy the following year. As a result, in 1952 Robin was selected by the Scottish Committee of the Arts Council of Great Britain (later to become the Scottish Arts Council) for a touring exhibition called 'Eight Young Contemporary Scottish Painters'. A group of oils of country scenes more under the influence of Kokoschka from this period include *Otter Hunt*, the sunny *Summer Morning* [fig, 2.5] and *The Countryside* [fig. 2.6], painted in vibrantly rich colour. These are particularly interesting British paintings of their period in their amalgam of atmospheric landscape with embedded figures.

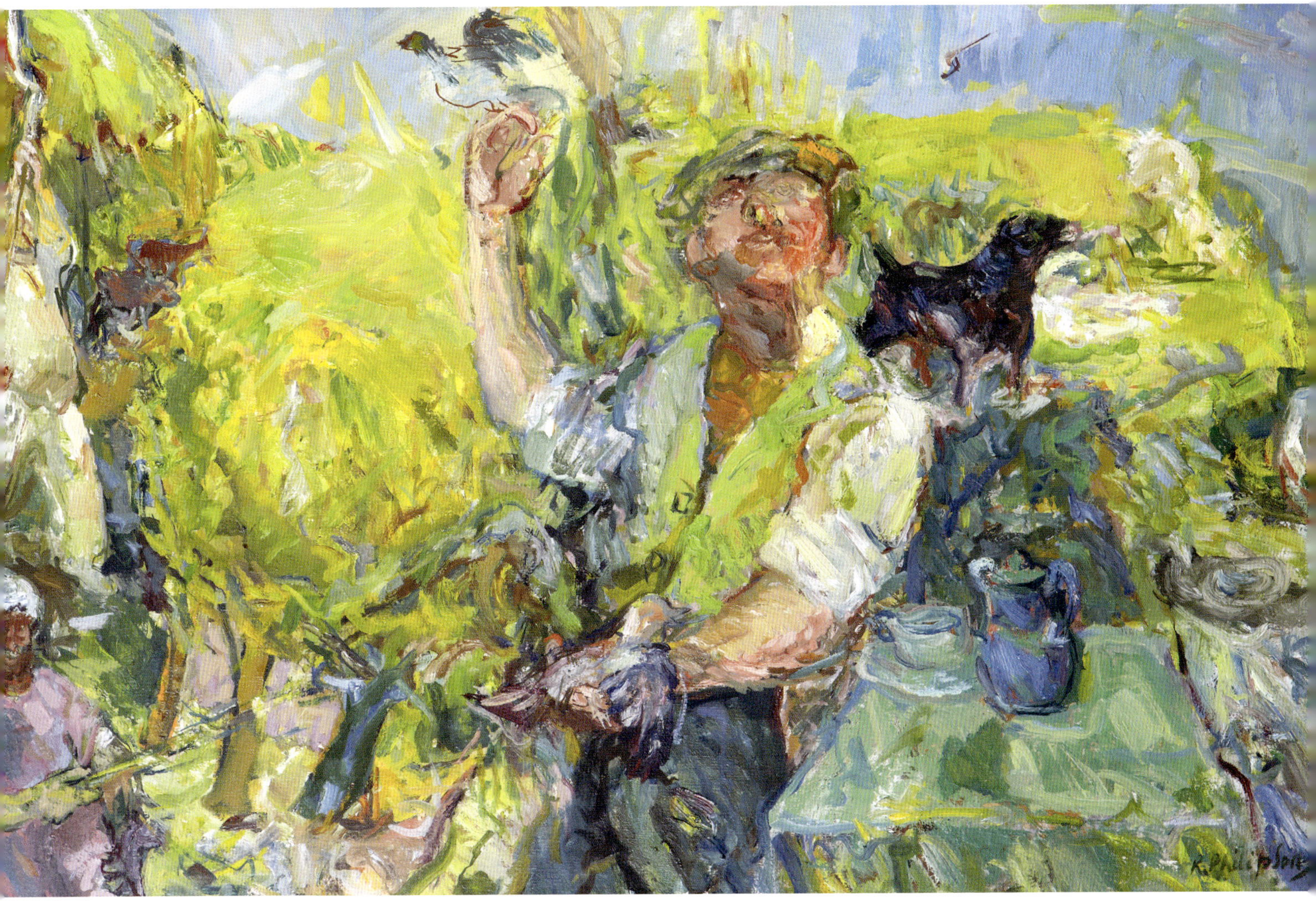

FIG. 2.5
Summer Morning
1952 / oil on canvas / 62 x 96 cm
City Art Centre, City of Edinburgh Museums & Galleries • photo: Antonia Reeve

▸▸ FIG. 2.6
The Countryside
1954 / oil on canvas / 82 x 102 cm
courtesy of Duncan R. Miller Fine Arts, London

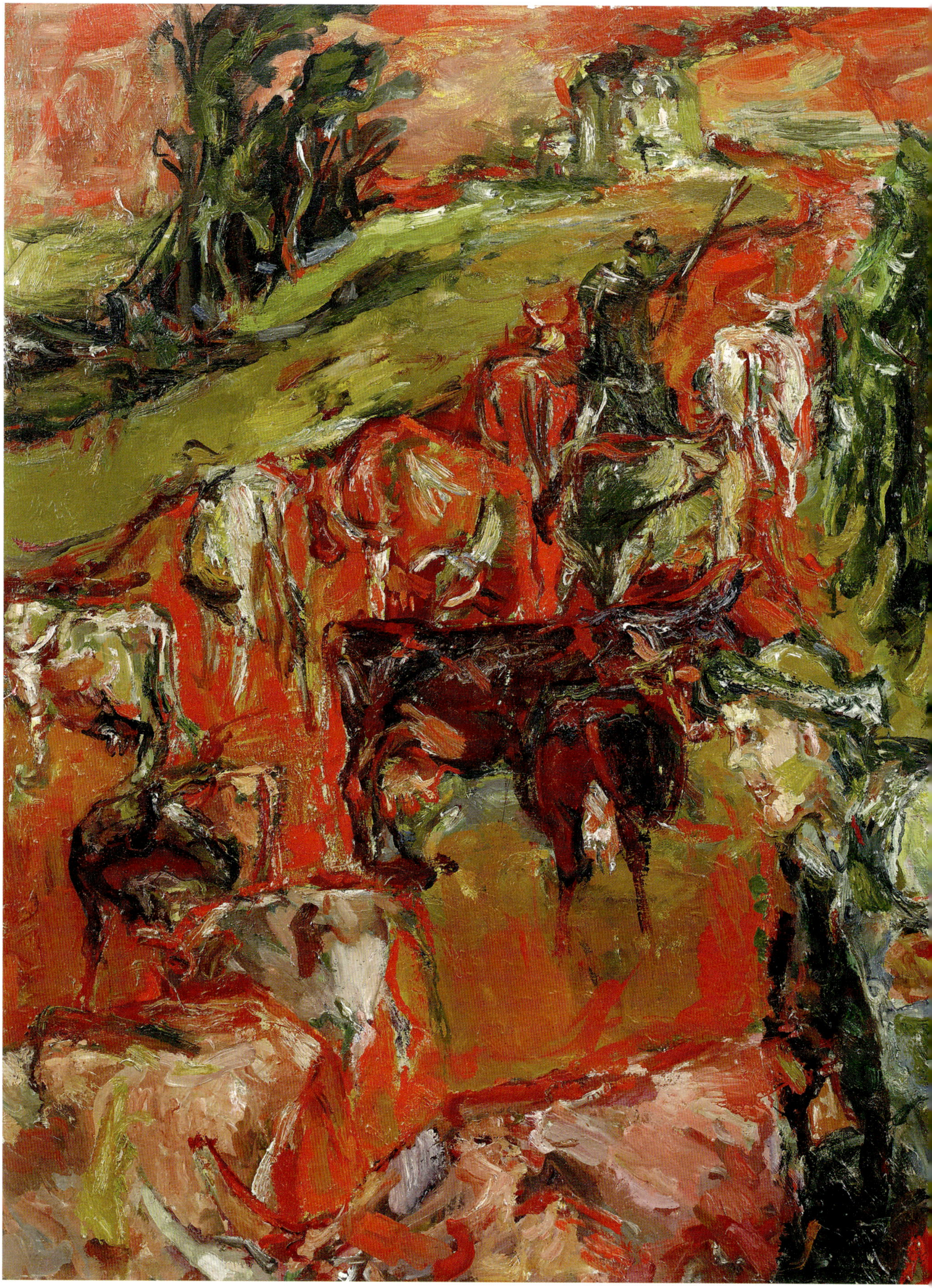

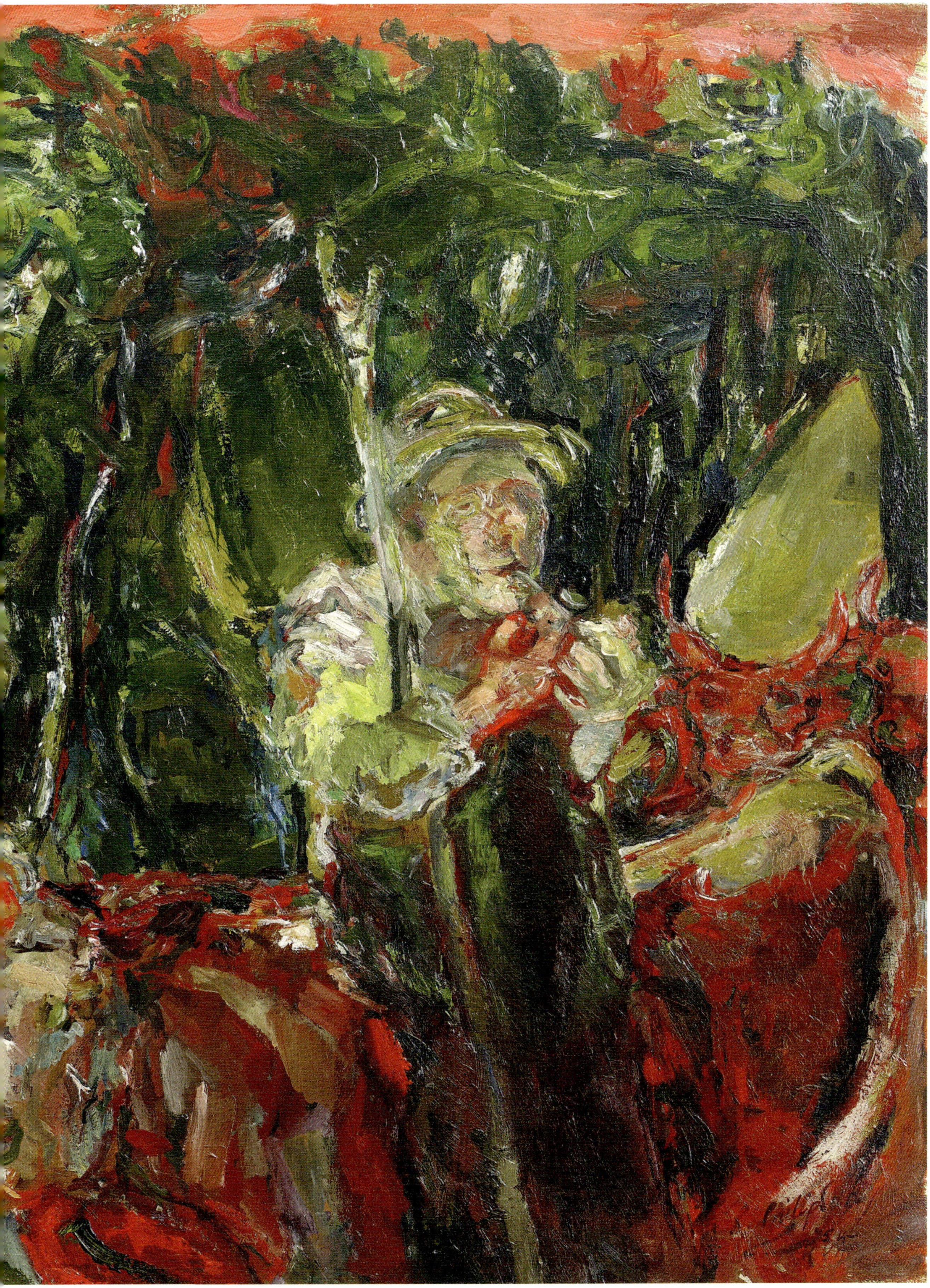

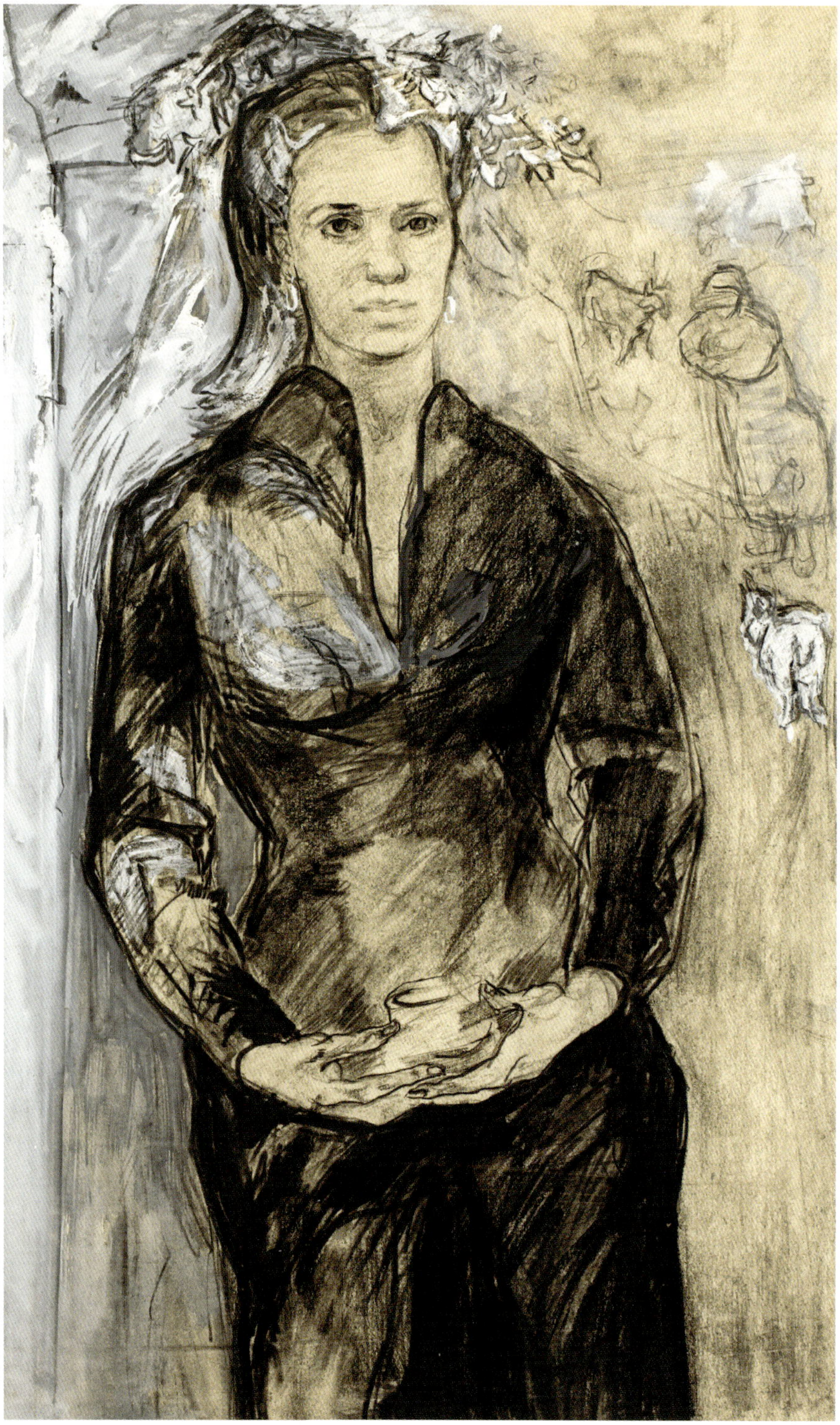

FIG. 2.7
Study for Brenda: Spring Portrait
1951 / chalk and gouache on card / 63.5 x 40 cm
private collection • photo: Antonia Reeve

▸ FIG. 2.8
Brenda: Spring Portrait
1951 / oil on canvas / 102 x 61 cm
private collection • photo: Antonia Reeve

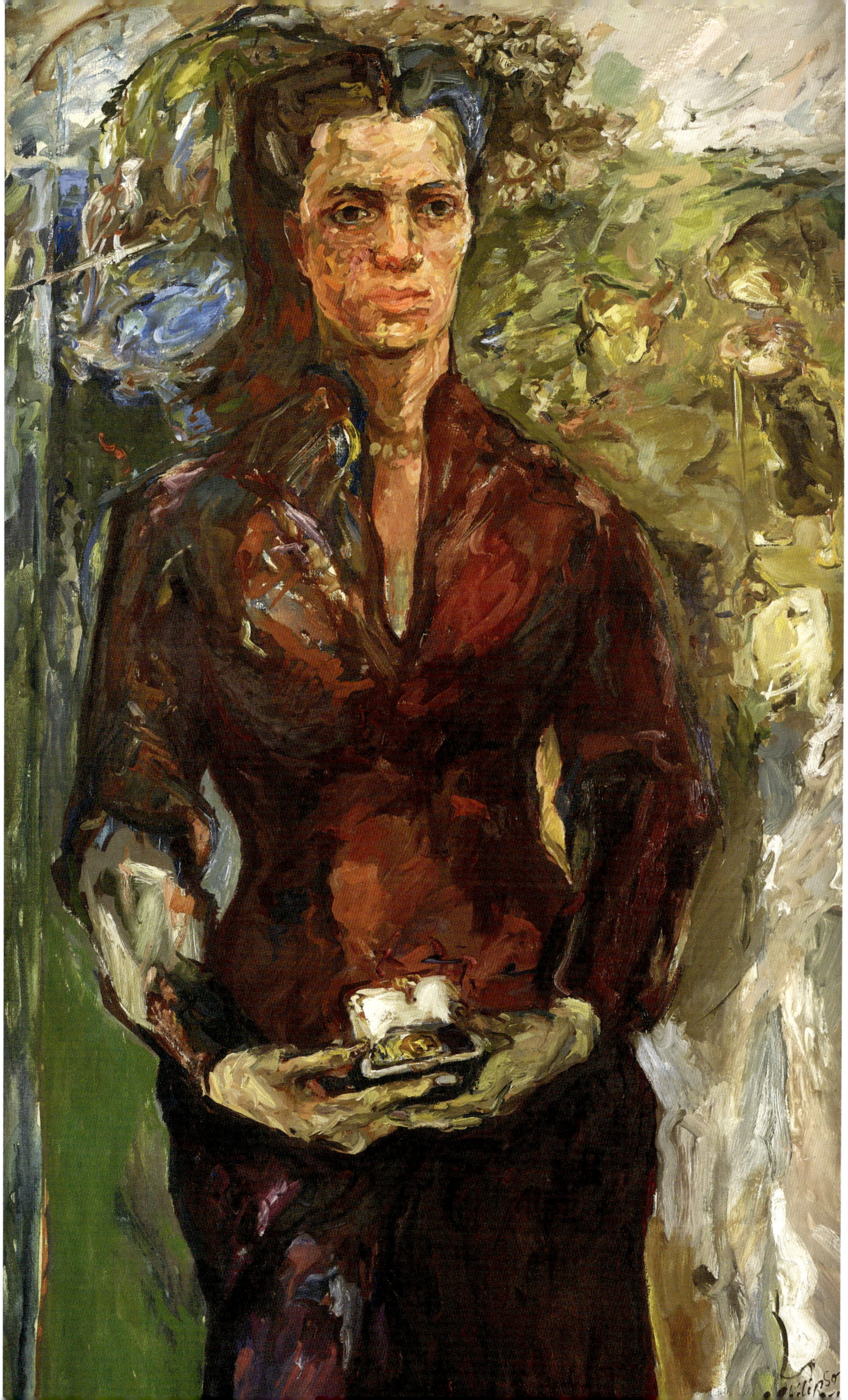

Also from 1954 is Robin's now celebrated view of Edinburgh Castle from his north-facing College studio which applied the freedom of his watercolour studies to a work in oils [fig. 2.1].

Brenda preferred a more neo-romantic approach to painting, whether a subject piece or a still life. Many of her paintings evoke a dream world and show the lasting influence of her former tutor, John Maxwell, and her admiration for Marc Chagall. She had exhibited with the SSA from 1951, the RSW from 1953, the RSA from the following year – when she won the Keith Prize for her oil, *Two Figures* – and also with the Women's International Art Society in London. As an employee of the EEA in the early '50s, she was engaged by Edinburgh Corporation to provide a mural decoration for Peffermill School in south-east Edinburgh, a commission which continued the pre-war tradition of art in Edinburgh schools [fig. 2.9].[7] The Italianate mural depicted a village wedding. Only a photograph of it has survived as it was painted over in the 1960s and the school was later destroyed by fire, but her palette can be imagined – reds, pinks and browns, greens, whites and a degree of blue. She was by now well known and respected in local art circles, and would be awarded the RSA's Guthrie Award in 1957 for her lyrical painting.

By now both were firmly establishing their careers as professional painters. The 1953 RSA exhibition had included, alongside a typical figurative painting of tinkers plus two landscapes, Robin's expressionist portrait of Brenda, *Going to the Garden Party*, painted with a passionate de Kooning brutalism in an autumnal palette [fig. 2.10]. His work was now raising interest, and in 1954 Aitken Dott's Scottish Gallery

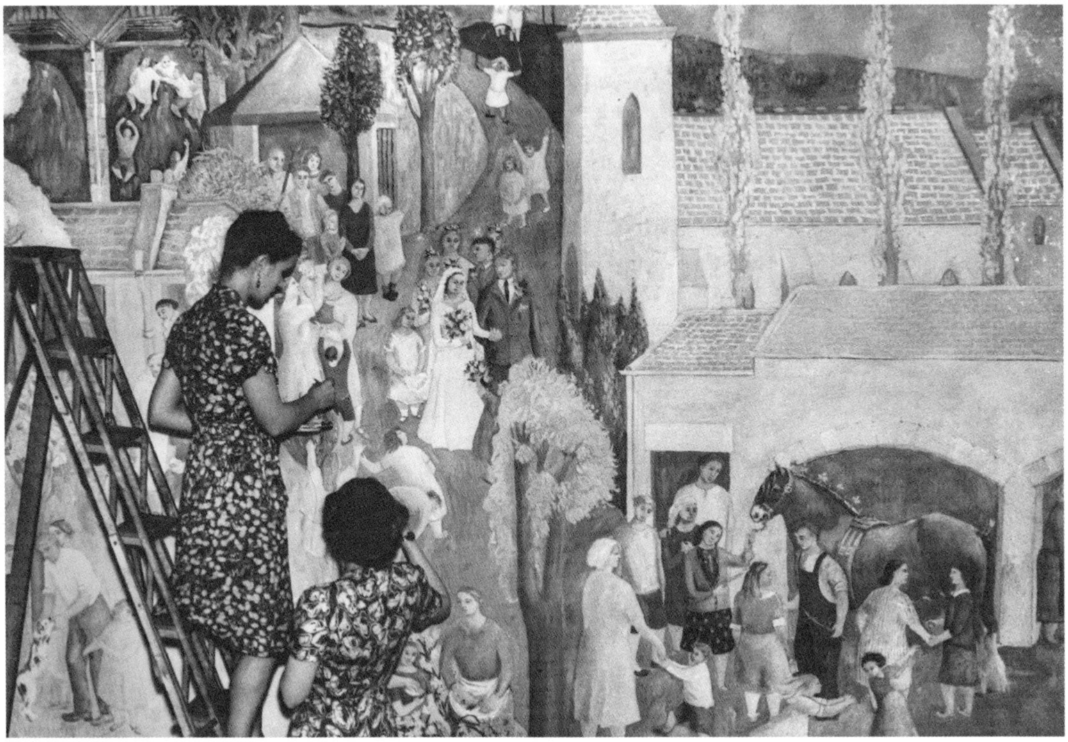

FIG. 2.9
Brenda (left) and unknown artist painting the mural at Peffermill School, *c.*1955
private collection

► FIG. 2.10
Going to the Garden Party
1952 / oil on canvas / 111.7 x 83.9 cm
National Galleries of Scotland
photo: Antonia Reeve

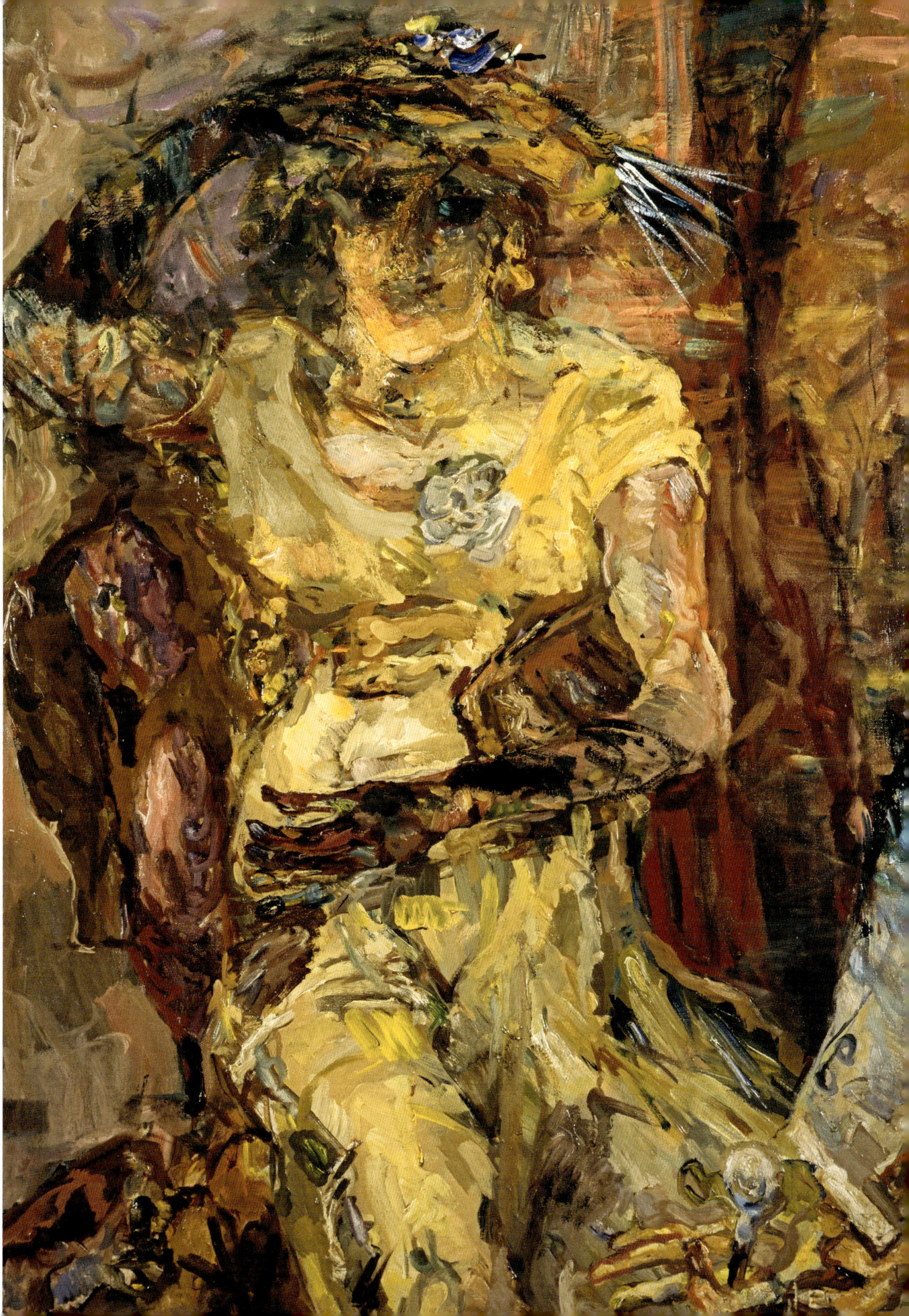

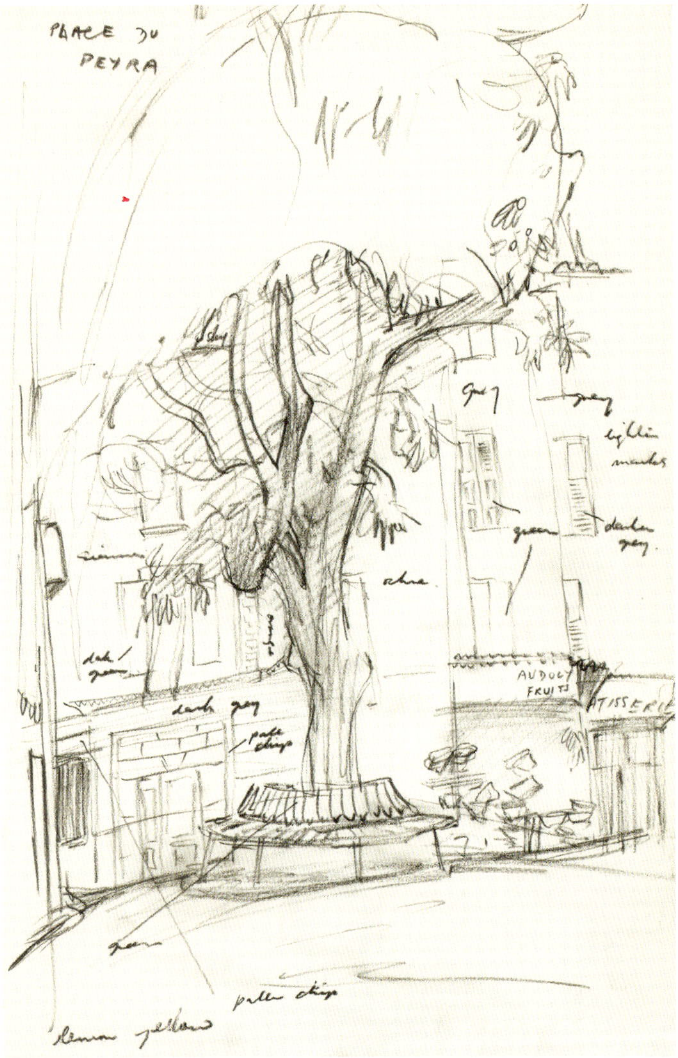

FIG. 2.11
Study of Place du Peyra, Vence
*c.*1957 / pencil on paper (sketchbook) / 37 x 23.5 cm
private collection • photo: Antonia Reeve

in Edinburgh offered him his first one-man show. He was also part of 'Six Scottish Artists' in a show sent by Aitken Dott to Canada and participated in a mixed show with Gillies and Redpath at the Crane Gallery in Manchester. A mixed show with Aitken Dott the next year would include both Robin and Brenda: 'Recent Paintings by Joan Eardley, Brenda Mark, R. Henderson Blyth, William A. Burns, David A. Donaldson, Robin Philipson'.

The 1954 one-man show was modern and progressive, and included such paintings as *The Countryside*. Robin's former tutor, Robert Westwater, reviewed it in October on BBC radio – the Scottish Home Service's *Arts Review*. He referred to him as a 'romantic painter, even a latter-day fauve' preoccupied with the effects of climate on landscape, and an artist who painted with passion, producing expressionist work whether landscape or still life. Westwater commented on the paintings of cockfights, inspired by what the artist had witnessed in Burma during the war, 'the ferocity and fatal scurry' of the fowl. He noted, however, that at times the ambition outweighed the result. He was above all 'a firm colourist', if addicted to 'rather obvious schemes'.

In the mid-1970s Robin would mention to Maurice Lindsay that Bobby Henderson Blyth should be thanked for the cockfight idea, spotting it as a foreground detail in a 1946 painting of Robin's of a villager and a soldier enjoying a game. This was an 'action subject' that Robin had first sketched in Burma in a 1943 watercolour, *Angami Nagas*. In his quest for subjects through which to explore expressionist ideas, Robin latched on to this as one to develop, with its rich potential and emotional power, and it would become one for which he would become well known. It was the first instance of a thematic approach, and themes would continue to provide a grounding for his ideas.

At the same time Soutine's fowl studies may be mentioned as a source for the early cockerel paintings, and of course the cockerel is a symbol of France. Over the years Sax Shaw and Robin would tease one another about which of them had first come up with the idea of the cockfight, and certainly Shaw had designed an elegant tapestry of cocks fighting for Dovecot Studios in 1950.[8] Like the Philipsons, Sax and Maisie Shaw were devotees of French culture, visiting the country most summers. In July 1950, for example, they had all holidayed together in France.

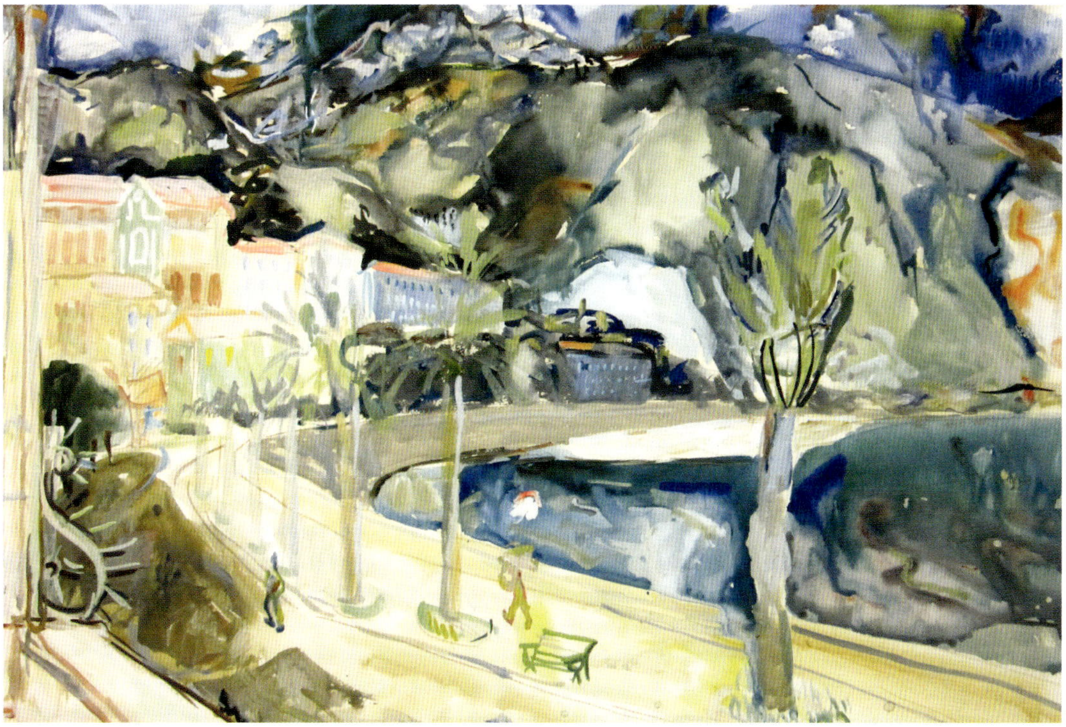

FIG. 2.12
Menton
1950 / gouache on paper / 36 x 54 cm
private collection • courtesy of the Scottish Gallery

From Paris they headed south, visiting Aix-en-Provence, taking in the local festival exhibition at Les Amis des Arts on the Cours Mirabeau, plus the Musée des Tapisseries and the local casino. Robin and Brenda were very taken with the town of Menton [figs 2.11, 2.12], and returned there several times over the years, motoring over in their Austin. On at least one occasion they rented a house there with the artist Nora O'Brien (known as Nobbie) – one of the regular Saturday morning crowd back home – and her husband, the French scholar Charles Chadwick (Chad), a fine cook who produced delicious meals for everyone.[9]

Having fixed on his subject of cockfights, Robin researched it in considerable detail. A sketchbook in the Philipson family archive contains not only drawings made of town squares and landscapes in the south of France but also close studies of live and dead poultry. Back home he visited a local poultry research unit where he could study the movements and colour of cockerels, finding their actions mesmerising but 'fiendishly difficult' to capture [fig. 2.13]. Notes made by Jack Firth in the early 1990s mention that the first recorded painting of a cockfight was executed in 1952.

Robin's 1954 one-man show drew on a supply of paintings and drawings from the previous two years and certainly included an oil and a watercolour both entitled *Fighting Cocks* [fig. 2.14] plus a watercolour called *Fighting Cocks: Prelude*. The remaining thirty-six works were landscapes and townscapes, including a view of Edinburgh in Coronation Year, still lifes, figure studies – a nude study plus one of bathers – and several of animals. The fresh landscape watercolours clearly show his teacher's influence. Among the particularly joyful and freshly atmospheric paintings from these times are the views of Gardenstown visited with Gillies in 1953

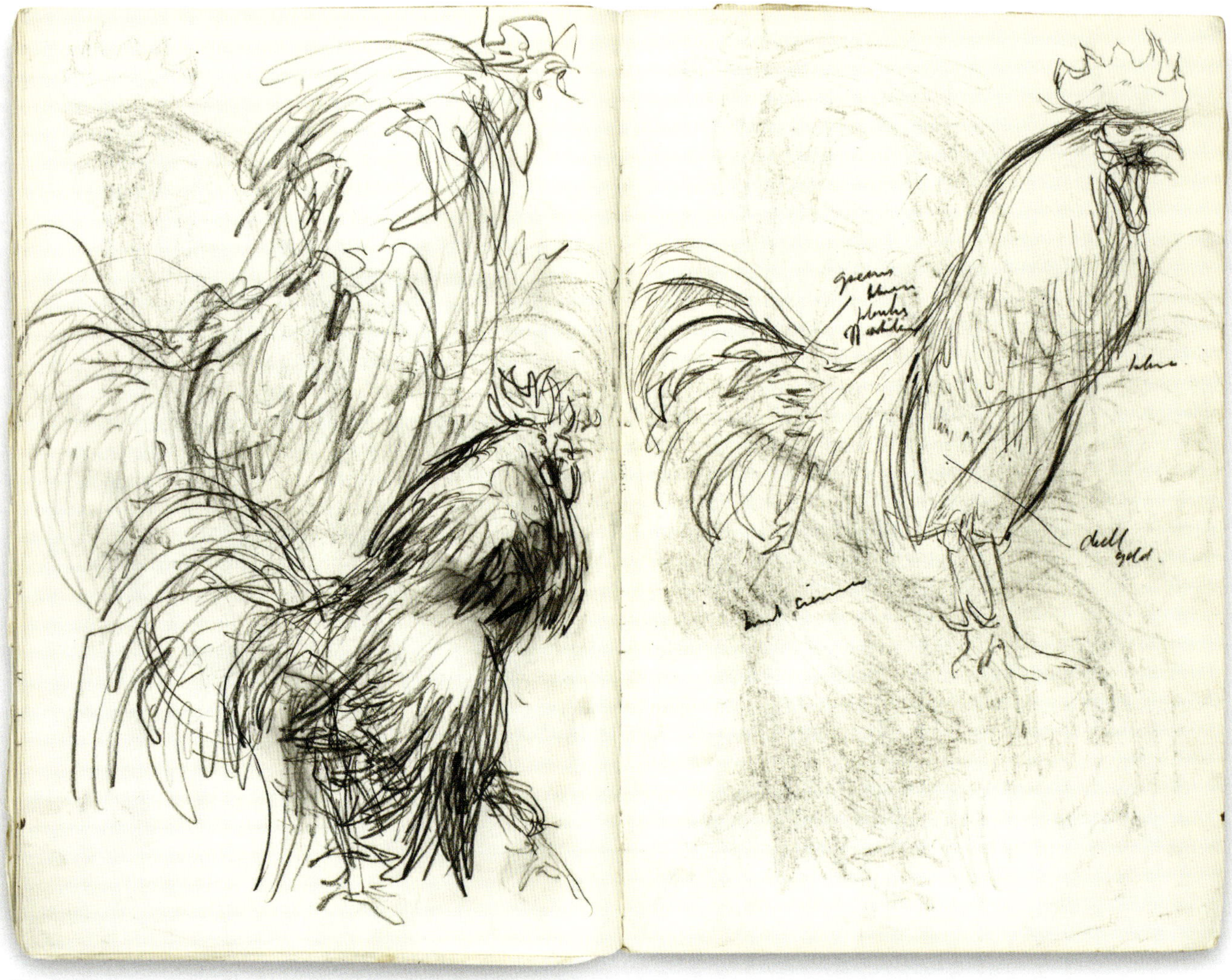

FIG. 2.13

Studies of Cockerels

*c.*1957 / pencil on paper (sketchbook) / 37 x 47 cm

private collection • photo: Antonia Reeve

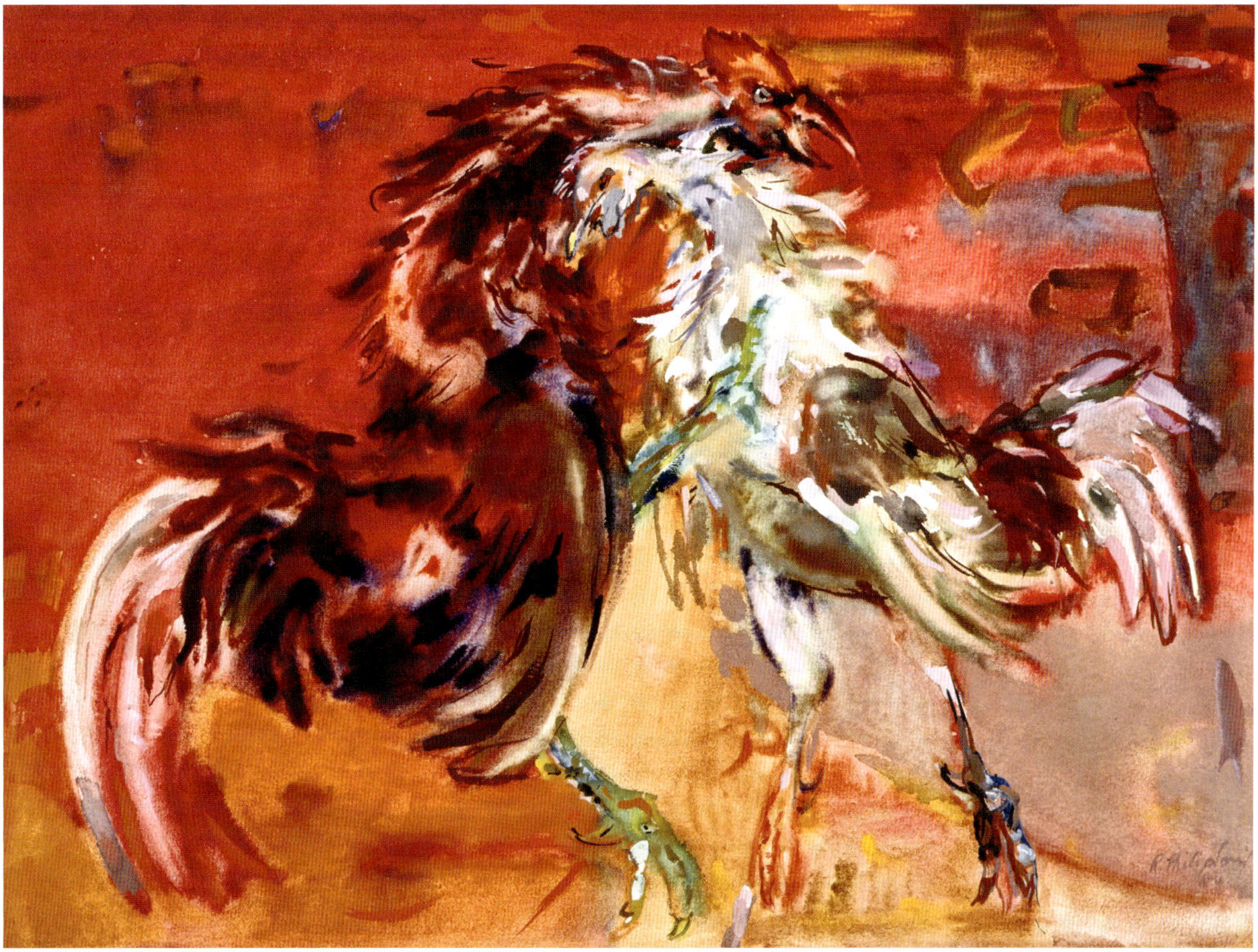

FIG. 2.14
Fighting Cocks
1954 / watercolour on paper / 50 x 66 cm
private collection • photo: Antonia Reeve

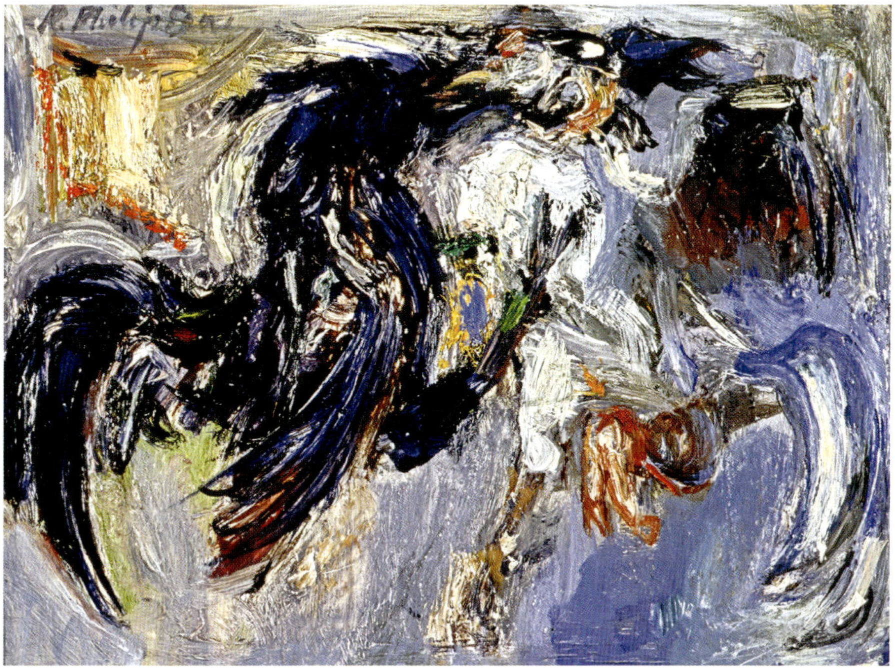

FIG. 2.15
Fighting Cocks
*c.*1961 / oil on canvas / 15 x 21 cm
private collection • photo: Antonia Reeve

[figs 2.16, 2.17]. With Brenda, Robin also enjoyed exploring coastal locations ranging from Fife to Cornwall and France.

Following his election in 1952 as an Associate of the RSA, Robin was elected a professional member of the RSW in 1955. That summer, the Philipsons as usual headed for France, with Robin visiting Paris studios on behalf of the SSA to research a display of paintings by Nicolas de Staël at its 1956 exhibition. The figurative paintings from shortly after the visit are vigorous, with form coming second to impassioned brushwork. But it was the cockfights which, in their majesty and rawness, provided a match between subject and energised brushstrokes [fig. 2.15]. Robin continued to paint cockfights into the late 1960s and far beyond, returning to use it as a motif in the 1980s. As discussed in a later chapter, it would be celebrated as a 'recurrent and significant theme'[10] in an important touring exhibition of 1970 curated by Bill Buchanan of the Scottish Arts Council.

If the Cockfight paintings kickstarted the idea of adopting a theme, a parallel cathedrals 'series' – as it soon became – opened up a new way of working a painting. Although familiar with, and indeed to an extent inspired by, Monet's celebrated studies of Rouen cathedral, Robin wanted to cut his own cloth and find new meaning and expression for a traditional subject. Initial studies of the formal architecture of French cathedrals, and especially Gothic window tracery viewed from the exterior, gave way gradually to an interest in the glass itself [figs 2.18, 2.19]. Interiors were at least as dynamic, and he produced a number of rose

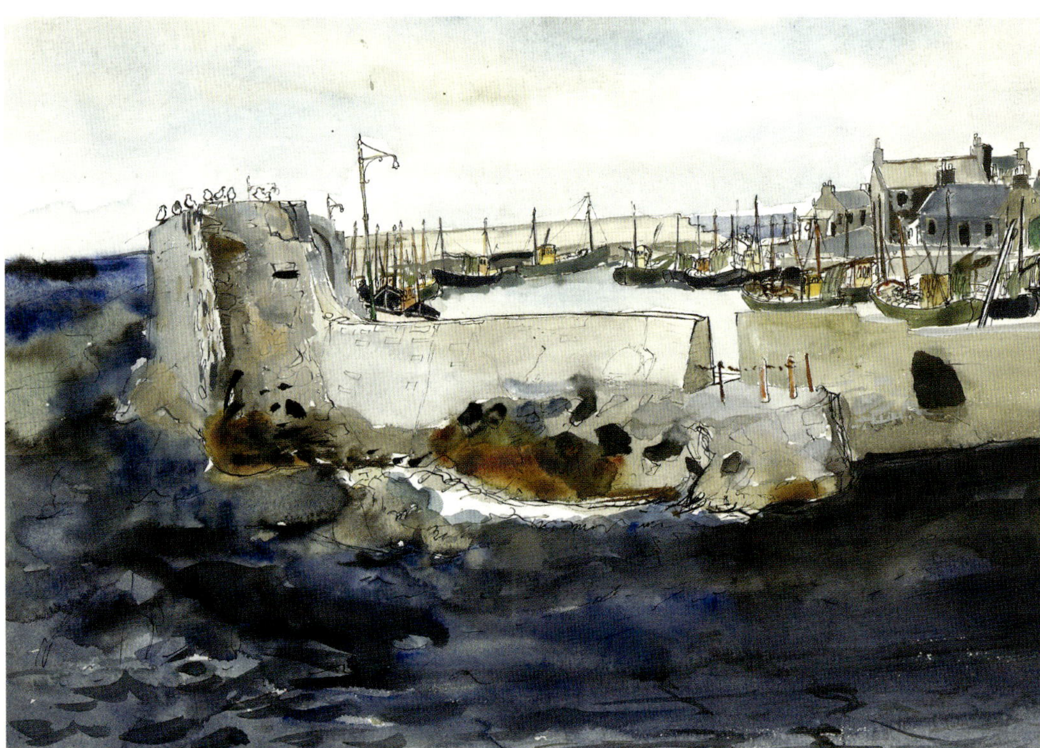

FIG. 2.16
Macduff Harbour
1953 / ink and watercolour on paper / 35 x 49 cm
private collection • courtesy of the Scottish Gallery

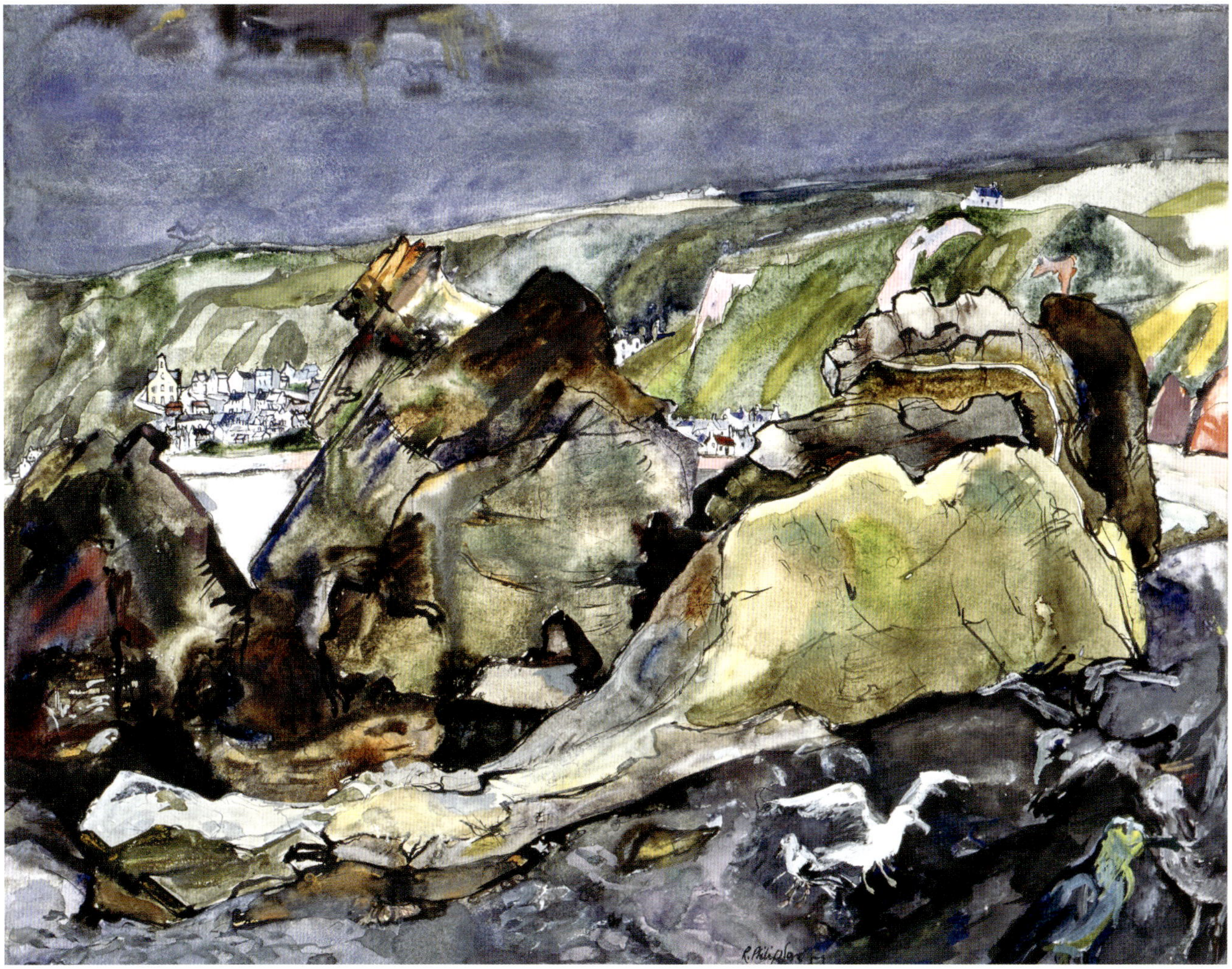

FIG. 2.17
Rocks at Gardenstown
1953 / watercolour, gouache, ink and gum Arabic on paper / 50.5 x 63.5 cm
National Galleries of Scotland • photo: Antonia Reeve

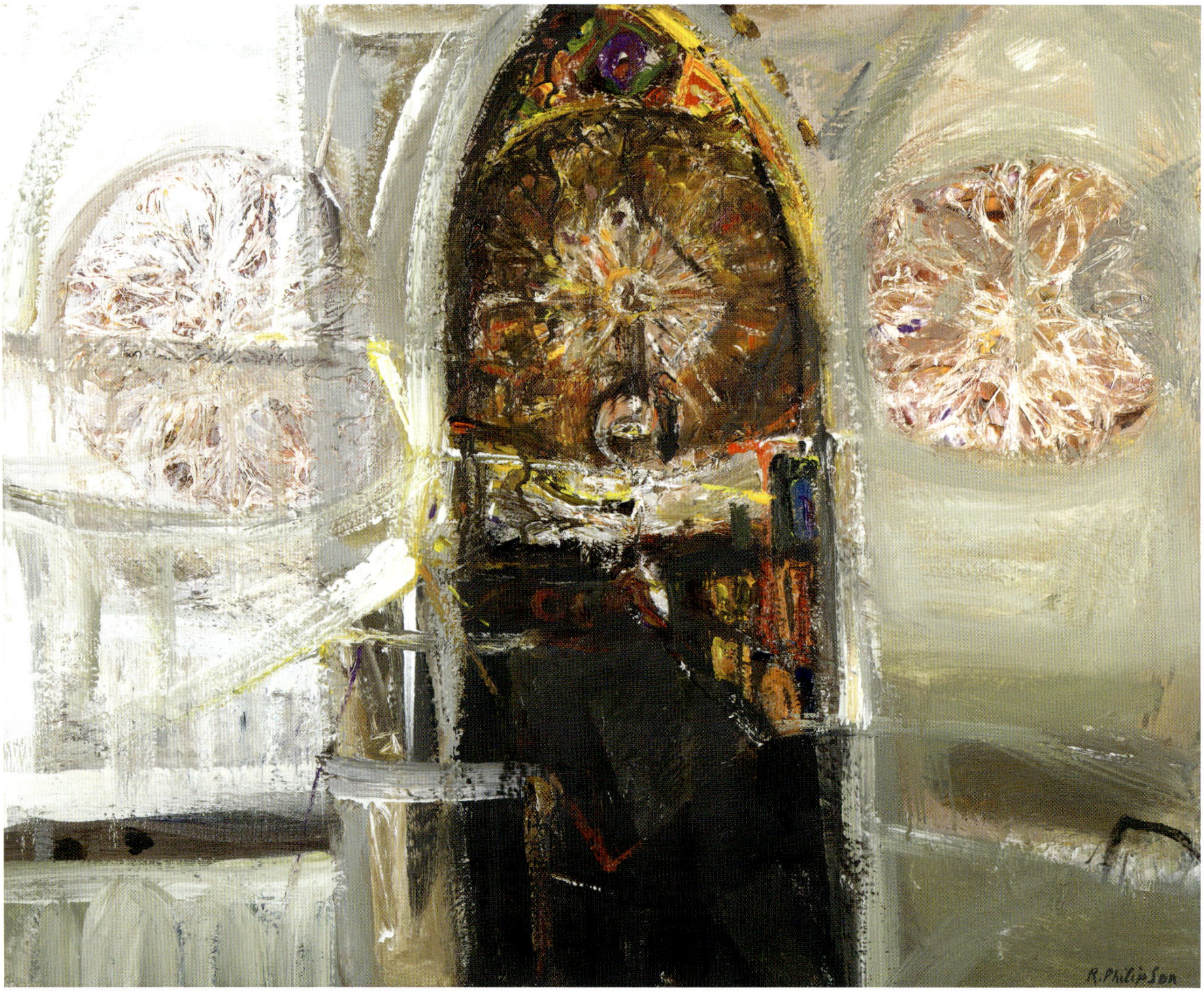

FIG. 2.18
Three Windows
*c.*1963 / oil on canvas / 62.2 x 74.6 cm
Dumfries Academy, on loan to Gracefield Arts Centre • photo: Mike Bolam

▸ FIG. 2.19
Cathedral, Red
1961 / oil on canvas / 183 x 101.6 cm
National Galleries of Scotland • photo: Antonia Reeve

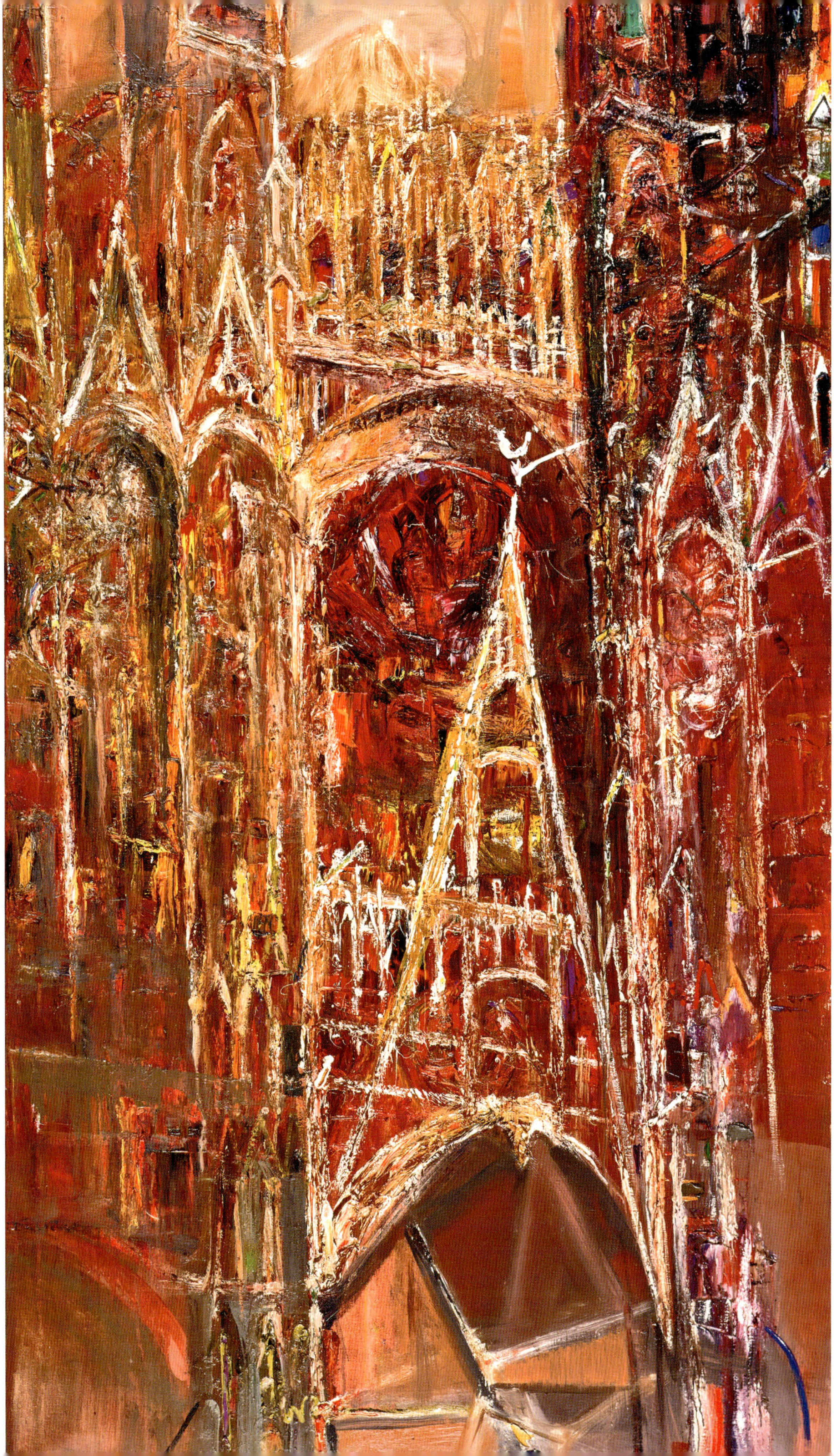

window paintings which were entrancing works in light and space. They were the result not only of his first-hand experience of the form and splendours of churches in northern France, notably Amiens, during summer vacations but also of conversations with Sax Shaw. Robin's fascination with the ways in which light was coloured by stained glass was also in his nature, going back even to his childhood delight in those translucent Rowntree Fruit Gum sweets.

It was difficult to capture the complete experience of an interior bathed in glorious colour if he continued to work in his recent brutalist way. Keeping an overall composition, Robin started to plan his canvas by subdividing it into areas, each with its own value and arrangement and not least often brilliant, powerful colour. This allowed a positioning of several complementary views of an interior and the source of its light, the traceried window, alongside each other to communicate its character: the whole as the sum of many parts. It was a consciously structural approach where light illuminates an interior from several directions as a multi-dimensional perspective is presented. By working within an underlying structure Robin was free to indulge his growing taste for expressing complicated colour and texture relationships to explore times of day.

As themes were found, Robin was increasingly participating in open exhibitions. In 1956 the Walker Art Gallery announced the John Moores painting exhibition to replace the pre-war Liverpool Autumn Exhibitions, with the first show to be held in 1957. This was to be an exhibition of painting 'embracing the best and most vital work being done today throughout the country'. Robin decided to enter in the 'open' category. The judges were the painter and art historian Lawrence Gowing, critic and writer Eric Newton and two curators, Sir John Rothenstein of the Tate and the Walker's own director, Hugh Scrutton. More than two thousand entries were submitted, with 181 paintings selected. Although Robin was not awarded a purchase prize – those went to Jack Smith, Victor Pasmore and Ceri Richards – Liverpool's collections did acquire, as a gift from Sir John Moores, the oil *Edinburgh in Summer*, which is a view from the Calton Hill, a favoured vantage point for sketching of Robin's [fig. 2.20]. The success of the first John Moores exhibition meant it would be repeated two years later and thereafter become the British painting biennale. In 1959 Robin again entered the competition, and this time he would win the third prize of £300 jointly with Ceri Richards. The invited artists included William Scott (1913–1989), Carel Weight (1908–1997) and Redpath. Newton chaired the selection panel, with Alan Bowness from the Tate, André Chastel, Gabriel White and Scrutton. Newton was a supportive critic of Robin's from this time. In May he reviewed the RSA annual exhibition for the BBC magazine *The Listener*, calling Robin's 'big visionary interpretations of Gothic cathedrals' the 'most ambitious exhibits'.[11]

By the late 1950s Robin's paintings were being seen not only in England but also in France. 'Five Scottish Artists' had been shown at the 1957 Menton Biennale (in part thanks to Robin's encouragement), while he also sent work to Nice as part of the 'Edinburgh-Nice' exhibition of 1958 at the Galerie des Pochettes to celebrate the twinning of the two cities. During their 1957 French holiday with Sax and Maisie they met Jean Cocteau, then supervising the painting of his mural in Menton's town hall. They were amazed to find a working artist so impractically, if elegantly,

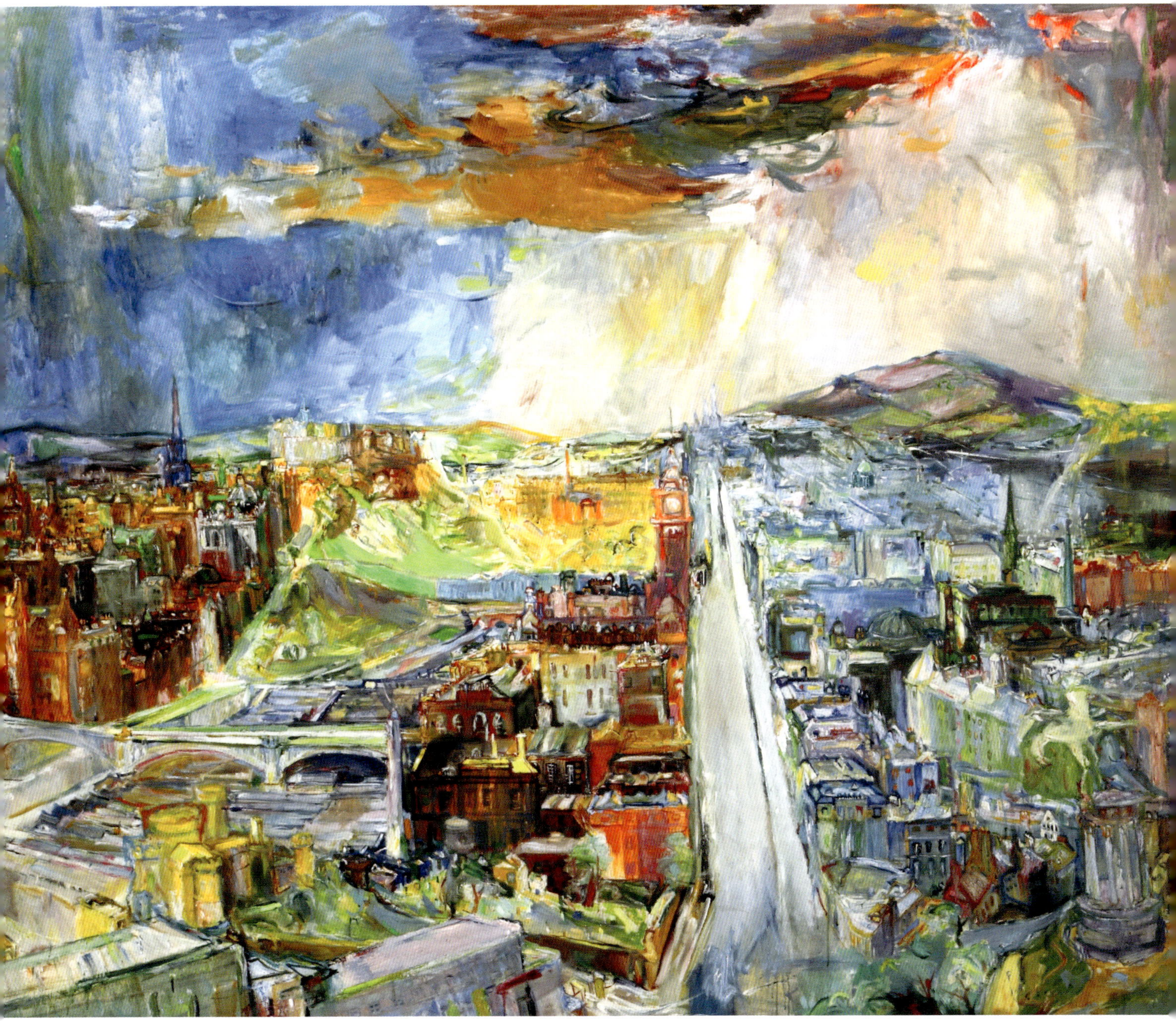

FIG. 2.20
Edinburgh in Summer
1956 / oil on canvas / 183.5 x 213.5 cm
National Museums Liverpool • photo: Public Catalogue Foundation

dressed head to toe in white, but Cocteau had in fact hired an elderly local artist to do the practical work.

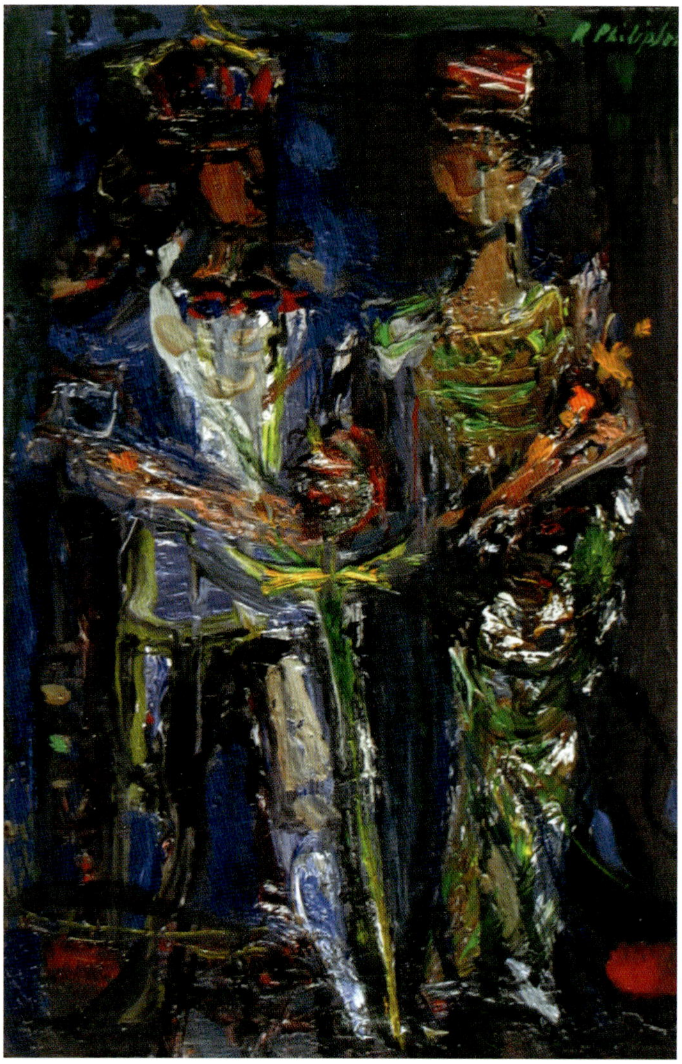

FIG. 2.21
King and Queen
*c.*1962 / oil on board / 27 x 17 cm
private collection • courtesy of the Scottish Gallery

Back in Scotland, Aitken Dott had helped negotiate Robin's inclusion in these mixed shows, and again presented a one-man exhibition at the Scottish Gallery in 1958. This time forty works were shown, and they included many devoted to another theme, kingship, as well as cockfights and still lifes and also the first of his cathedral paintings. Following such exposure, he was invited to take part in a group exhibition at the University of Nottingham's art gallery in May 1959. This show (which also showcased work by Maxwell) included five oils and five watercolours. The Philipsons had visited Tuscany in the summer of 1958, enjoying Italian culture and especially the art of Florence and Assisi. His subjects included landscapes, a still life of roses plus *Deep Sea* (an oil) and *Forest Pool* (a watercolour study), where colour and free technique represented the natural landscape. Armour seen in the Bargello in Florence had inspired the concept of kings on horseback, with two works in oil and watercolour included in this first show in England. Robin would recall that the armour, a symbol of 'man's obsession with conflict and prowess in arms', had taken possession of him.[12] The exotic set designs and paintings of Anton Clavé, whom he had met in Paris, also influenced the king paintings [fig. 2.21].[13] Conflict, as already witnessed in his cockfighting images, would reappear in the following decade under a different guise.

The watercolour *Equestrian Kings* was lent to Nottingham by Dr John Roberts. A lecturer in botany at the University of Edinburgh and a collector of contemporary works on paper, 'Jack' Roberts happened to be a neighbour of Johnston Douglas, of the printers Harley Brothers at 19 St James Square in Edinburgh. Harley's was a long-established firm which printed commercial products such as leaflets and labels, but in 1956 Douglas had been asked by a friend in the paper trade if he might print a colour lithograph for John Piper.[14] Douglas was aware of recent French developments in printmaking. In Paris the firm of Mourlot Frères, printer to Picasso and the École de Paris, was using similar equipment to that found at Harley's and this encouraged Douglas to embark on a new field of modern art printmaking. He also met Robert Erskine, then running the St George's Gallery Prints studio in London and, with Erskine's encouragement, set about bringing artists on board. Eleven prints by Piper would be printed at Harley's between 1956 and 1959; other English artists taken on in 1957 were Alistair Grant and Michael Ayrton (these two were the first artists to work in person with the printers at St James Square), Bernard Cheese and Terry Frost.[15]

Robin's role in developing Harley's output would be to bring in local artists, and these included himself. In 1957 he met Johnston Douglas through the College evening classes in printmaking with which Douglas was by now involved [fig. 2.22]. Robin soon became engrossed in printmaking and was fired by its technical challenges. His first print was *Fighting Cocks: Prelude*, which was pulled in an edition of fifty-nine, and in the same year *Roses* was printed in an edition of fifty [fig. 2.24]. These related to paintings already made which he would show in Nottingham two years on. Importantly, he also introduced Anne Redpath (1895–1965) to Harley's, and her print *Cocktail* came off the press the same year. Redpath herself played a role in the development of this key printmaking studio by suggesting to Douglas that he might approach the Scottish Committee of the Arts Council (the forerunner of the Scottish Arts Council) to discuss funding for its Scottish artists. As a result, the Committee agreed to purchase £1,000 worth of lithographs if it were to be involved in the selection of the artists. The sum of £500 would be advanced, with the rest supplied when its list of prints were fully editioned. This increased Harley's real potential as a base for good Scottish art printmaking.

The list of artists who became involved is impressive, and with Robin's help the Committee and firm chose well. A number of artists were his colleagues or former students at the College of Art [fig. 2.23]. David McClure, a former student, after

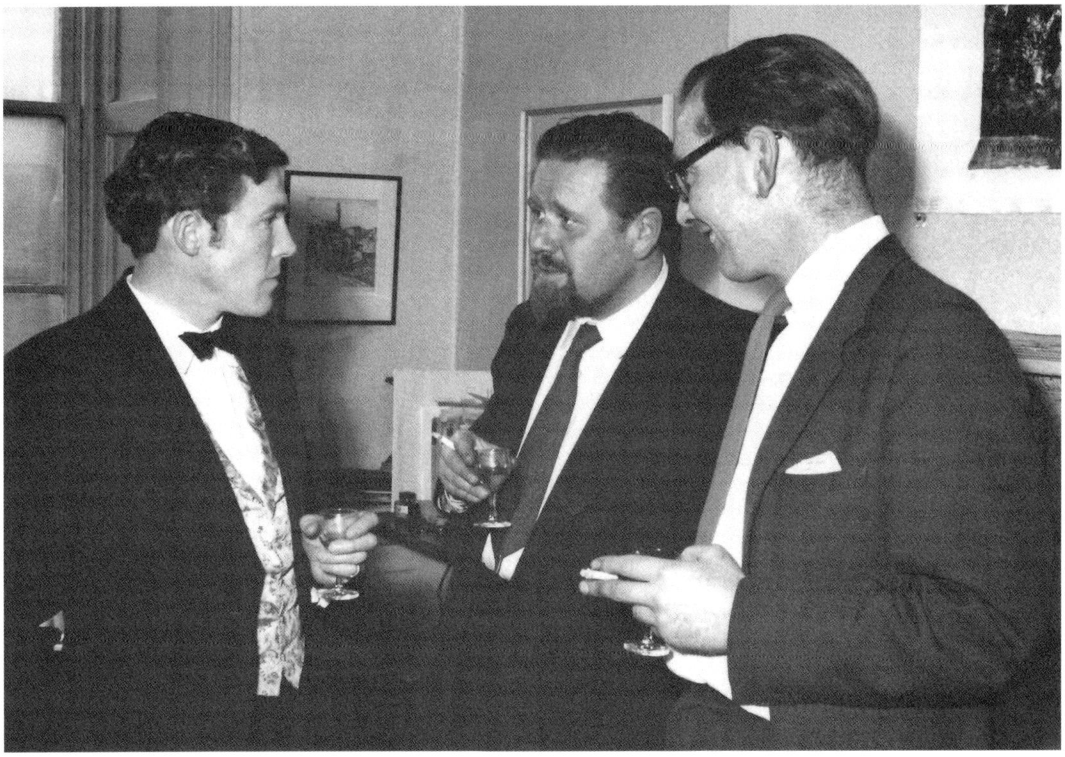

FIG. 2.22
Robin (left) with Michael Ayrton and Johnston Douglas at Harley Brothers, Edinburgh, 1958
private collection • photo: Ronald Wilkie

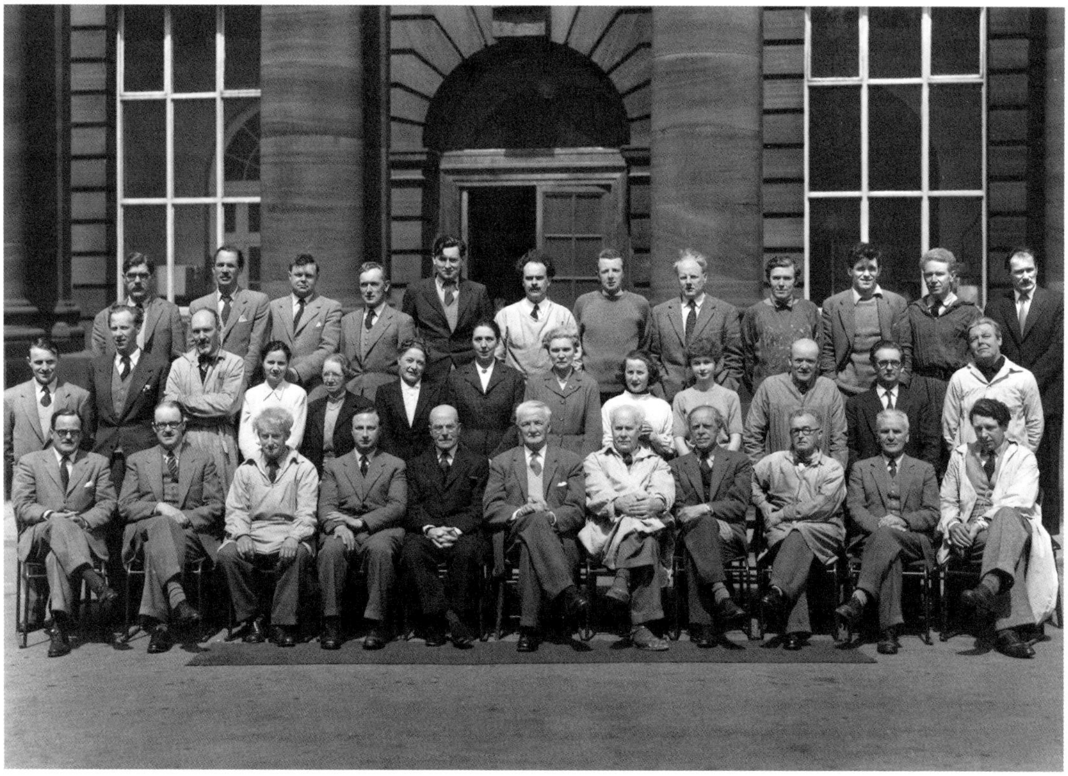

FIG. 2.23
Edinburgh College of Art staff, 1957–58, with (front row) William Gillies, Dr T. Elder Dickson and principal Robert Lyon seated third, fifth and sixth from the left and (back row) Robin, John Houston and James Cumming standing fourth, fifth and seventh from the right
Records of the Edinburgh College of Art, uncatalogued material, University of Edinburgh • photo: F.R. Yerbury & Son

some teaching at the College in the 1954–55 session, had recently joined the staff of Duncan of Jordanstone College of Art in Dundee. They remained friends, and Robin had shown a joyously coloured double portrait of him with his wife Joyce at the RSA in 1955 [fig. 2.27] for which a number of fine preparatory pencil studies were made [fig. 2.26].[16] Other artists producing prints included Elizabeth Blackadder (born 1931), her husband John Houston and David Michie, all former students who were now teaching part-time in Lauriston Place. Another contributor was the stained glass artist Willie Wilson (1905–1972), also a College colleague.[17] Redpath made a total of six prints in 1957 and 1958, and in 1958 a further three prints of Robin's were editioned, of which *King* is probably the best known [fig. 2.32]. First issued in an edition of seventy-five, it was also printed in a tiny edition of five for Green and Abbot, furnishing contractors to the British Railway hotels: this was in a second colour variation, with pale green replacing the magenta of the first printing. The other prints he made were *Peasant* [fig. 2.25], in an edition of seventy-five, and *Compôte of Fruit*, in an edition of seventy.

Using graphic values and colour to realise an idea sat in stark contrast to the demands of oil painting or watercolour. Although Robin taught drawing in both day and evening classes at the College, such an entrée to the values of printmaking was exciting and lasting. He would henceforth design his own Christmas cards to be printed in the College for the rest of his life; from the late 1960s, when he was more influenced by Pop Art and notably by Peter Blake (born 1932), these often contain a reference to a recent event or record the family [fig. 2.28]. He focused

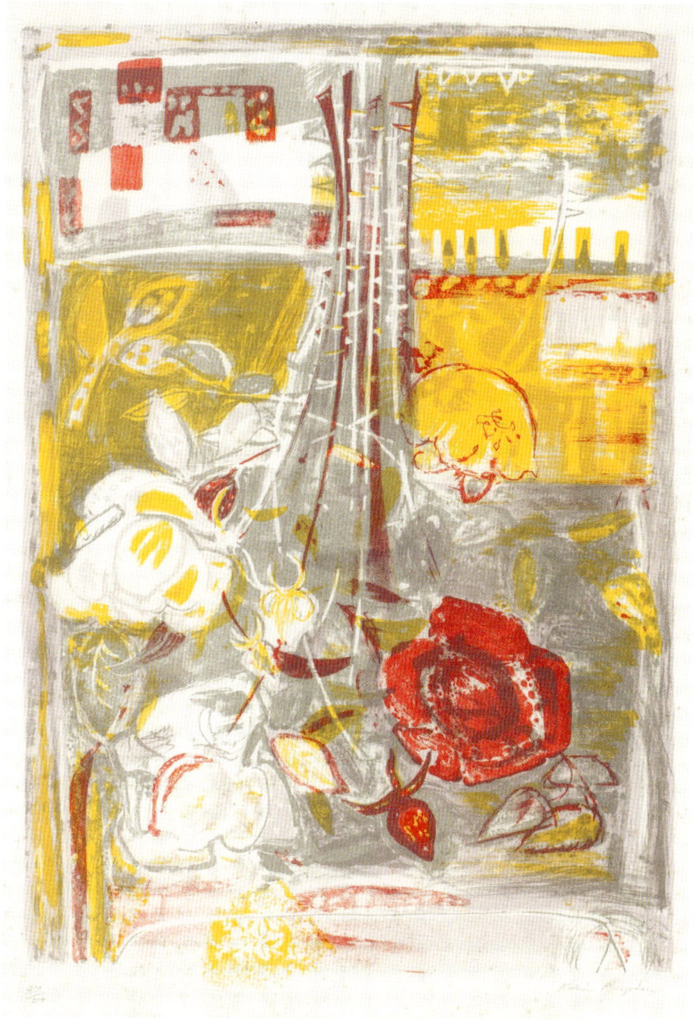

FIG. 2.24
Roses
1957 / lithograph / 64 x 43.3 cm
private collection • photo: courtesy of Bonhams

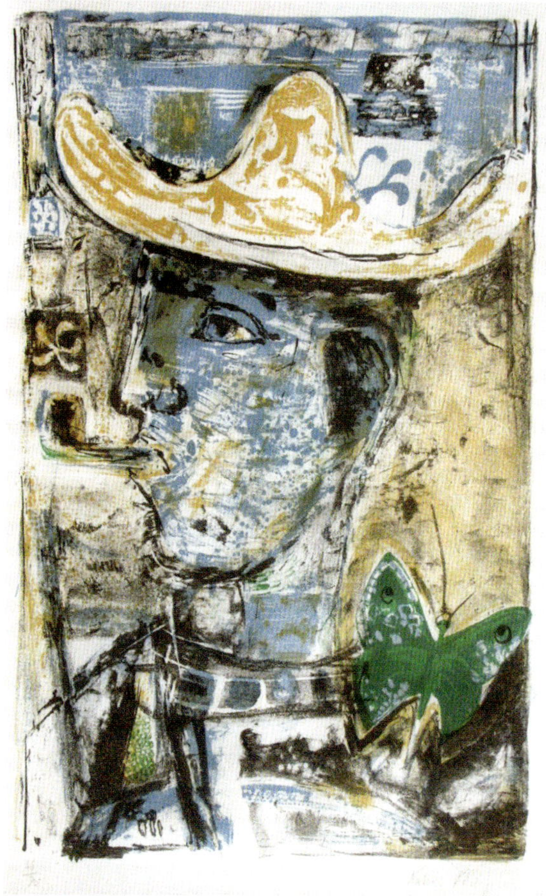

FIG. 2.25
Peasant
1958 / lithograph / 45 x 28.7 cm
private collection • courtesy of the Scottish Gallery

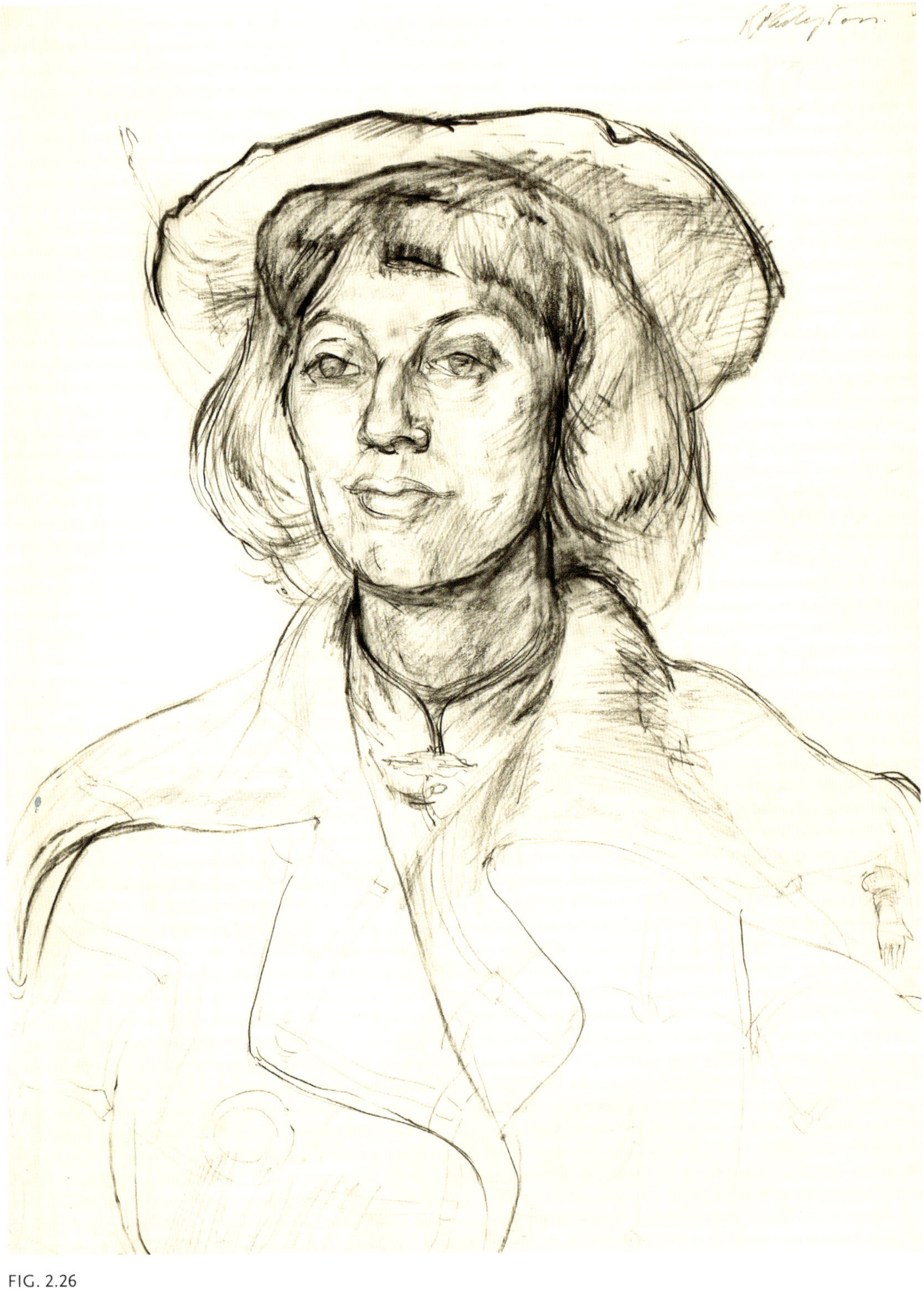

FIG. 2.26
Study for Portrait of David and Joyce McClure
*c.*1954–55 / pencil on paper / 54 x 40 cm
private collection • photo: Antonia Reeve

▸ FIG. 2.27
Portrait of David and Joyce McClure
*c.*1954–55 / oil on canvas / 127 x 102 cm
private collection • photo: Alan Richardson

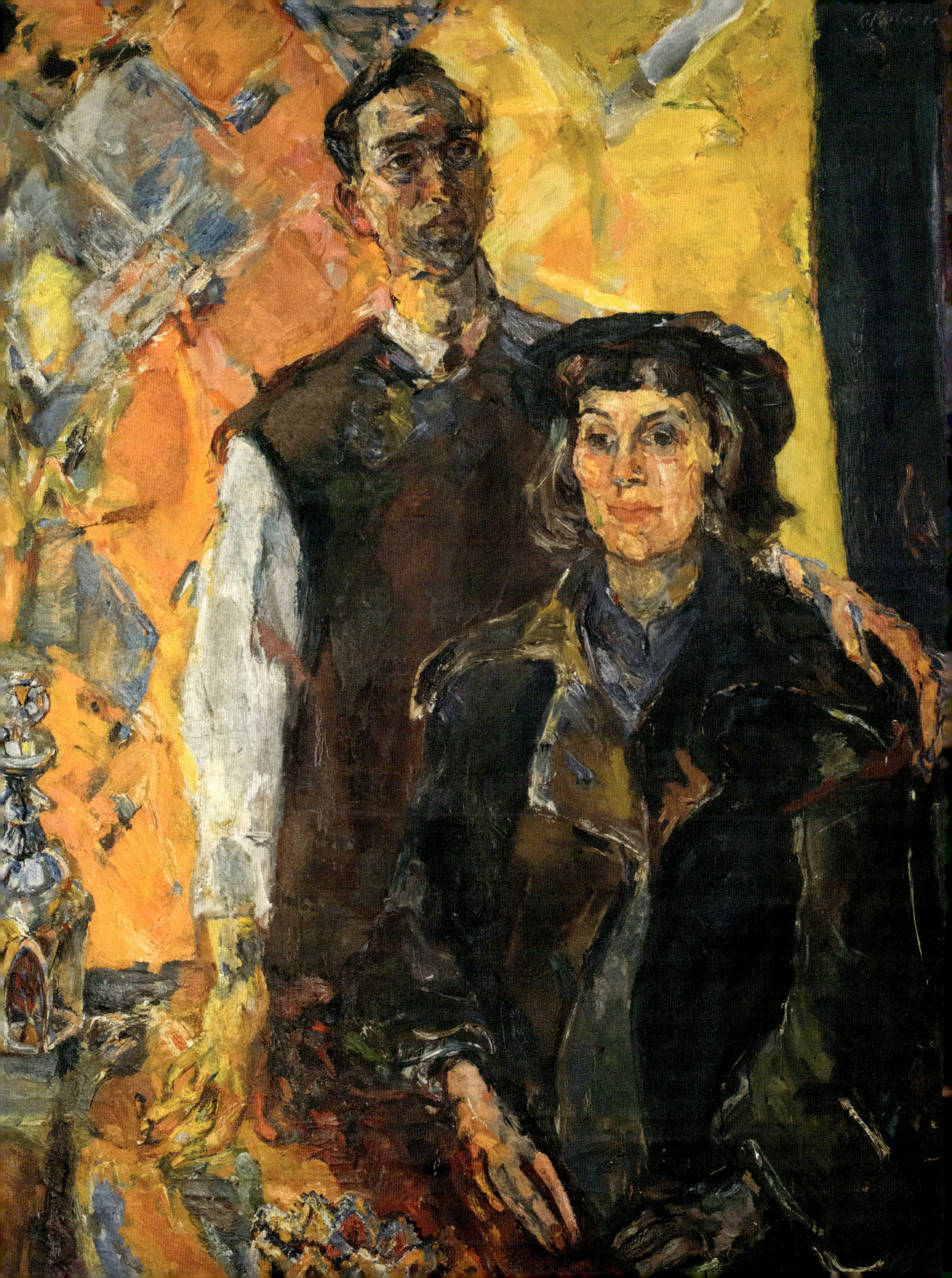

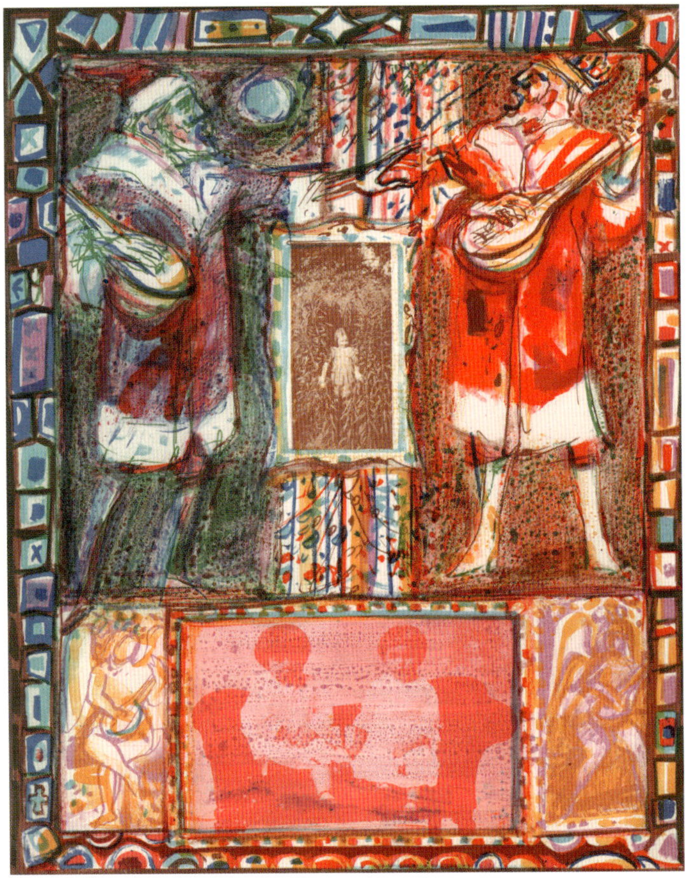

FIG. 2.28
Robin and his second wife Thora's Christmas card for 1972: the design incorporates a photograph of young Thora taken by her brother Henry and one of Phyllis and Robin when young
private collection

on the importance of pure colour in design, and, as a result of his early Harley work, was invited by the Edinburgh International Festival's committee to design the ticket brochure, poster and souvenir programme [fig. 2.29] for the 1958 Festival. His key motif was a drummer member of the town guard, which appeared on the cover of the programme alongside the Scott Monument, printed by Harley in red, yellow and black, and inside as a one-colour black image. Its success led to a repeat commission for 1959, and, unlike later Festival designs, a different image was required [fig. 2.30]. This time it was more directly festive – a trumpeting harlequin and his horse, which was printed on the souvenir programme cover and poster in a smart colour mix of sugar pink, orange and black, and an equestrian image in subtle shades of grey and black on the ticket brochure cover. A more vibrant design, the harlequin was particularly successful; but no further Festival designs would be made. A full set of advertising was designed each year, ranging from posters to a quite new mode of commercial art, the car sticker. His work for the Festival led directly to a private commission from the poet Margaret Tait to design the jacket for her anthology *The Hen and the Bees* (1960), in which a honey palette was chosen to match the title [fig. 2.31]. His graphic work also included designing bookplates for other friends, including Maurice Lindsay. All were printed by Harley.

While it was in Robin's nature to be ambitious for his art, it was always important for him to work closely with friends. Jack Roberts was just such a one, and another key friend in these years was Robert Scott Hay (1904–1965), a man he may have met through Harley's. Scott Hay hailed from Edinburgh and had joined the Langholm textile company Reid & Taylor in 1933 after serving an apprenticeship with Adam Paterson in Haddington and with Dr Oliver of Galashiels, 'the great doyen of the woollen industry'. He had taken charge of the company's design and production on the early death of its managing director, Fred Graham. Through the war the firm, which produced fine twisted cloth for men's suiting, had been forced to turn out khaki cloth. As managing director after the war, Scott Hay knew that competition from home and abroad for quality suiting would be fierce, and he worked tirelessly to keep Reid & Taylor ahead of the game.

It may seem curious to mention Reid & Taylor here, but for several years either side of 1960, design was hugely important to Robin. He and Robbie Scott Hay

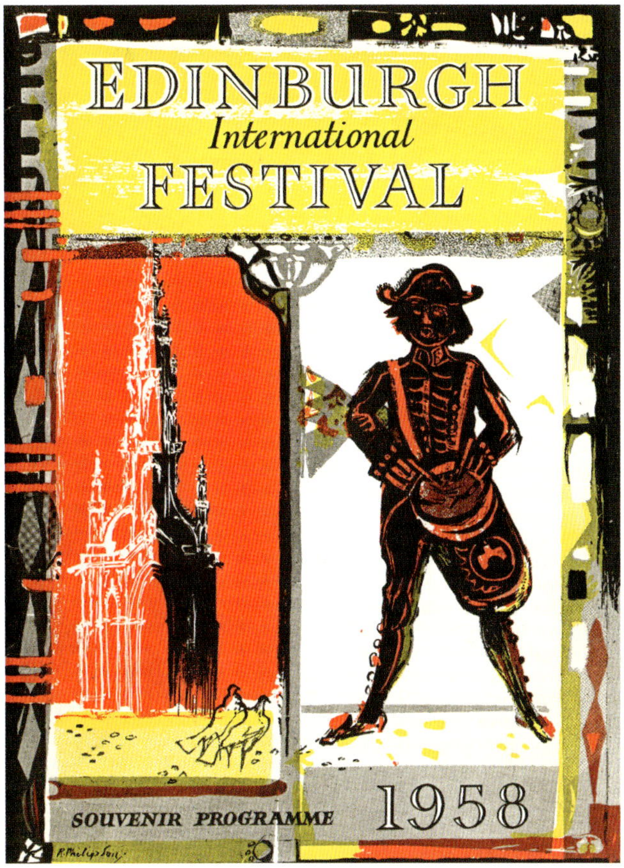

FIG. 2.29
Cover for the souvenir programme, 1958 Edinburgh International Festival, 25.7 x 18.3 cm
private collection • photo: Antonia Reeve

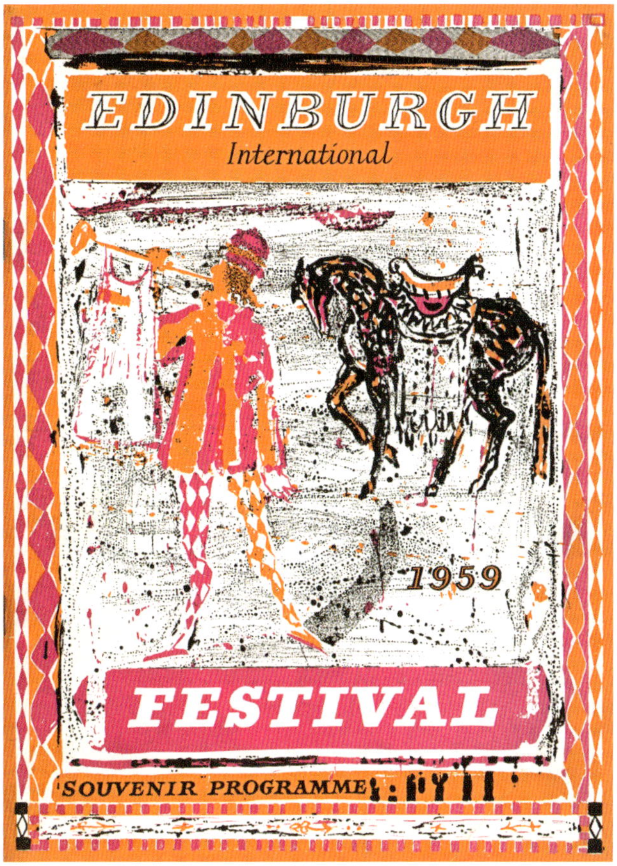

FIG. 2.30
Cover for the souvenir programme, 1959 Edinburgh International Festival, 25.7 x 18.3 cm
private collection • photo: Antonia Reeve

enjoyed debating colour, its use in art and its application in design. In December 1959 Scott Hay invited him to a weekend conference at the Lockerbie House Hotel on 'Quality and Design' with three British cloth manufacturers. While the intention was primarily to emphasise the value of selling 'fine quality, well designed' woollen and worsted cloths to trade representatives, this was a key seminar with guest speakers Sir Albert Richardson, lately president of the Royal Academy, directors from Aspreys and a London psychiatrist, Dr W.P. Kraemer. Robin attended with Jimmy Cumming, with each registered under his private address – a sure indicator of personal commitment. Now Robin was seriously broadening his perspective with studio experiences in printmaking and design practice.

The 1950s had been a decade in which Robin's career had expanded in different directions as new challenges were sought and associations and friendships forged. By 1960, his art was to be found in public art galleries in Liverpool, Middlesbrough and Aberdeen (the last a print), plus the collections of the Contemporary Art Society and educational authorities in Yorkshire, Nottinghamshire and his own Dumfries. In 1959 he had participated in the Stirling Festival Fortnight and a Christmas group exhibition in Newcastle upon Tyne. And, as a direct result of works seen at Aitken Dott's in 1958, he was also signed up with the London dealer Lillian Browse for a one-man show in 1960. In addition, his public profile was also blossoming in the media, from an article on his art by D. Cleghorn Thomson published in Germany's

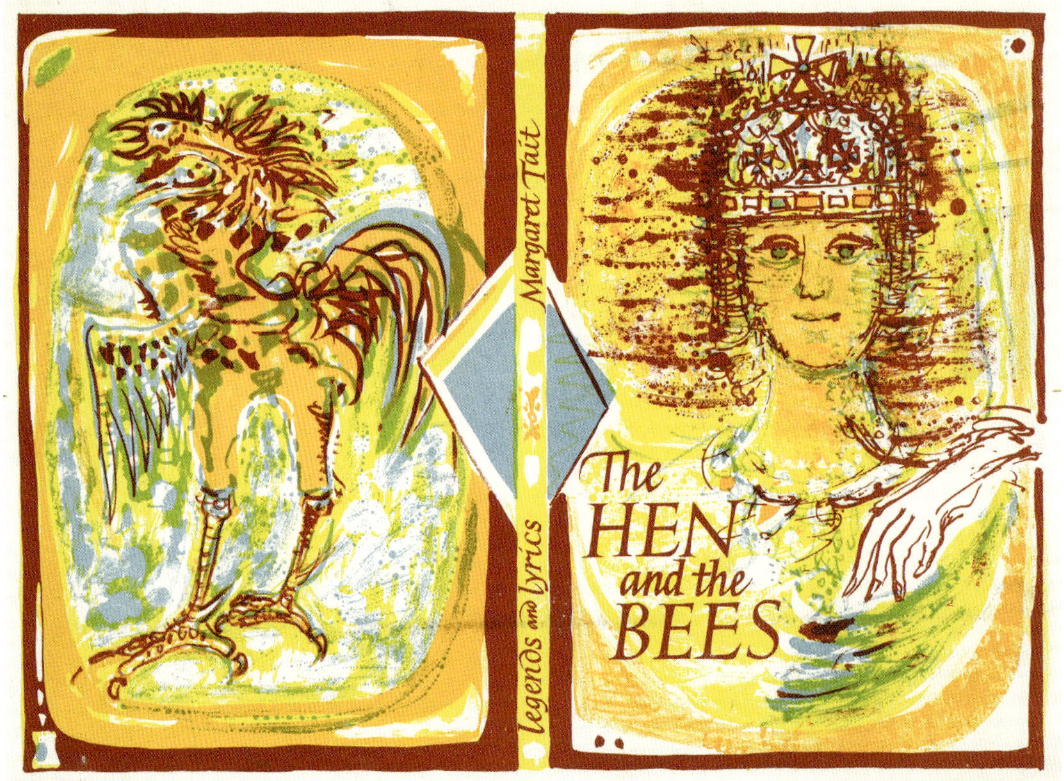

FIG. 2.31
Book jacket for *The Hen and the Bees* by Margaret Tait, 1960, 19.1 x 17.8 cm
private collection • photo: Antonia Reeve

Die Kunst in 1958 to radio interviews broadcast in Scotland, and even in Finland. This was also the age of the British public being introduced to the arts through television documentaries, with Huw Wheldon's *Monitor* series remaining the best known. In 1959 the BBC in Scotland, on the recommendation of Bill Gillies or Elder Dickson, invited Robin to talk to camera on the subject of 'Distortion' in an innovative television arts series called *Counterpoint*. This was followed by a discussion filmed with Dr Tom Honeyman, Glasgow Art Gallery's director, called 'Look at This' and in 1960 by a programme on the collection of fine French nineteenth- and twentieth-century paintings donated that year by Alexander Maitland to the National Galleries of Scotland. Here were paintings by Courbet, Picasso, Rouault, Vuillard and Bonnard which gave Robin the chance to talk passionately about them from an artist's perspective. Although the interview had made him apprehensive, the experience proved enjoyable for all concerned, and he was found to be a natural communicator. The producer of *Counterpoint* was the poet George Bruce (1909–2002), who immediately became a member of the Philipsons' circle. Through the making of both films, Robin also got to know National Gallery of Scotland curator Colin Thompson (1919–2007), then preparing to open the Gallery of Modern Art at Inverleith House. Thompson was one of the last national curators to have trained as a painter, and a professional rapport was soon established.[18] With all such varied interests and activities life was indeed full.

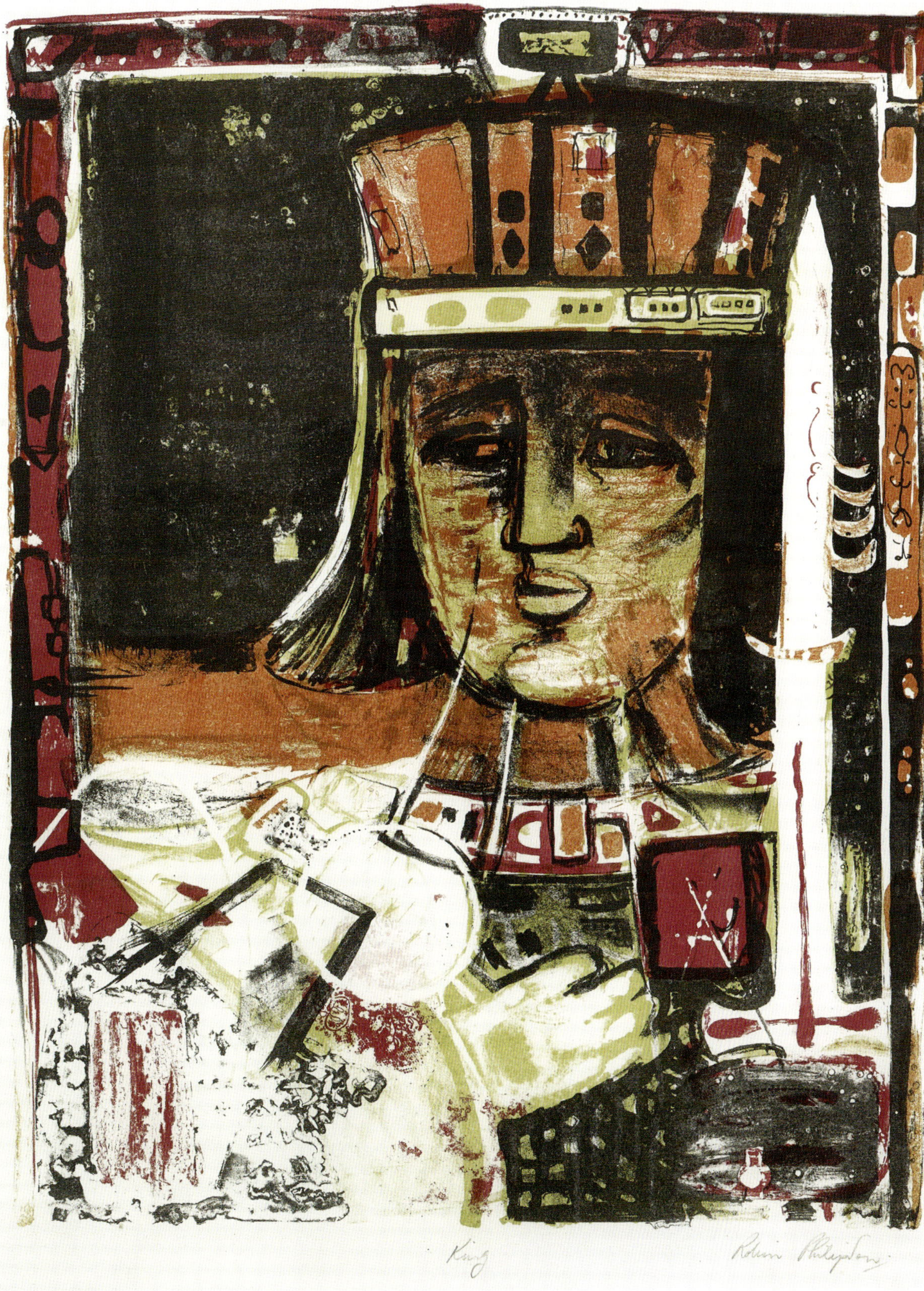

FIG. 2.32
King
1958 / lithograph / 58.3 x 43.2 cm
private collection • photo: courtesy of of the Scottish Gallery

3 NEW WORLDS

In late May 1959 an order was placed for a new car – this time a Morris Oxford Saloon de Luxe in off-white with smart red leather upholstery[1] – and, as soon as their teaching finished, Brenda and Robin set off for their annual summer holiday in France. The country offered the opportunity to visit exhibitions and explore the glories of cathedrals and their stained glass, and generally to enjoy the culture again. This holiday provided a good diversion for them both as Brenda had not been in good health for much of the year. In the autumn she was diagnosed as having a brain tumour, and in January 1960 had her first operation. Hospital visits and a second operation would follow, but on 20 September she died. She was only thirty-seven years old.

The year 1960 also brought major changes on the professional front. A little hesitatingly, Bill Gillies had been appointed Principal of the College and his vacated post of head of D&P was advertised in the spring. Robin applied in June, was appointed, and took up the post on his return from France. In his application he referred to his teaching experience as 'having worked in all subjects'. As an assistant his teaching had included still life, life painting, anatomy and mural painting. His application specifically referred to his development of the teaching of anatomy. He was known for the thoroughness of all his teaching, and in anatomy he had all his students draw the skeleton and apply the muscles stage by stage. As part of their rigorous training they were required to study the extraordinary museum collections of the University's medical school. Another area of teaching he had developed in the 1950s was in mural work where, following the departure of Rosoman, he had introduced painting on plaster for third-year students to give a more authentic experience.

Only a couple of weeks before Brenda's death, Robin had moved into the dedicated studio of the head of D&P. It is one of the largest and finest in any art school, facing north with a majestic view of Edinburgh Castle through the generous window – giving an even more glorious vista than the one that he had painted from the main D&P studios in 1954. He would have been glad at this time especially to have this good and private space. Bill Gillies was a huge support, continuing to shoulder some of the D&P work for some weeks of the autumn term. In October, with the worst (or perhaps was it the best?) possible timing, Robin's long-planned London one-man show opened at his new dealers Roland, Browse and Delbanco. The show was of cockfights and cathedral paintings already gathered in the studio, and thankfully it was well received. Robin's art was never easily produced, but Eric Newton,

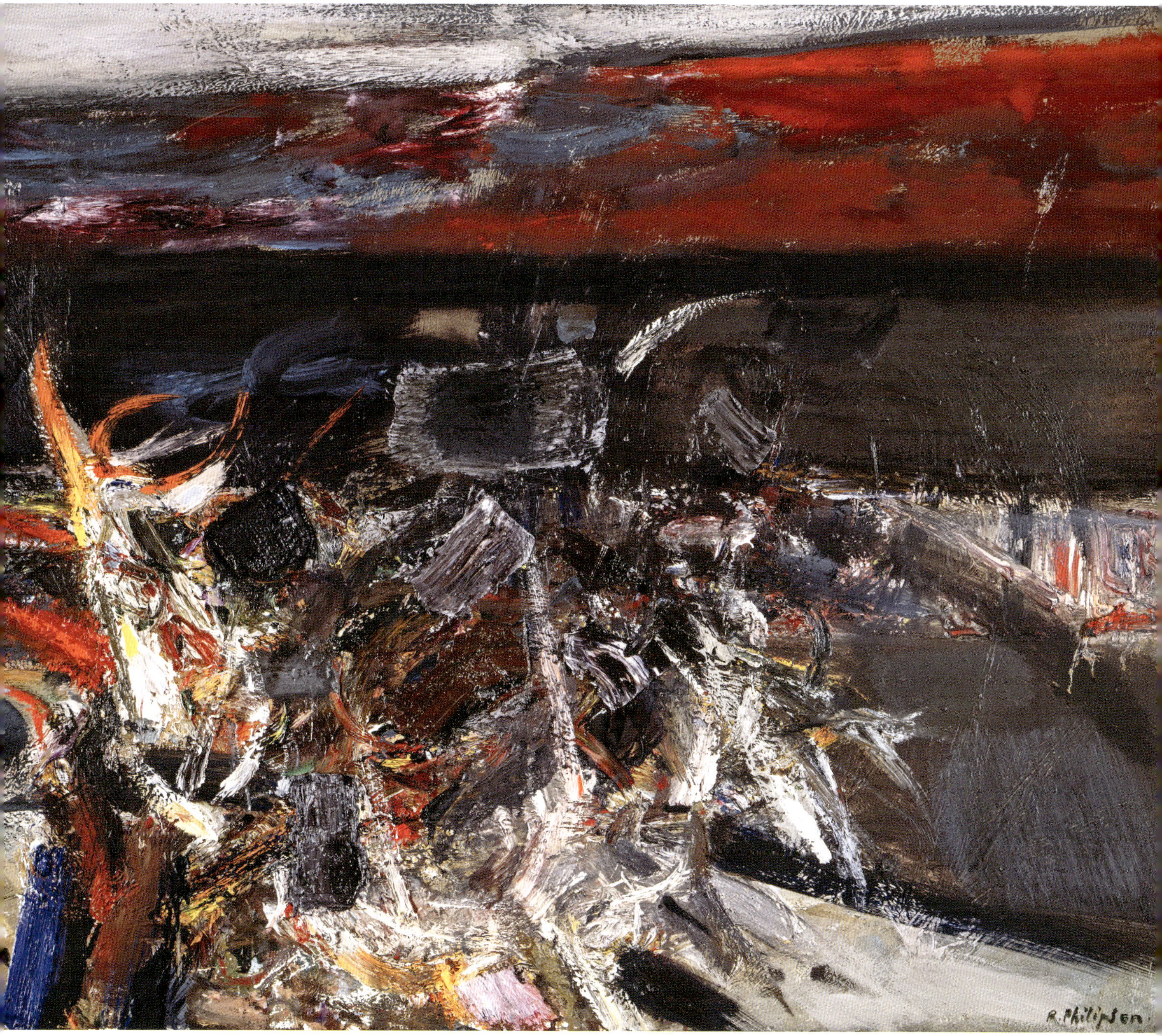

FIG. 3.1
Burning at the Sea's Edge
*c.*1961 / oil on canvas / 63.5 x 76.2 cm
National Galleries of Scotland • photo: Antonia Reeve

who had encountered his painting at Liverpool, wrote in *The Manchester Guardian* that his approach to picture-making was 'as a duck is a born swimmer'; he found him to be a painter of 'great courage and fluency ... but also an artist with the urge to explore the full meaning of the themes he makes his own'. His technique was considered expressionist, and he was said to have it in him 'to go on building on his early promise'.[2]

These words may have been supportive but naturally Robin had been rocked by Brenda's death, and his art would reflect his grief for some time. Only two paintings were shown at the RSA in 1961 – one a cockfight and the other *Rose Window and Fallen Warrior*, its very title symbolic of his feelings. There is a bleakness in the relatively few paintings produced during this period, and for a full year plus we find no sense of an artist looking for fresh subjects to explore. Gone were the rhapsodic landscapes of the mid-1950s with their flickering paint strokes and the joyous colour streaming across a cathedral interior. Watercolours darkened, and an oil painting such as *Burning at the Sea's Edge* [fig. 3.1] is a sombre, brutal and heartfelt response to the landscape. Cockfights continued to be painted, sometimes to express anger. He was supported by his closest friends, including Jimmy Cumming, Sax Shaw, Bill Gillies and Robbie Scott Hay. He had encouraged Scott Hay's design ventures through the summer of 1960, and their friendship would be mutually supportive through the following few years.

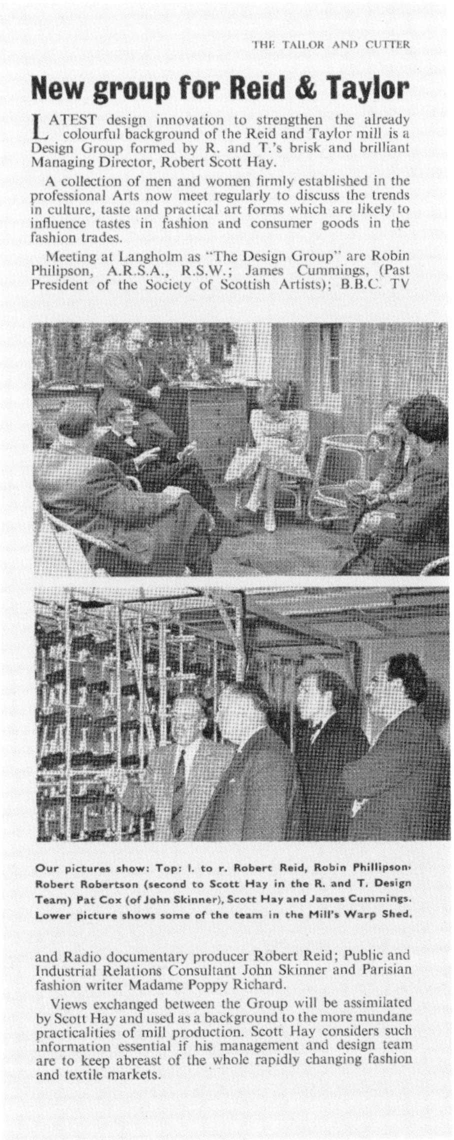
THE TAILOR AND CUTTER

New group for Reid & Taylor

LATEST design innovation to strengthen the already colourful background of the Reid and Taylor mill is a Design Group formed by R. and T.'s brisk and brilliant Managing Director, Robert Scott Hay.

A collection of men and women firmly established in the professional Arts now meet regularly to discuss the trends in culture, taste and practical art forms which are likely to influence tastes in fashion and consumer goods in the fashion trades.

Meeting at Langholm as "The Design Group" are Robin Philipson, A.R.S.A., R.S.W.; James Cummings, (Past President of the Society of Scottish Artists); B.B.C. TV and Radio documentary producer Robert Reid; Public and Industrial Relations Consultant John Skinner and Parisian fashion writer Madame Poppy Richard.

Views exchanged between the Group will be assimilated by Scott Hay and used as a background to the more mundane practicalities of mill production. Scott Hay considers such information essential if his management and design team are to keep abreast of the whole rapidly changing fashion and textile markets.

Our pictures show: Top: l. to r. Robert Reid, Robin Phillipson, Robert Robertson (second to Scott Hay in the R. and T. Design Team) Pat Cox (of John Skinner), Scott Hay and James Cummings. Lower picture shows some of the team in the Mill's Warp Shed.

FIG. 3.2
The meeting of the Design Group at Reid & Taylor, December 1960, from *The Tailor and Cutter*, January 1961
courtesy of the National Library of Scotland

As the London show opened, Reid & Taylor's new range of twill twists was launched. It was called the 'stained glass collection' and followed discussions involving Robin. Scott Hay was a Sunday painter, and, according to the official, persuasive publicity, the range was inspired by his own visits to Paris and seeing the glorious glass in the Sainte-Chapelle. The reflection of stained glass in the cloth was subtle, an ultrafine line of rich colour ensconced between the neutral-toned weaves. Writing in *The Observer*, columnist Katherine Whitehorn neatly referred to the tweed's richness of colour being 'fined down to pinpoint size, the total effect subdued, but the feeling of deep colour underneath remains, like wine in a casserole, or a friend'.[3] Colours were modestly used to provide a hue, a thread of light, to the weaving, but the new theme of stained glass was advertised by suppliers as 'an apt analogy for the glowing colours' in Reid & Taylor's twist suiting bunch no. 46, created 'by craftsmen for craftsmen'.[4]

For a couple of years Robin was not only new to School management but also deeply involved in this design factory. In January 1961 the trade journal *The Tailor and Cutter* was able to report the first meeting of the new 'design group' at Reid

& Taylor the previous month [fig. 3.2]. Scott Hay had brought together men and women 'firmly established in the professional Arts' – and key among them were Robin and through him Jimmy Cumming (as the retired president of the SSA). The group also included a London BBC colleague of George Bruce, Robert Reid, the Paris fashion correspondent for *The Scotsman*, Poppy Richards, and industrial relations consultant John Skinner. A field of grain, a painting by van Gogh or a single flower could provide the right tone for the discussions. Scott Hay also built up a private collection of Scottish art, which included sculpture by Benno Schotz, paintings by Penelope Beaton, Bill Baillie, Henderson Blyth, Elizabeth Blackadder and Jimmy Cumming, and of course paintings by Robin, whose *Cathedral, Red* [fig. 2.19] appears in the background of press photographs.

Such meetings were accompanied by conferences that included an international forum held in late November 1961. The setting again was the Lockerbie House Hotel, with a tour of Reid & Taylor following a sherry party in the home of Scott Hay – always a man of immense generosity – and lunch at Langholm Town Hall. The long list of delegates shows that speakers came from Germany, the Low Countries, France, Switzerland and Scandinavia. The programme cover's wording gives the convivial nature of the gathering: 'food eaten, wine drunk, words spoken – a visit to Langholm by the special guests'. These were days of welcome, talk and pleasure, and they provided a useful (and fruitful) diversion for some participants.

Apart from the colour debates, the most significant contribution made by Robin was the idea of establishing an art gallery at Reid & Taylor's mill. First opened in time for the 1961 conference, it served as both an exhibition space and the works' canteen: food for the spirit as well as the body for the mill's 200 workers. Before the opening, Scott Hay declared that the gallery was intended to 'develop in Reid & Taylor employees, from chairman to apprentice, the love of Scottish art in all its various manifestations, but principally to cultivate appreciation of the painter's art'.[5] Built in stone faced in red cedar, the simple, rectangular building had a large picture window at either end, with one facing the lawns and the other looking on to the river. The two long walls were left for a display of Scottish modern art. Comittees were established, with one consisting of patrons such as artists MacTaggart, Willie Wilson and William Thyne, the head of a long-established Edinburgh family printing business, and the other a working committee chaired by Scott Hay which included Robin, Jimmy Cumming, John Skinner, John Packer, Robert Robertson and Iain MacIntosh. MacTaggart, as president of the RSA, was invited to open the gallery officially on 14 April 1962, when he declared it to be an historic occasion, with the gallery the first of its kind in Scotland and possibly in Britain.

The opening show was a mixed one, some twenty-one paintings from Robin and Cumming plus those fellow artists they had persuaded to contribute: Bill Gillies, of course, Baillie, Blackadder and Houston, Joan Eardley (1921–1963), Redpath, David Donaldson (1916–1996), Henderson Blyth, McClure, Michie and John Kingsley Cook (1911–1994), head of the College's School of Design and Crafts. Although now largely forgotten, the Gallery, as it was first known, became a popular Borders venue for Scottish art, serving the community as much as the company, showing professional art and playing host to local art clubs. It gladly employed Robin as its lead programmer and often its curator, with the national press noting that its international visitors came from across Europe, Japan and America.[6] Within its first year Earl Haig joined Jimmy Cumming and Robin in advising on appropriate exhibitions. In its second year the Gallery was renamed 'The Factory', an appropriate name and also a nod to Andy Warhol's New York studio. Tom Pannell (later to be director of the Glasgow School of Art) was hired as its in-house exhibitions curator: he consulted Robin for ideas, which included showing a selection of around twenty modern Scottish paintings from the collection of Dr Robert A. Lillie.

Robin's work with textile companies varied through this decade. One 'thread' of his interest was his participation, via Robbie Scott Hay, with the Scottish Woollen Designers' Group based in Galashiels. Although never a key player in the group, Robin maintained an outside interest in its activities and debates and occasionally helped organise Edinburgh meetings. In November 1962, for example, he set up a visit and introduced a discussion for the Group's members at Dovecot Studios in Corstorphine, west Edinburgh, with Elder Dickson and Archie Brennan – Dovecot director of weaving (born 1931) – also being involved. Arranged at short notice, it followed a recent suggestion from Harry Jefferson Barnes (1915–1982), director and part-owner at Dovecot on top of his day job at Glasgow School of Art, that Robin design a tapestry.[7] Robin was interested ('I would like very much to have a try at designing a tapestry'[8]), but regretted he was under pressure to prepare for an exhibition the following April. Jefferson Barnes reluctantly accepted that Robin's workload ruled out his participation but asked that the idea should be carried to some future date – he wanted this to be a tapestry coming not from an interpreted 'exhibition painting' but from a fresh design, as this would be exciting and essential.

By this date the first in-depth published commentaries on Robin's art were being written by Elder Dickson, who in 1947 had risen within the College to become its deputy principal. More than any other colleague or critic, he was responsible for positioning Robin within an intellectual context and for setting him securely on his course towards academic ambition. Sydney Goodsir Smith wrote a piece on Robin for *The Weekend Magazine* of *The Scotsman* on 20 May 1961 and Elder Dickson published two articles on his former student in *The Scottish Art Review* in 1961 and in *The Studio* the following year. In these, Dickson suggested that the new cathedral theme had been deliberately chosen for its antithesis to the cockfights, which had transfixed 'one horrible moment in time'. The paintings of interiors were intended to open up the way to 'the serenity, wonder and stillness surrounding mankind'.[9] He equated Robin's subject switch from conflict to peace as being parallel to, if not consciously inspired by, Pascal's 'anguish before the *silence eternal des espaces infinis*'. Colour and structure were now fully integrated with 'artistic necessity'. Robin had developed a 'characteristic pictorial scaffolding' dependent on one of two 'large static units enriched and supported by subordinate rhythmic systems of form, colour and *facture*'.[10]

Such coverage in widely read art journals gave Robin added confidence and at the start of 1962 he could also celebrate his election as a full academician of the RSA, an institution in which he would play an important role. In personal terms he found happiness with the friends who supported him after Brenda's death. A particular friend from this time was Thora Clyne (born 1937), appointed by

Bill Gillies to assist him in his new responsibilities. Thora, from Caithness, had graduated in 1960 in Fine Art at the College.[11] She had taken Robin's classes in anatomy and still life as part of her Fine Art degree, and on gaining a postgraduate scholarship was given a Graham Street studio (now the site of the Hunter Building). On completing her postgraduate year in June 1961, she was awarded a three-month travel scholarship. She had thought of visiting Pont-Aven in Brittany on her own before Robin suggested she might care to join him on his planned summer visit to Italy. First stop was Venice, before they moved on to San Gimignano, Arezzo and Florence and finally Milan, where they were invited to stay with Robbie and Margie Scott Hay at their flat – Scott Hay always made a point of attending the fashion collections in London, Paris and Milan. Thora spent the rest of the summer painting and drawing in Edinburgh and back home in Caithness. The impact of Italy, and especially the glorious Byzantine art to be found in Venice and Torcello, was revelatory. Venetian churches struck Robin as having (as had the Gothic cathedrals of France) 'beautifully lit spaces – they gave me a great desire to recreate all their visual aspects simultaneously, taking in their inspired intricate rhythms and richly saturated colour.'[12] The influences of this visit were to be seen in Robin's painting over the next decade in paintings of exotic interiors gloriously clad in golden and jewel colours.

Thora and Robin were married at St Bernard's Davidson Church in Henderson Row on 31 March 1962. Jimmy Cumming was best man and Bill Gillies a witness. From this time, new subjects began to appear in Robin's painting. Alongside cathedral interiors the first of his paintings of odalisques, to provide a theme through the 1960s and 1970s, came off the easel in 1962. *Odalisque with Mirror* from that year [fig. 3.6] is one of several which have the dense rawness of a Frank Auerbach portrait and is one of the most expressionist works of the period. Vigorously modern works using a wide colour palette, at least three of these early odalisque pieces were bought by Robbie Scott Hay, with one destined as a gift to a Japanese colleague. One had been shown at the RSA in 1962, and among the other three new paintings exhibited was *Coronation and Crucifixion*, the first of Robin's paintings that specifically depicted the keenness of human suffering and, like his cathedral works, bringing more than one image into focus. He was increasingly interested in how to narrate a story or explore a range of emotions, and it has been said that *The Burning* [fig. 3.4], a mixed-media piece on paper, was his first work to do so. Here, Robin had accidentally discovered the strength of serial imagery when he placed single paintings alongside one another and clearly saw their connection.[13] A triptych, originally framed in silver for the 1963 RSW exhibition, this work links to ongoing cathedral imagery but is also on the verge of abstraction. It announced a series of semi-abstract oils devoted to landscape and burning from these years, of which one of the finest is *Burning at the Stake* of 1962–63 [fig. 3.3]. Here, a synthesis of imagery, including a rose window, is expressed through vigorous brushwork and finely orchestrated colour. The density of hot and cool colours is accentuated by contrast with dark, neutral tones, reflecting something of the textile debates at Langholm. This triptych was followed by a diptych, *Burning in a Wasteland* [fig. 3.5].

However energised these works are, the tension also embedded within them in part reflected Robin's early years as head of D&P, which were not particularly easy. The movement among British students to have more autonomy in their studios

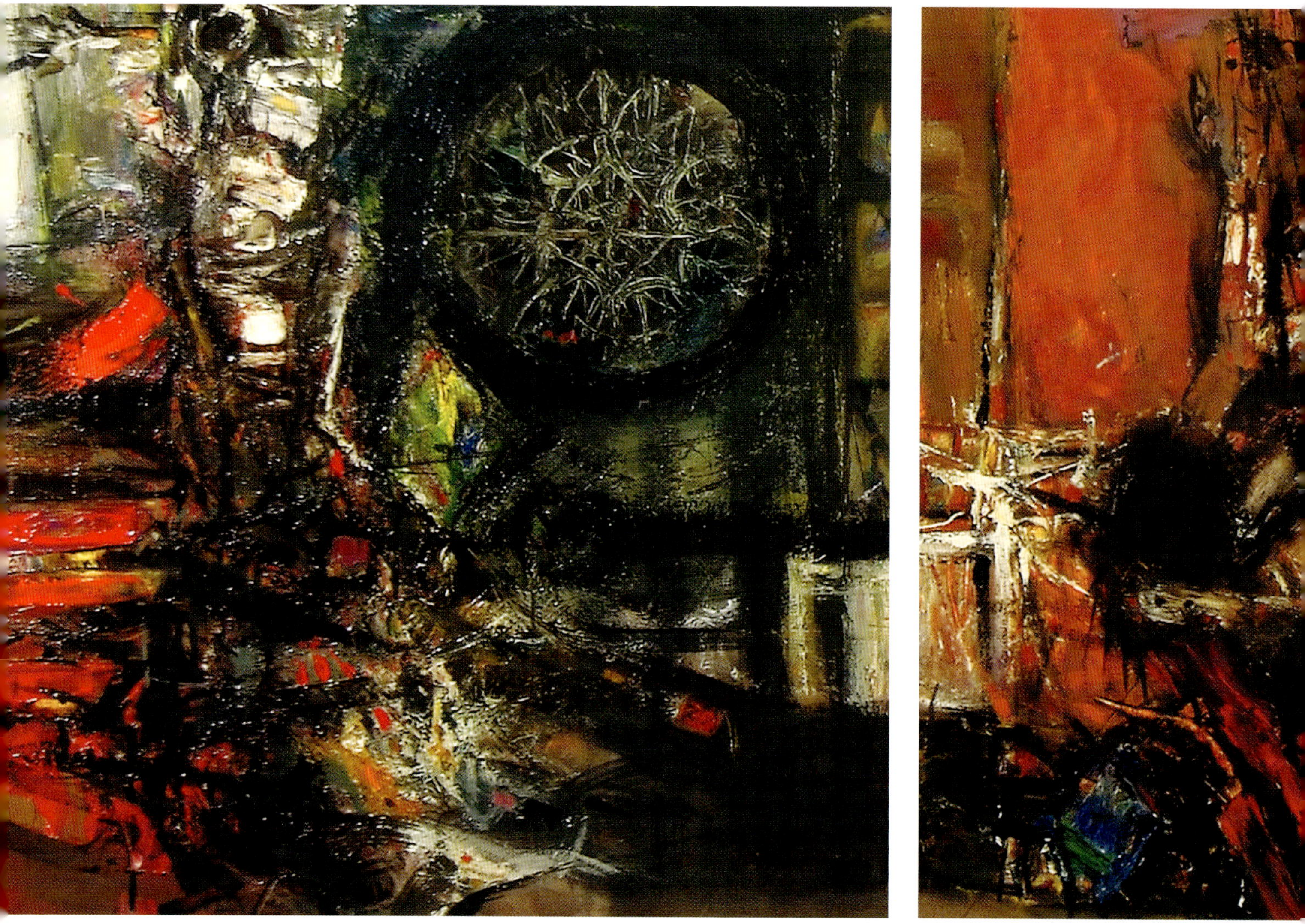

FIG. 3.3
Burning at the Stake (triptych)
1962–63 / oil on canvas / each panel 76 x 76 cm
Aberdeen Art Gallery & Museums Collections

▸▸ FIG. 3.4
The Burning (triptych)
1963 / watercolour, pastel, gouache, black chalk on paper / each panel 137.2 x 81.3 cm
National Galleries of Scotland • photo: Antonia Reeve

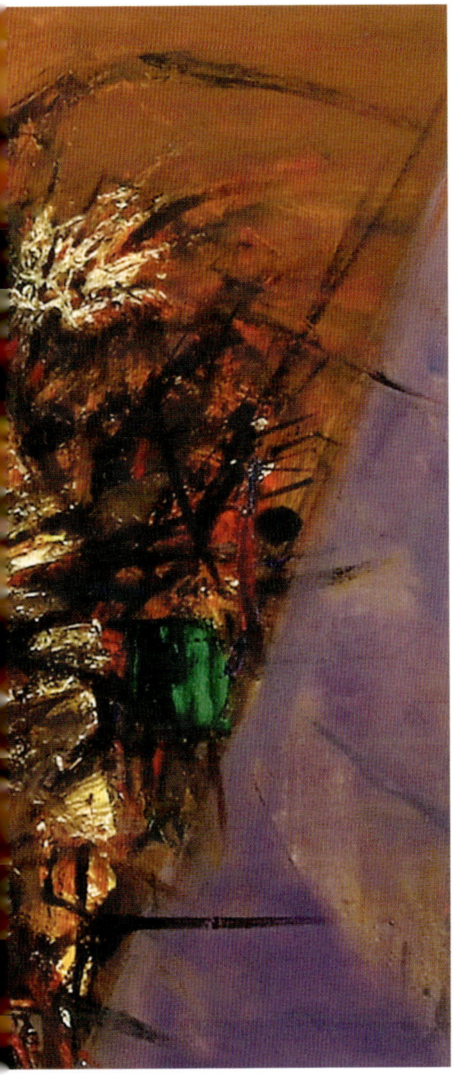

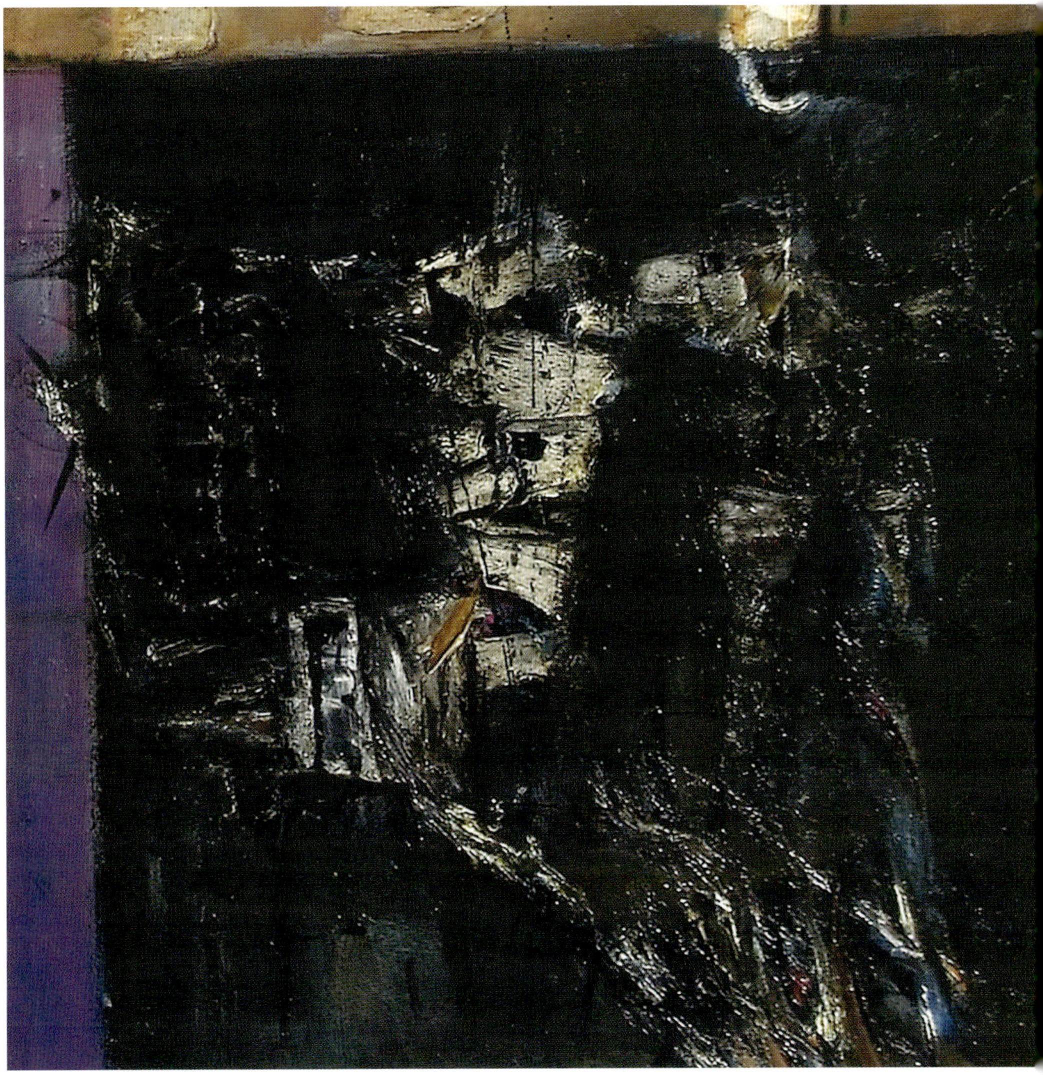

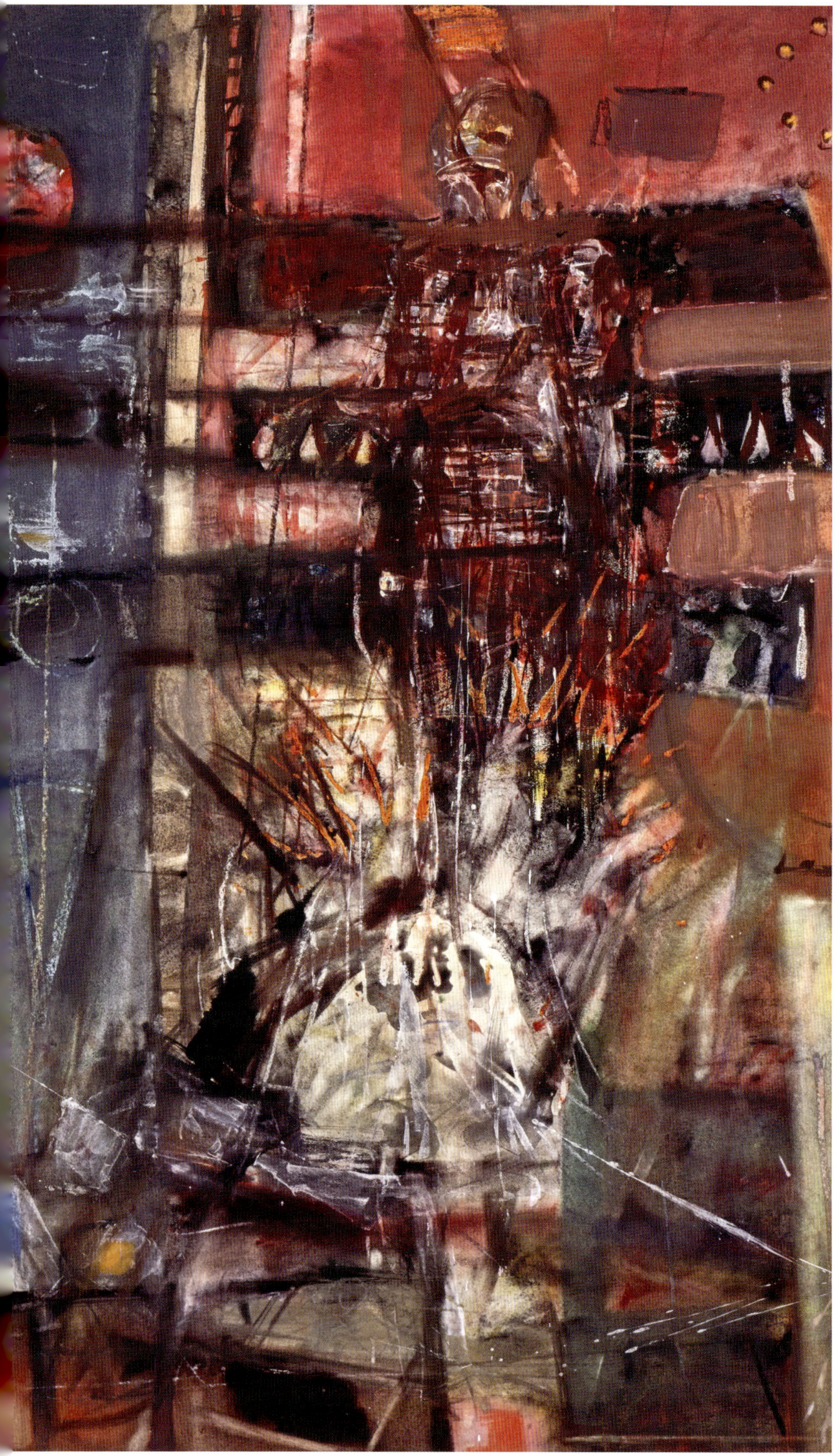

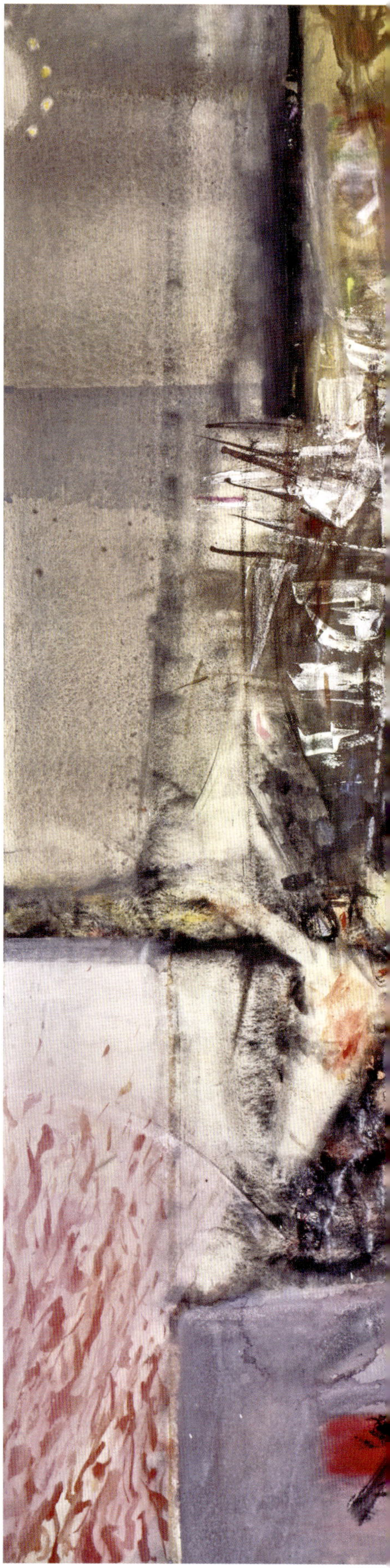

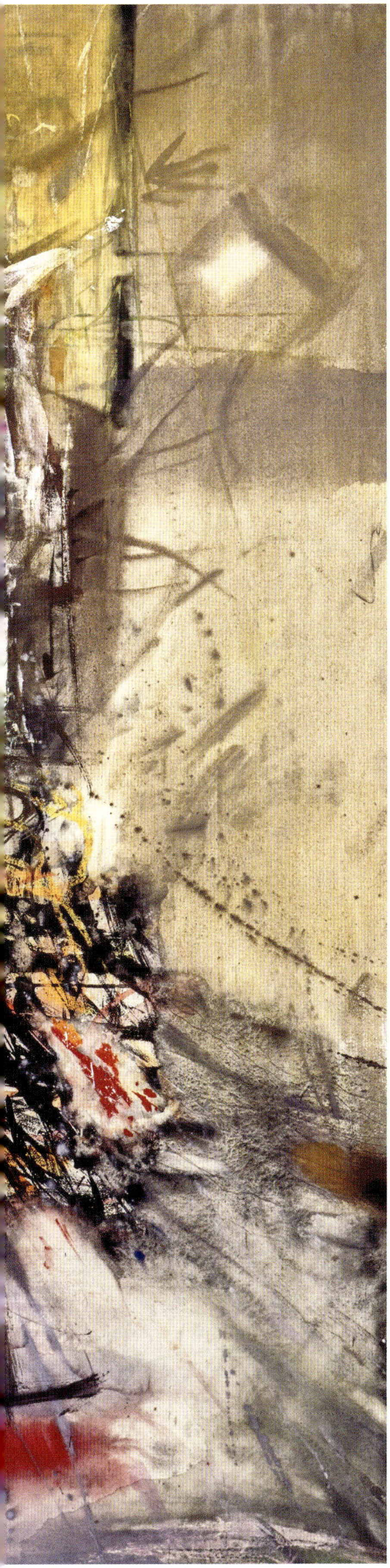
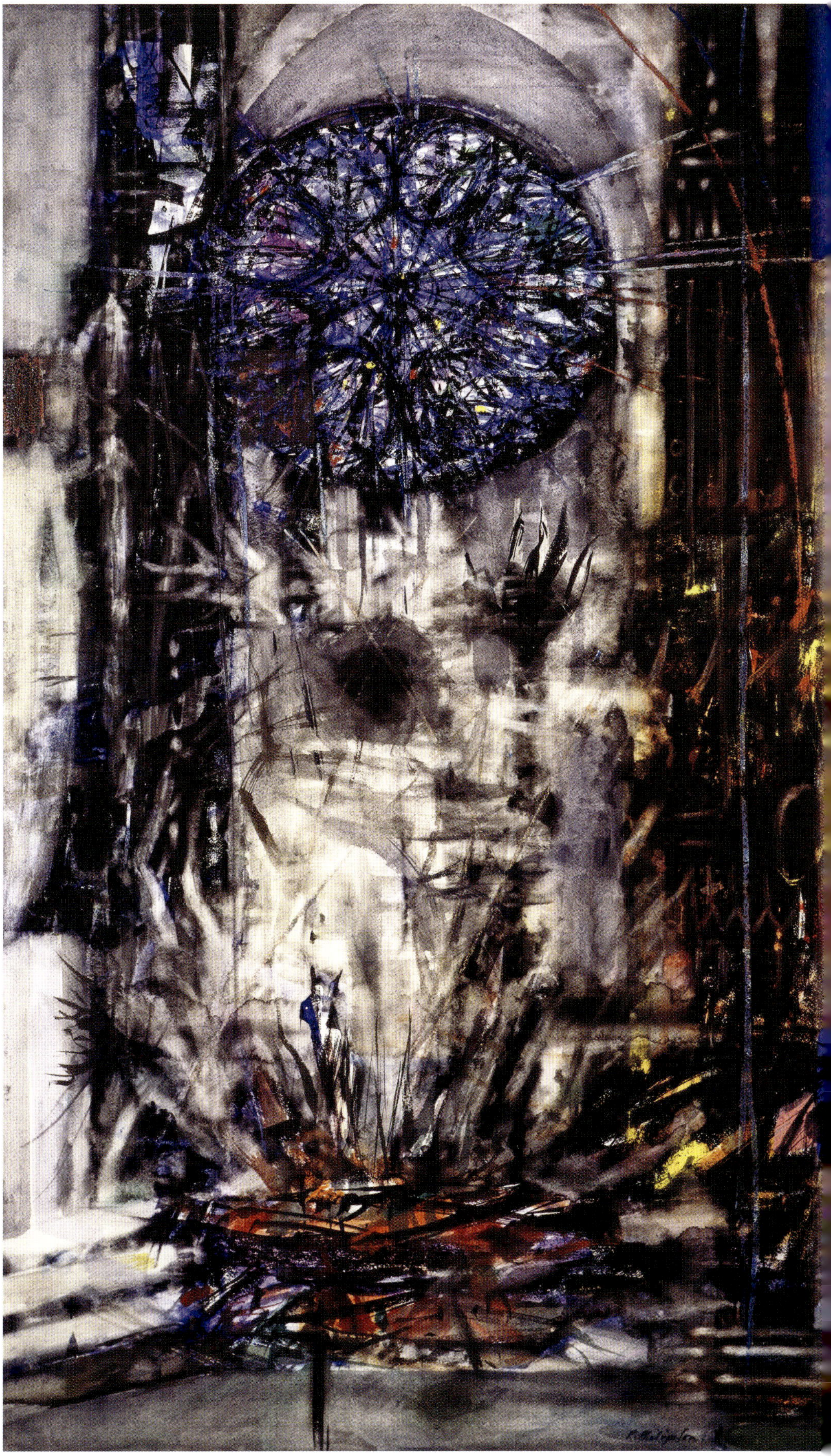

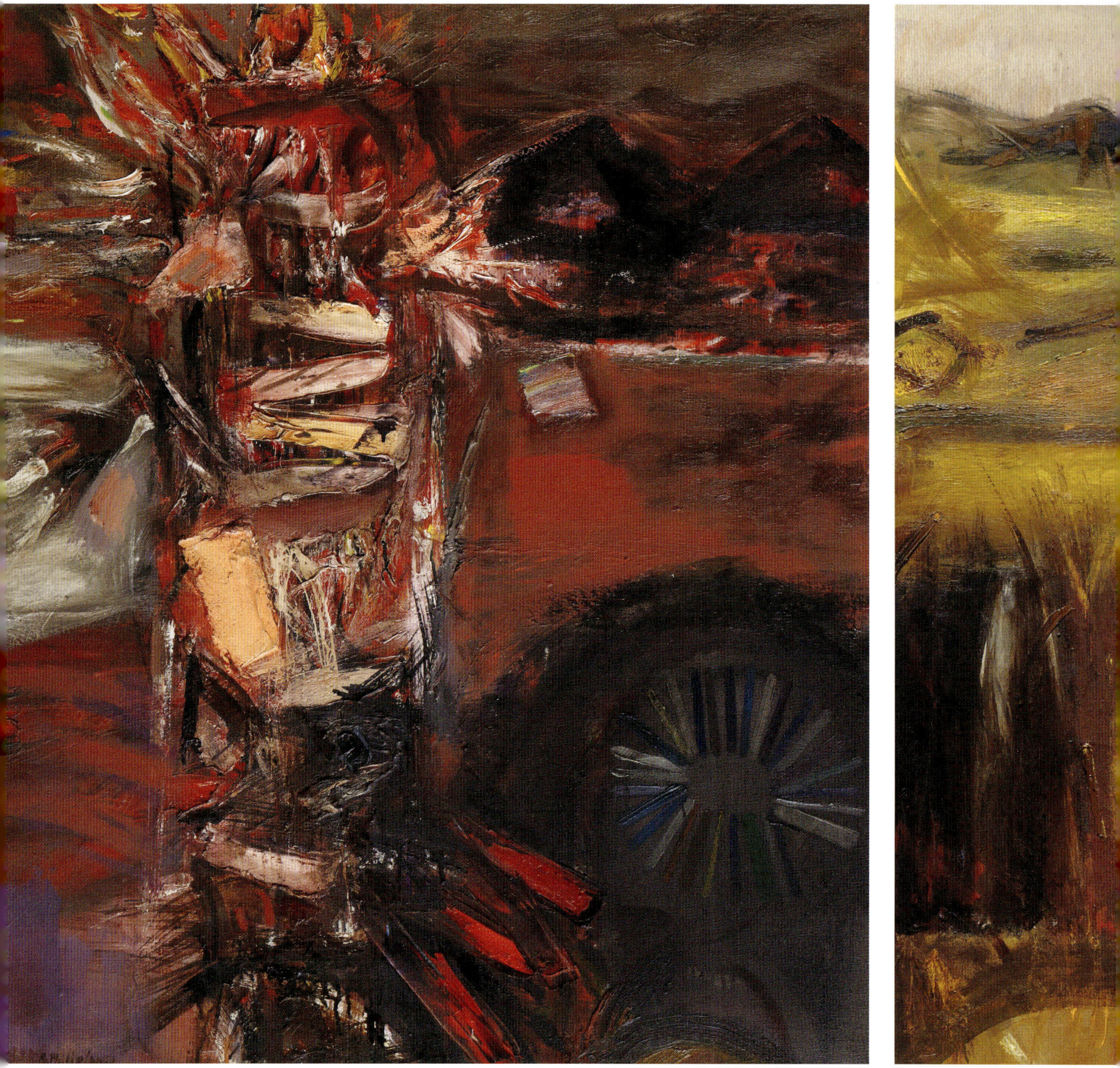

FIG. 3.5
Burning in a Wasteland (diptych)
1963 / oil on canvas / 91.5 x 76.2 cm and 91.5 x 126.7 cm
City Art Centre, City of Edinburgh Museums & Galleries • photo: Antonia Reeve

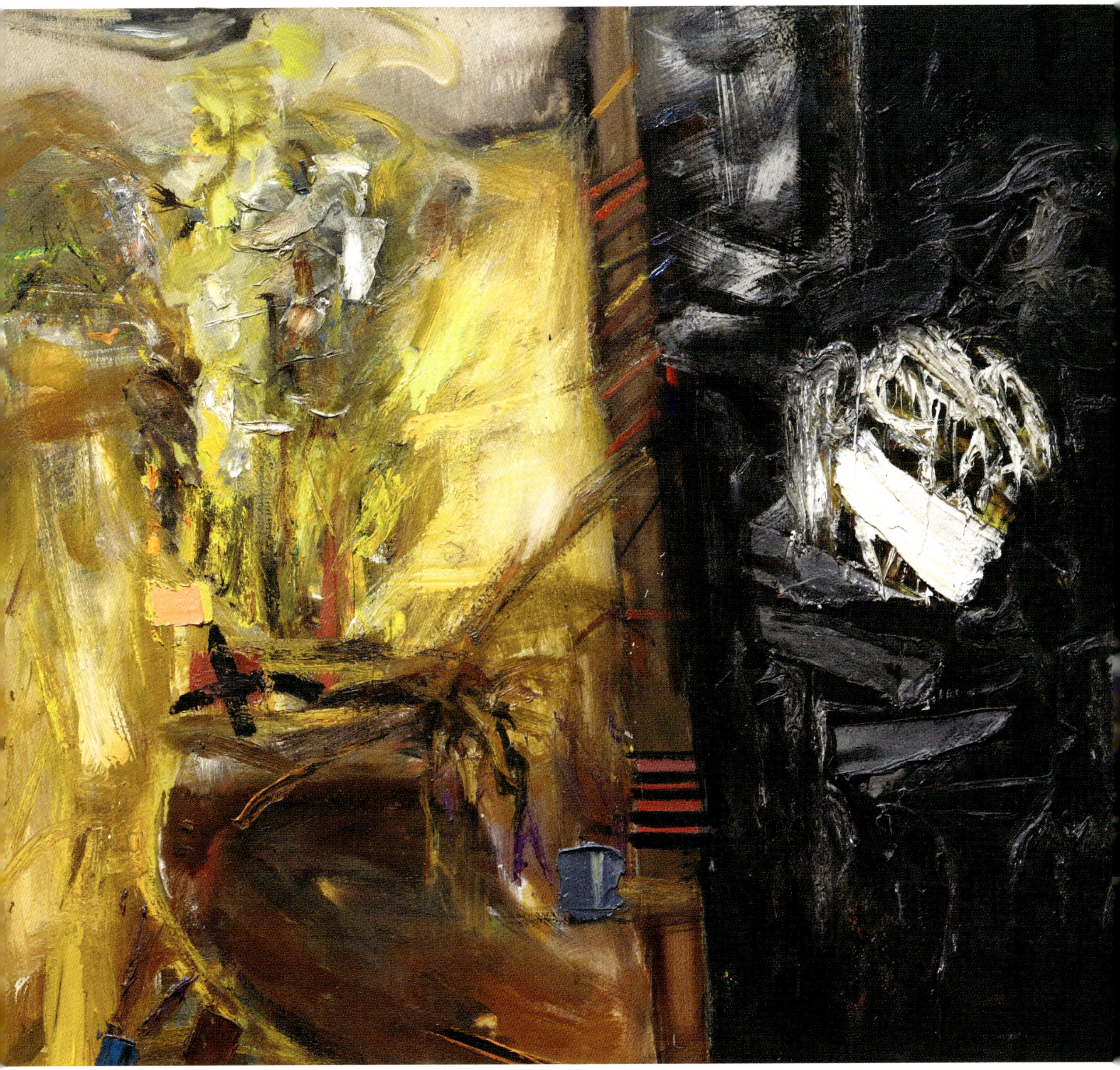

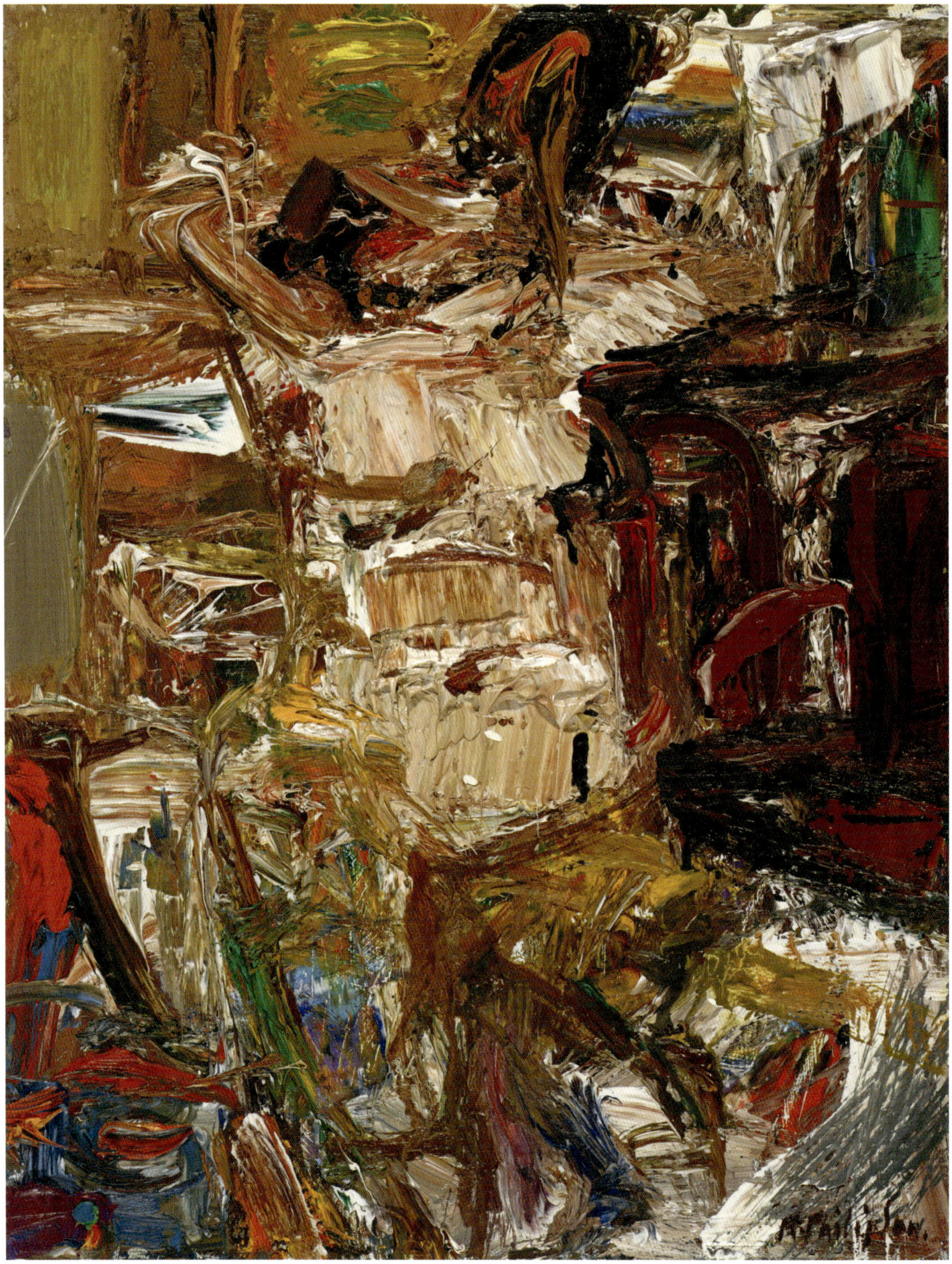

FIG. 3.6
Odalisque with Mirror
1962 / oil on board / 40.6 x 30.5 cm
National Galleries of Scotland • photo: Antonia Reeve

was also felt in Edinburgh. Robin firmly believed in the importance of working through a strictly traditional curriculum, and this was in line with policy across the Scottish art colleges. He initially stood firm in the face of protest, with his views endorsed by the College Board of Governors.[14] The College's Annual Report for 1961–62 referred to 'a large body of teachers such as ourselves [who] hold resolutely to the belief that a sound academic training in life drawing and life painting is fundamental to the training of the artist'. Working with Professor Romanes of the University's medical school, Robin introduced advanced anatomy as a final-year class in 1961. While maintaining life painting, life drawing of heads and life drawing in the curriculum, the College prospectus for 1962–63 shows them to have been relegated to final-year, not third-year, teaching, thereby reducing core instruction in earlier years. Mural painting, where Robin's former class was now taken by Jimmy Cumming, continued as a third-year subject and was briefly offered as a final-year class in 1962 before reverting to a third-year class – and this arrangement continued right through the rest of the 1960s under Robin's leadership. Another of Robin's principal innovations was the introduction of a practical course in 'grounds' from 1962, a legacy of his own valued early help from Charlie Howison.

Overall, the continuing emphasis on academic precision and detailed practical instruction seemed old-fashioned, even dull, but some students from that time have since acknowledged that it did give them a full skillset. Robin was also behind new cultural opportunities being offered to the students. Replying in late 1964 to a letter from Graham Smith (later to become a professor of Art History at St Andrews) on the role of the art historian in art education, he underlined what was now on offer to Edinburgh's students – visits to concerts, film discussions and debates on 'matters concerning creative activity'. Art histories were being taught at first- and third-year level, with the format changing from passive lecture-attending to tutorials and seminars 'which we hope will become a very lively and exciting part of the curriculum'. By the late 1960s the College prospectus emphasised the open choices available to a student: '[while] students are divided into small groups working under the guidance of a lecturer, students are given considerable freedom to plan the allocation of study time'.[15]

As noted, the winter of 1962–63 had been particularly busy, with much to celebrate. A painting, *Fighting Cocks, Grey*, had been purchased by the new Scottish National Gallery of Modern Art, the first painting of Robin's to enter the national collection. On top of everything, he was now much in demand as a speaker to art societies, especially in southern Scotland. Thora was teaching part-time at the College, leading design drawing classes on Wednesdays and Thursdays plus a Thursday evening class, and she would teach there for thirty years. To free up daylight time for his own painting, Robin took several evening classes, as he always had, in addition to his teaching and administration within the School. His commitment to Reid & Taylor also regularly took up time, with one of their exhibitions, presented that February, devoted to the work of fourteen women artists, including Thora, Mary Armour (1902–2000) and Anne Redpath. Meanwhile, plans for the development of D&P were also coming to fruition. Robin's personal interest in printmaking, plus his awareness of the need to keep abreast of modern practice, steered these expansions.

One goal was a new School of Printmaking which Hubert (Kim) Kempshall (born 1934) would be appointed to lead from autumn 1963. This School would be located next to a new School of Postgraduate Studies in property purchased at 37 Inverleith Place near the Royal Botanic Gardens. Both were up and running by the start of the 1963–64 academic year. D&P was a growth area in the College, and by 1965 as many as twenty-eight staff were employed in the School, with the majority of teachers working part-time.

Being the head of a painting school also involved Robin in many extramural educational activities. For example, Bill Gillies and he together served on the advisory board for Carlisle Art College in the mid-1960s – a school of particular interest, given Robin's Cumbrian roots. But art education by then seemed to be breeding advisory committees right, left and centre to modernise the curricula. Robin had no time for reporting panels involving non-practitioners who would lay down the rules. Rather, he believed change should evolve from within a School through open discussion among studio staff.

Despite being pulled in different directions by responsibilities, Robin would soon become one of the most prolific of all Scottish artists. In addition, throughout 1962 George Bruce had tried to pin him down to make a new film with Colin Thompson for the BBC's *Counterpoint* series on his own work, and this was eventually filmed in January 1963. His studio output accelerated from this time onward, with invitations to exhibit coming his way from commercial galleries such as the Stone Gallery in Newcastle. Lillian Browse, sensing that Robin's career was very much on the up, demanded that other commercial galleries should arrange to offer paintings strictly by agreement with her, his dealer in England. Through the winter Robin was working as usual towards his contributions to the annual spring society and RSA exhibitions at the Mound. Then, in March, Bill Buchanan – of the 'Arts Council Scottish Committee' – suggested Robin contribute to an Edinburgh Festival show that summer of 'Four Scottish Painters', alongside Redpath, Eardley and MacTaggart at the Council's gallery at 11 Rothesay Terrace. One immediate result of this show was the commissioning by architect W. Forbes Hutchison (whose office was at 4 Rothesay Terrace) of a five-panel mural piece for the entrance hall of the new Napier Technical College – the term 'mural' could mean art which took cognition of its architectural surroundings. Forbes Hutchison would also buy Robin's work for himself.

On top of this a fresh start was being made on the domestic scene. Thora and Robin had begun their married life in the St Vincent Street flat but soon decided they needed a different space and a garden. A flat in Gloucester Place was considered in November 1962. They also looked at a beautiful house in St Bernard's Row but it required too much work spent on it. Finally, a large detached house in Crawfurd Road in Newington was purchased in the late spring of 1963. This had a substantial garden to the rear plus a front garden and a garage and room for both their studios – Robin painted his watercolours at home and his oils at the College. Thora organised the move from St Vincent Street to Newington within weeks, even days, of their first visit to America in June.

March 1963 had been a particularly positive month. On the recommendation of

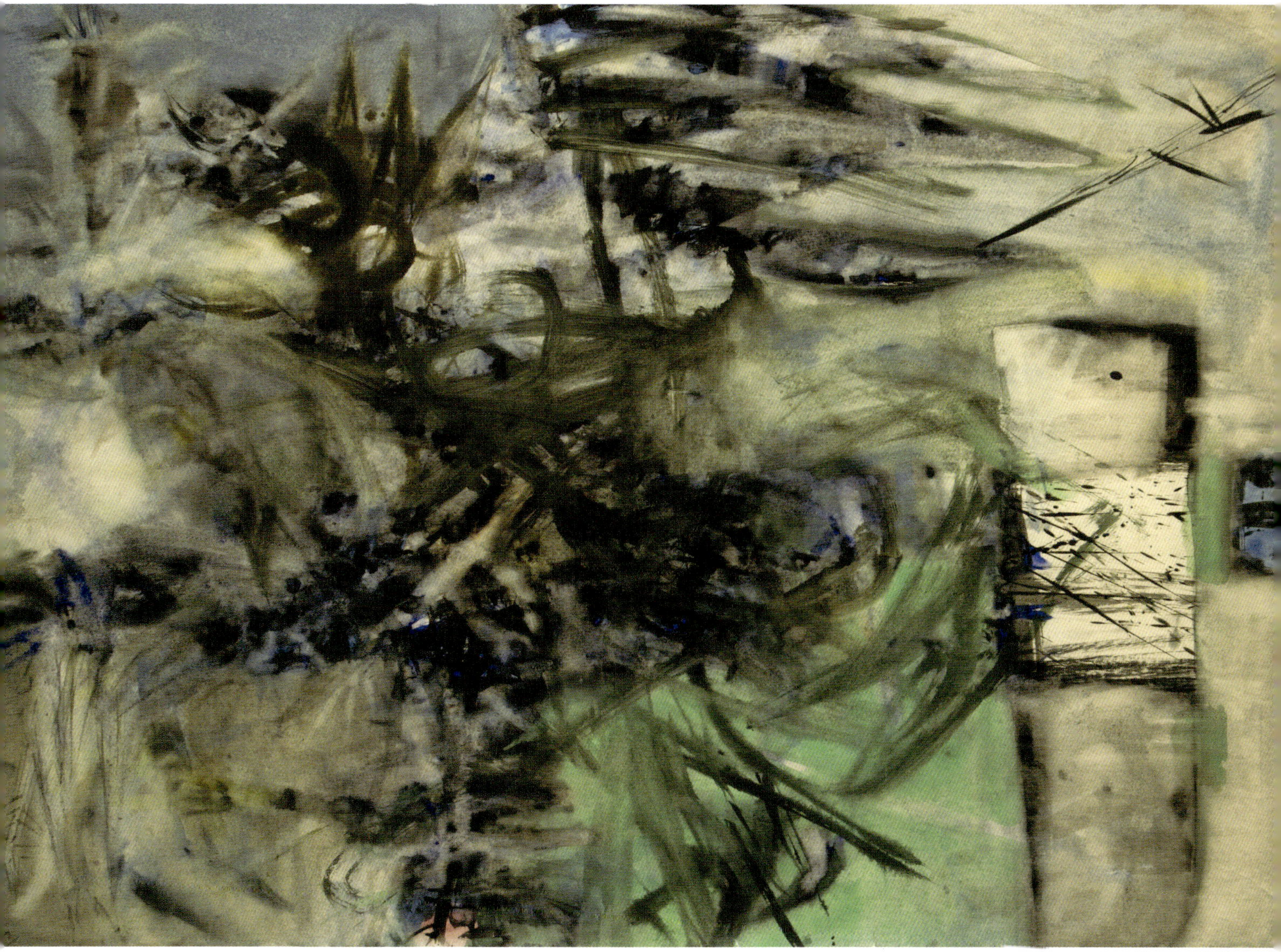

FIG. 3.7
Untitled
1963 / watercolour on paper / 64.5 x 92.7 cm
C.U. Art Museum, University of Colorado Boulder (63.313) • photo: courtesy C.U. Art Museum

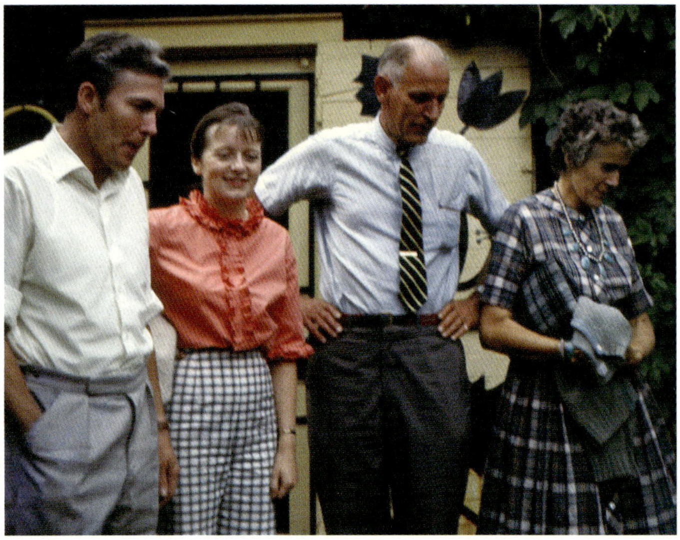

FIG. 3.8
Robin and Thora with Alden and Rue Megrew at the Megrew cabin, Colorado, summer 1963
private collection • photo: Annie Megrew

Katie Horsman, Robin had applied for a Fulbright Travel Grant to spend the summer as a visiting professor at the University of Colorado's School of Fine Art at Boulder. The summer programme of bringing visiting artists to work with senior and graduate students had been initiated by Alden Megrew, chair of the School of Fine Art and a friend of the director of the St Louis Art Museum. Previous visiting artists on the summer programme had included Max Beckmann (1949, the first visitor), Mark Rothko (1955), Richard Diebenkorn (1959) and Clyfford Still (1960). Bill Gillies supported Robin's application, describing him as 'a very much alive person, a good mixer, a fluent speaker and conversationalist',[16] while MacTaggart, as president of the RSA, supplied a glowing reference which not only mentioned his standing as 'one of the best known painters of the Scottish School' but also emphasised his communication skills – 'Mr Philipson is a gifted speaker and lecturer and has made frequent appearances on television where he is considered a "natural". He is a good "mixer" and in every way an excellent representative for Scottish art.'[17] The application was successful and Robin was appointed as Professor of Advanced Painting.

Success also came at home, where within weeks of the 1963 RSA show's opening, Robin's contribution to it attracted much interest, including praise for 'the very big one' (probably *Burning at the Stake*)[18] from the writer Naomi Mitchison, who invited him to her home in Carradale in June. However, by then Thora and Robin would be on their way to Boulder. Although no studio was formally on offer to visiting professors, Robin and Thora were given a studio next to the teaching studio vacated by a resident professor where they could show their own work. The work he produced was energised, and a watercolour was purchased by the University of Colorado [fig. 3.7]. Robin taught life painting from a model over two five-week sessions, with some time between to explore Colorado and New Mexico, including a memorable visit to Santa Fe [fig. 3.8]. Alden Megrew introduced Robin to the art of America's first people, which he found thrilling in terms of materials, colour, pattern and ritual – his first experience of a totally distinct culture. While in New Mexico they visited Chimayo, finding its church of El Santuario to be a small, simple structure made of rough wood and grass with an altar covered not in gold but yellow paint. Robin later remembered it as deeply inspiring, 'majestic, magnificent', noting with wonderment that 'crutches and other proofs of miraculous cures were lying about.'[19] The experience would inspire a number of paintings of church interiors and altarpieces in various cultures for over a decade [figs 3.9, 3.10]. During their American trip they also found time to visit New York City to enjoy its own vibrant culture.

On their return that September, the College students noted something of a

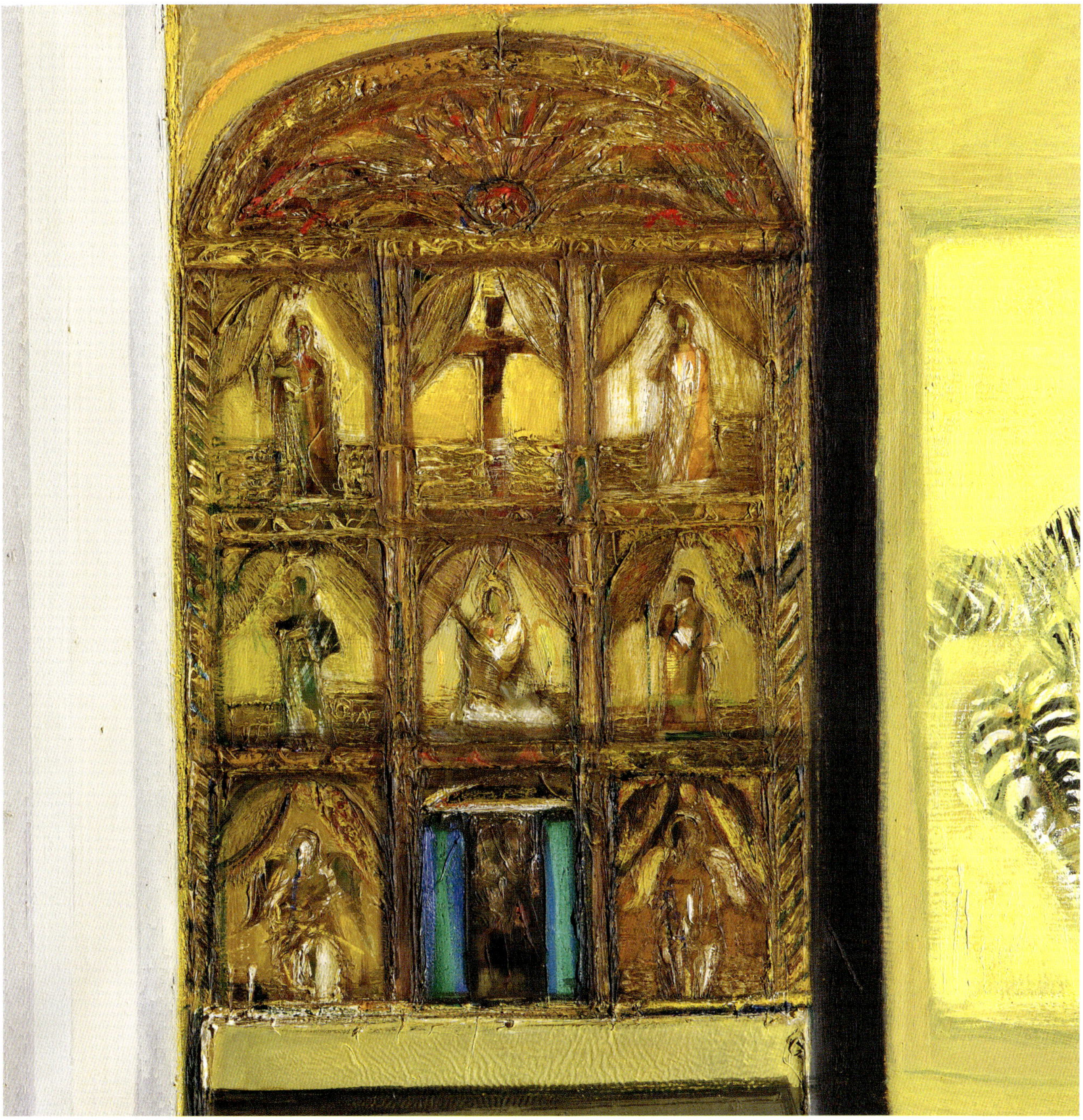

FIG. 3.9
Mexican Altar
1972 / oil on canvas / 49.5 x 49 cm
University of Aberdeen

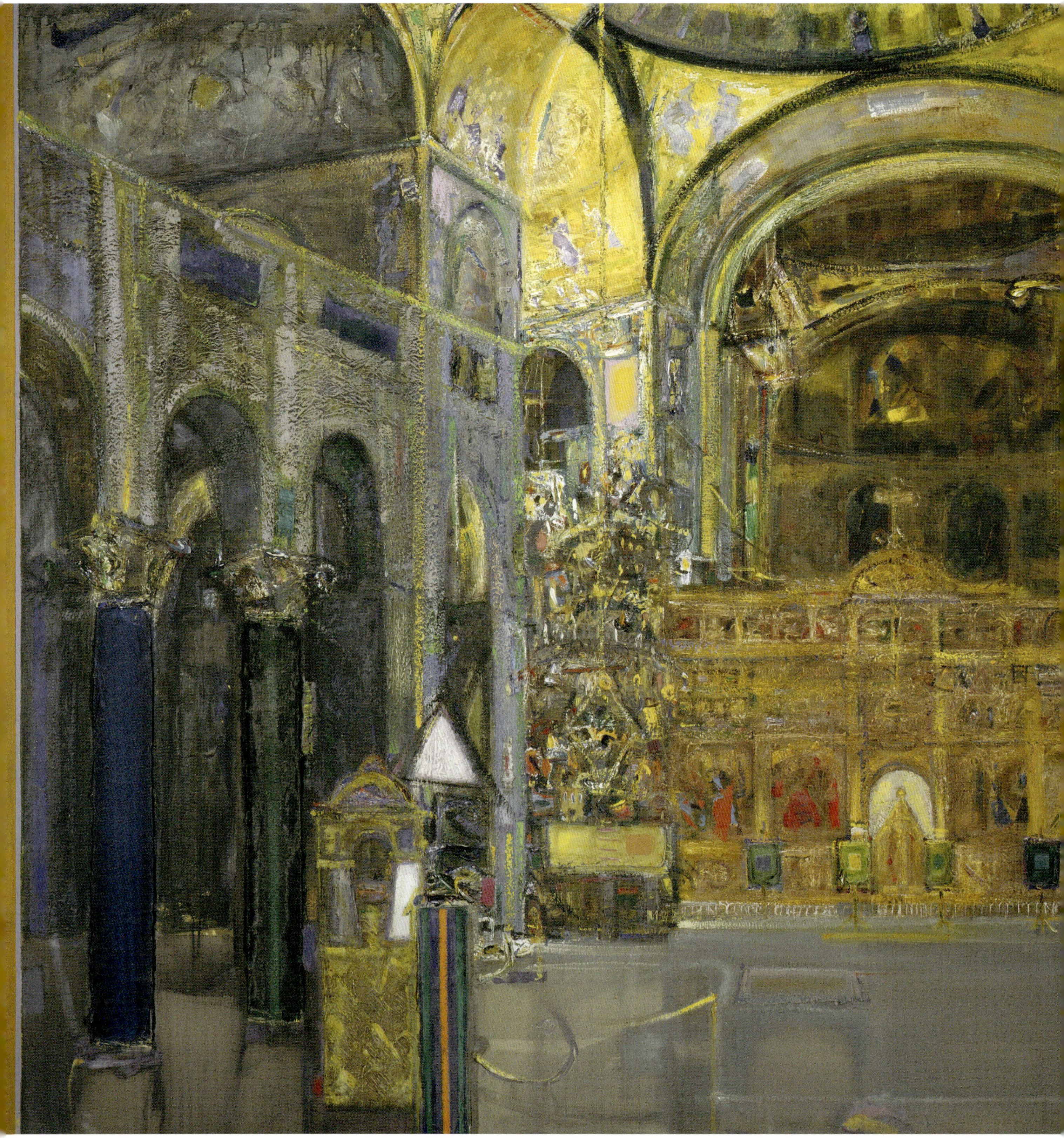

FIG. 3.10
Byzantine Interior
*c.*1975 / oil on canvas / 151.5 x 151.5 cm

change in Robin. He was now more casually dressed, sported blue denim jeans and a 'jazzy' cravat[20] in place of his customary smart bowtie, and, most noticeable of all, he had abandoned the long smock customarily worn by the College teachers in favour of a linen jacket – soon to become equally paint-spattered. The American culture and way of life had made a deep impression, not least on the scale and potential scope of painting. He had begun to think even more about the fundamentals of art, about materials and ideas, and a new phase in his career would soon be established. Meanwhile, some fruits of his visit were shown at London's Commonwealth Gallery that December in a display organised by Roland, Browse and Delbanco, who had included his paintings with Jimmy Cumming's work in a mixed show earlier in the year. The paintings' titles reflect his visit but none yet indicate a new direction: *Mexican Cockfight, Cross and Skirmish, Red Geese over the Tepee, Blue Totem* and *War Chant*. Mexican subjects would resurface as late as 1979, when the watercolour *Mexican Retable* was produced.

As a fully fledged Academician, Robin was happy to become involved with the RSA's loan exhibitions. Every August a major show was presented in association with the Edinburgh Festival Society. His time in the States meant that he had missed setting up the Chaïm Soutine show for the 1963 Edinburgh Festival but had narrowly caught it – and also 'Four Scottish Painters' – on his return to the city in early September. At the Academy he was involved in arranging loans for the Georges Braque exhibition the following year, corresponding from the College with the likes of Eric Estorick of the Grosvenor Gallery, Lady Hulton, Gabriel White at the Arts Council of Great Britain and the dealer A.J. McNeill Reid. Before that he had the opportunity to work on the Joan Eardley memorial display during the 1964 RSA annual exhibition.

Outside College hours Robin participated in many different activities, giving talks and attending committees. Due to his American trip he had had to postpone the opportunity to present the school prizes at Dumfries Academy until 9 July 1964 – an event which reunited him happily with his old art teacher, Jock Ramsay. As a token of thanks, Robin gave the school his painting *Three Windows* [fig. 2.18]. At this point, as a 'name' in the art world he remained reluctant to decline the many committee invitations, and gladly served on cultural committees such as the new Jean F. Watson art purchase panel of Edinburgh Corporation (today's Edinburgh Council) in 1964 and the following year the Royal Commission on the Fine Arts in Scotland – a membership which would be repeatedly renewed over the coming fifteen years. The British Council also knocked on his door and he gave freely of his time there too. But special time was also saved for spending with Bill Gillies who, following the death of his surviving sister Janet in 1960 and mother in 1963, was now living alone in Temple, Midlothian. It is a token of the widely felt affection for Gillies – and of Robin and Thora's natures – that, along with others such as the painter Helga Chart, they developed a weekend habit of taking a casserole dish and a bottle of good wine to Temple to keep him company. George Bruce, another of the circle, wrote an evocative poem entitled *Soup and Sherry* to commemorate his own visits to his Temple friend. These were days which they all would remember for a very long time.

4 THE ACADEMIC ARTIST

America affected Robin's art in different ways. The honesty and freedom of its indigenous art and the sheer scale of the Colorado landscape (and of recent American painting) struck him with force and would question preconceived notions of the limitations of easel painting. Exploring materials and the technical construction of painting became of paramount importance as he looked to find new ways to communicate meaning in his work – almost but never quite to the point of replacing representation. The exceptions are several works on paper from 1964 and 1965 which delight in free form and colour purely for their own sake [figs 4.1, 4.2]. Nonetheless, in his works on canvas he set out to look for ways to sustain a variety of textures and tonalities as well as images, and also to find a method of giving a degree of transparency to parts of a painting and a sense of layering. Japanese paper provided the means to do so, but affixing it also forced him to rethink the qualities of his paints. While a coating of thick white oil paint was still wet, he worked on an image, 'a very strong statement in light and dark'[1] before gently rolling over it a sheet of lightly textured Japanese paper. Some colour glazes were then applied over the surface, which might not yet be dry. Robin was also keen to find a suitable way of affixing gold leaf to his canvases. Although the College had regular visits from Rowney and Winsor & Newton representatives to discuss stock for the shop and to demonstrate new products, he chose to consult local paint manufacturers Craig & Rose, a firm widely famed for its red paint used on the Forth Bridge. They suggested he try vinyl toluene, which dried quickly. In 1964 he also began to use it in place of linseed oil as a binding medium for his pigments. Craig & Rose also prepared some oil paints for him, famously mixing a beautiful, clear and sonorous blue which was used from this time on and was called by many a 'Philipson blue'.

Examples of Robin's painting of the early 1960s – his exploration of angry fire alongside calm watercolours of odalisques – were seen in his second show with Lillian Browse in May and June 1964, but the results of his 1964–65 experiments were premiered in a major exhibition at the Scottish Gallery at the 1965 Festival. In retrospect this would turn out to be a key one, bringing together new work in mid-career as he approached fifty. By this date he already had works in no fewer than twenty public collections worldwide. As figurative, male-dominated works, the latest paintings took their cue from the idea of war and man's inhumanity to man, which he had personally witnessed during his Far East service in the 1940s. They are said to have been triggered by seeing one film in particular.

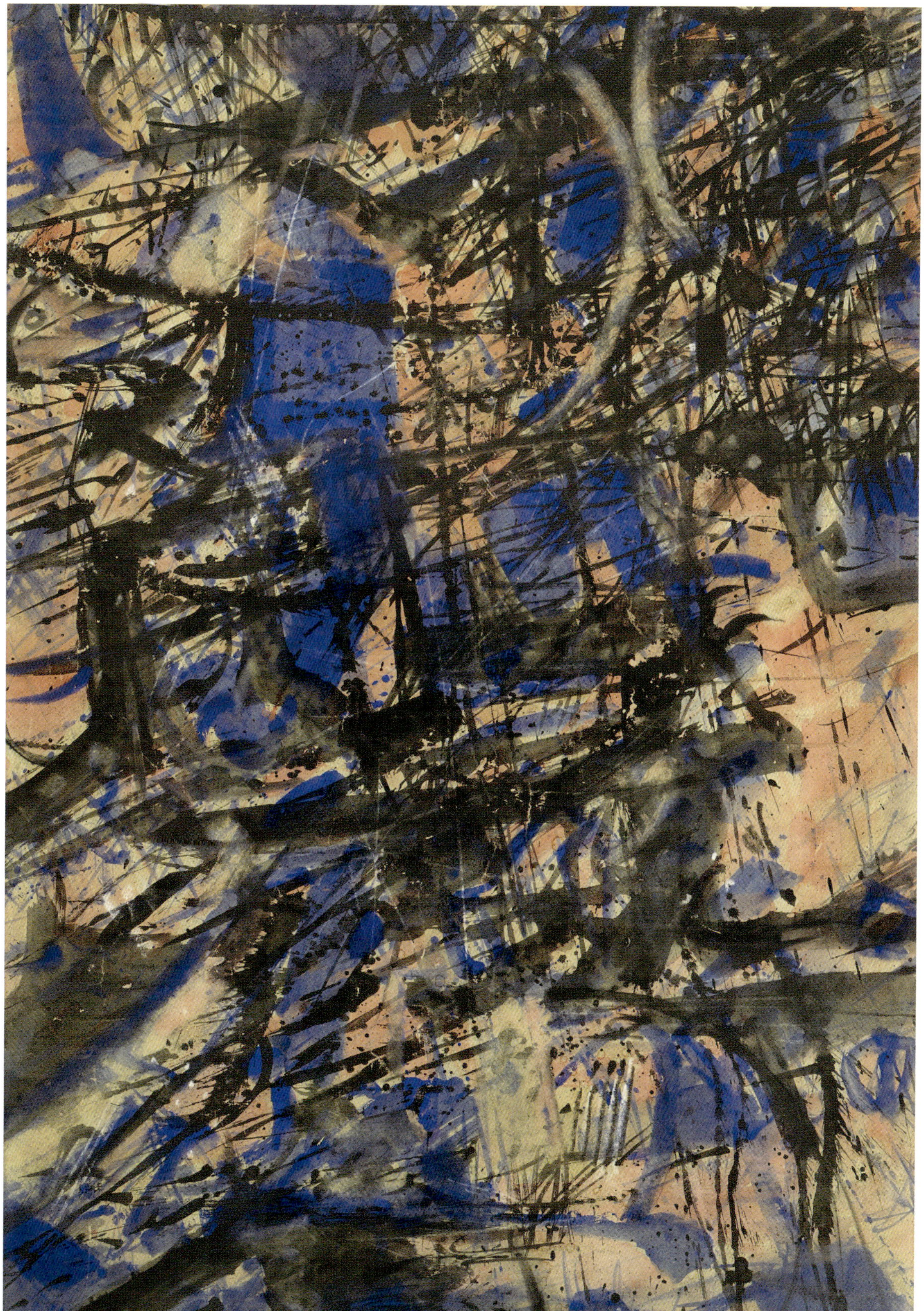

FIG. 4.1
Abstract
*c.*1964–65 / watercolour on paper / 73.5 x 50.5 cm
private collection • courtesy of the Scottish Gallery

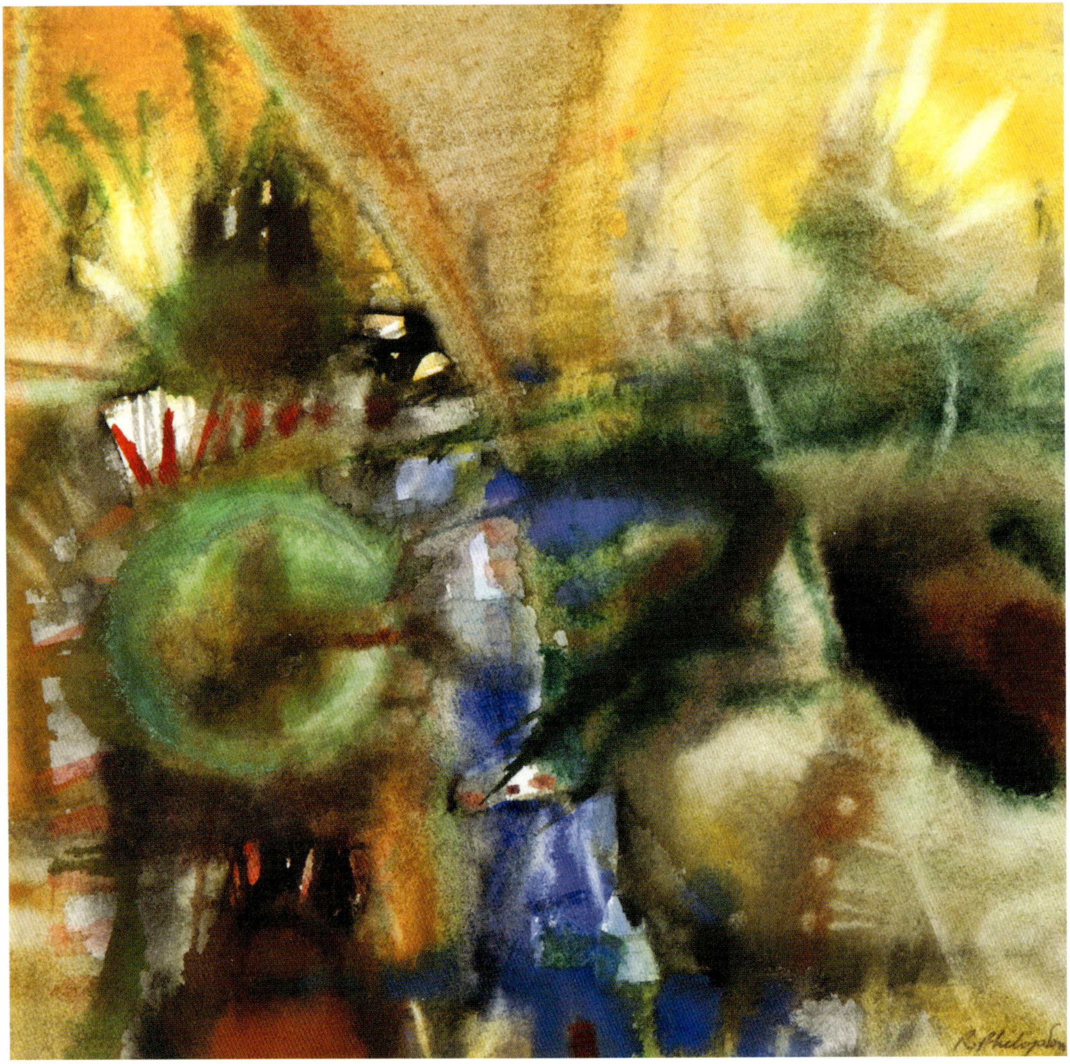

FIG. 4.2
Corn Dance
*c.*1964–65 / watercolour on paper / 17.5 x 17.5 cm
private collection · courtesy of the Scottish Gallery

In 1989 Robin remembered watching Joseph Losey's film *King and Country* and its cruel dragging of a young man through the snow: 'you saw them put a hood over his head, strap him to a post and shoot him – to a background of haunting Christmas carols on the soundtrack.'[2] He had found a subject where iconography could match the energy of his painting technique. But the new art was probably also triggered by his Colorado trip, and a sense of the wrongs in the clash of cultures which had built modern America.

He had prepared in different ways for these new paintings to be the most intellectual of his career. An artist whose ideas interested him was Aleksander Kobzdej (1920–1972). On a first visit to Poland in the winter of 1963–64, he had discussed the organisation and division of pictorial space on a canvas over several days with Kobzdej, a leading painter who was his counterpart at the Warsaw Academy of Art. Kobzdej had also followed a path from representational art – in his case a powerful Socialist Realism – to a material-based abstraction following six months spent in China, where monumental scroll paintings had made a huge impression on the

Pole, as had the Pollock paintings shown at the 1954 Venice Biennale.[3] Kobzdej was also interested in the idea of the triptych, with one of his key paintings concerned with politicising death: the triptych *Na śmierć czlowieka* (*For the Death of a Man*) would be painted in 1965, months after what has since become Robin's most famous work, *Stone the Crows*, and they both reflect their conversations. Robin and Kobzdej may well have talked of the Second World War and the horror of concentration camps, though only discussion on the making of art has been recorded. In his 'matter' paintings Kobzdej was exploring the status of paint, investigating texture and colour on their own terms, and incorporating 'foreign' materials such as wood, metal and plastic placed between bands of painted canvas. While connecting to such art and appreciating its potential, Robin never adopted such non-organic materials in his painting, nor did he take this route to its abstract extreme. Nonetheless, the discussions usefully encouraged resolutions in his own picture-making, and he also subsequently accepted the chance to exhibit in Warsaw in May 1967 as part of a show, '15 British Painters', organised by Richard Demarco at the Union of Polish Artists in Warsaw.

Although undated, *Stone the Crows* [fig. 4.3] was most likely painted in the late autumn of 1964. With its filmstrip scenes of advancing soldiers, a line of dead crows occupying the upper line, and its potent mix of squares of Japanese papers and thick pewter and mud-coloured oil paints vigorously applied with brush and knife, it was to be the painting most closely derived from the Losey film – although other works, such as the two versions of *Never Mind* [figs 4.4, 4.5], deal equally and more directly with military brutality. For *Stone the Crows*, Robin said he tried to find 'a more than usual mattness, using a lifeless, inert paint, to suggest the dullness of earth itself, the earthiness of the trenches and no-man's land, men in their thousands dying and becoming earth themselves'.[4] It also dealt with contrasts of war and peace: at the foot of *Stone the Crows* is an odalisque, the passive female form included in sharp contrast to the all-male action above – a hint of the physical pleasures of life in contrast to its pain. The appearance of the odalisque here may have been in response to the note from his twin Phyllis written on a poem she posted to him. The poem, *To 'My People' before the 'Great Offensive': The Threnody of Lieut. Eric Wilkinson* MC*, Leeds Rifles, killed in action October 1917*, had been published in 1916 in London in a slim volume called *Soldier Poets*. Its final stanza voices an affirmative resolution as the poet addresses his love from beyond death. This emotive poem is loaded with intense, dark images of the war in action and the first stanza in particular was picked up by Robin for his imagery in *Stone the Crows*:

> *Dark with uncertainty of doubtful doom*
> *The future looms across the path we tread;*
> *Yet, undismayed we gaze athwart the gloom,*
> *Prophetically tinged with hectic red.*
> *The mutterings of conflict, sullen, deep,*
> *Surge over homes where hopeless tears are shed,*
> *And ravens their ill-omened vigils keep*

The 1965 Festival exhibition with the Scottish Gallery was a mix of works on canvas, including *Stone the Crows*, and on paper; many had not been previously offered to either the RSA or the RGI. The new large oils on show were deliberately

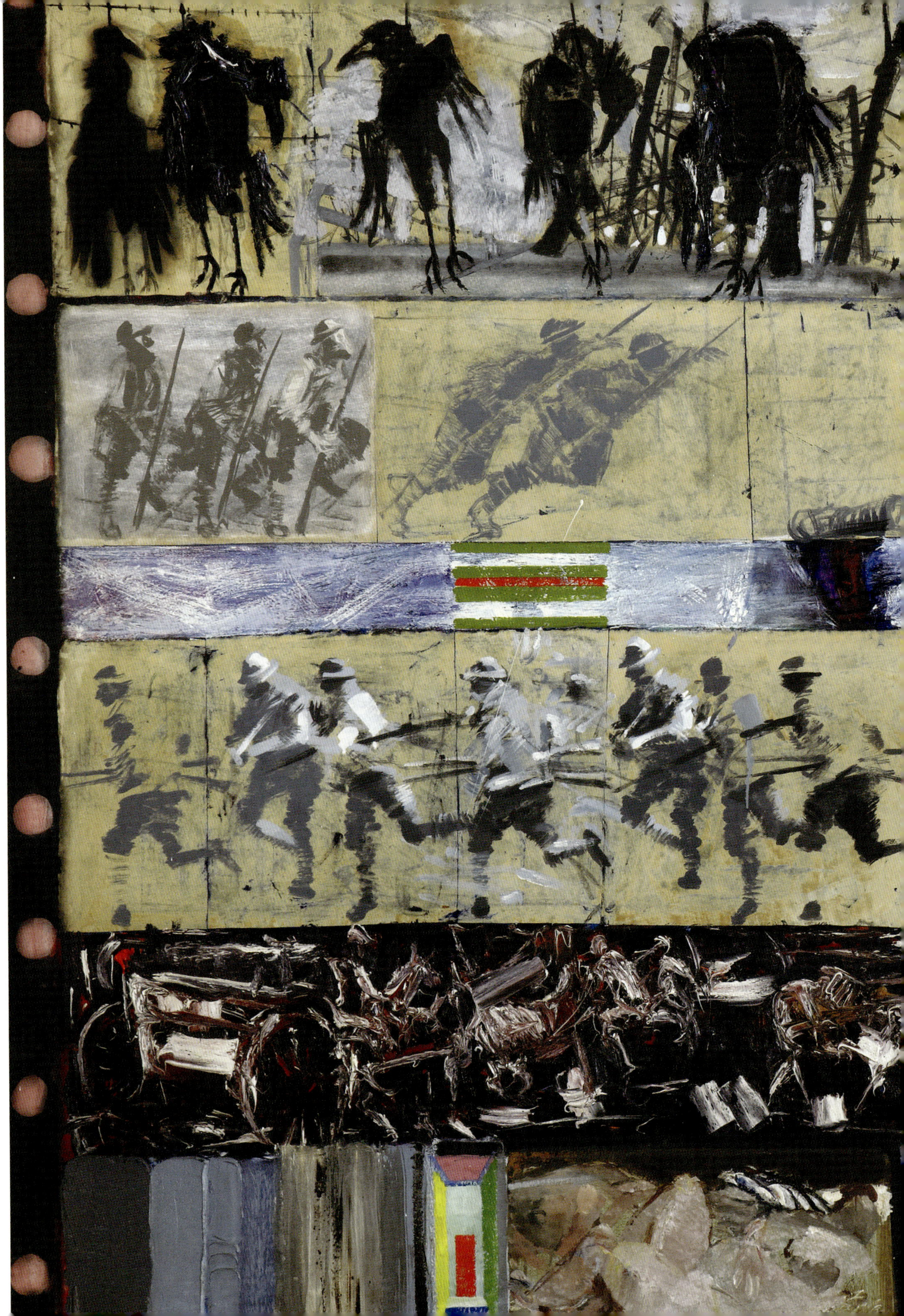

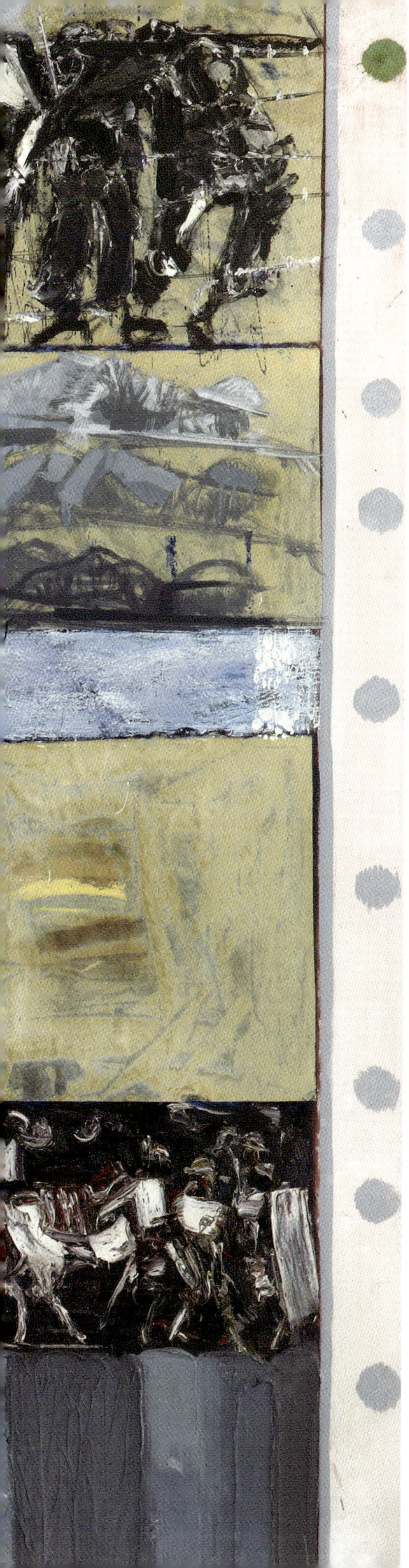

FIG. 4.3
Stone the Crows
1964 / oil and vinyl toluene with paper strips on canvas / 152.3 x 152.3 cm
Royal Scottish Academy of Art & Architecture (Scottish Arts Council Bequest)
photo: Andy Phillipson

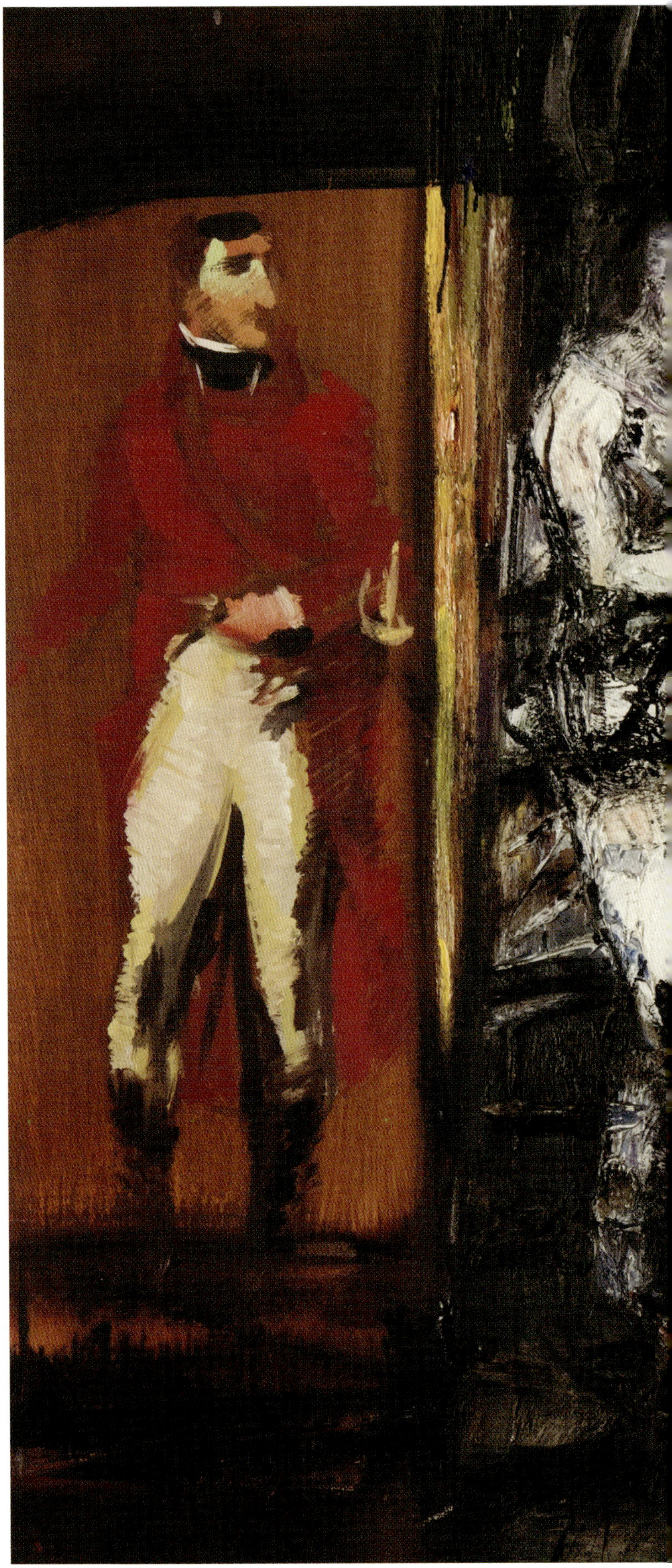

FIG. 4.4
Never Mind
1965 / oil and vinyl toluene on canvas / 91.4 x 121.9 cm
image courtesy of the Hunterian, University of Glasgow, 2018

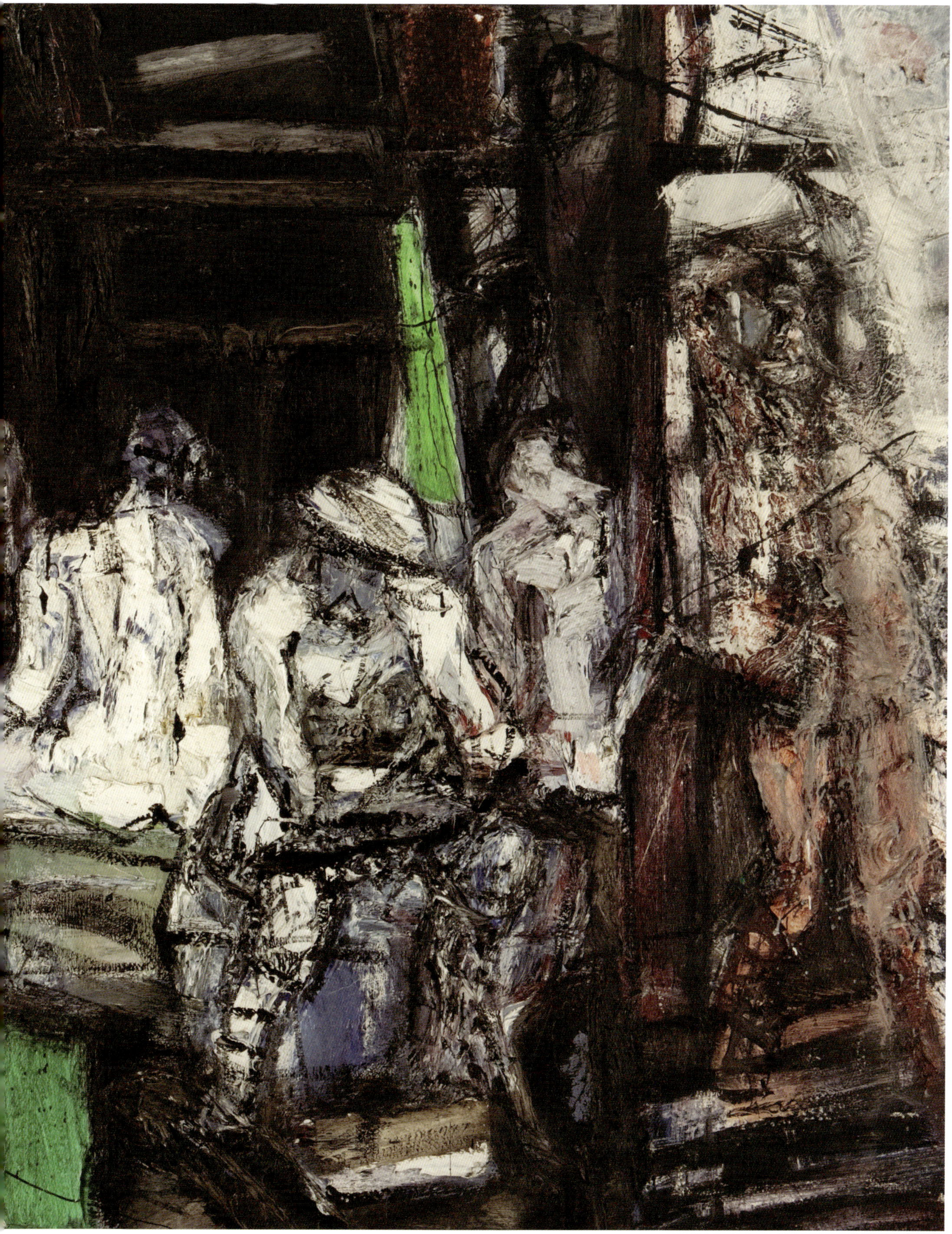

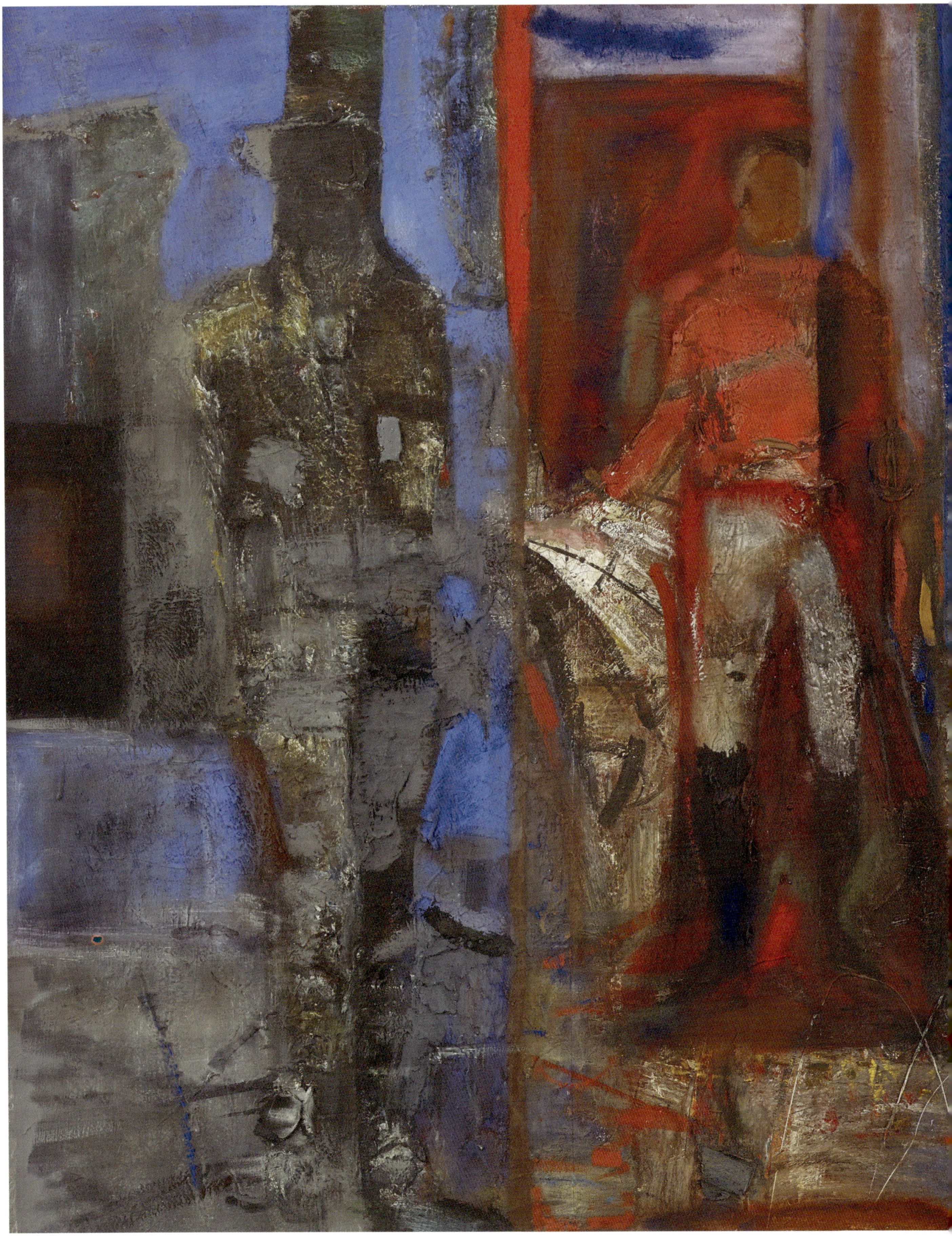

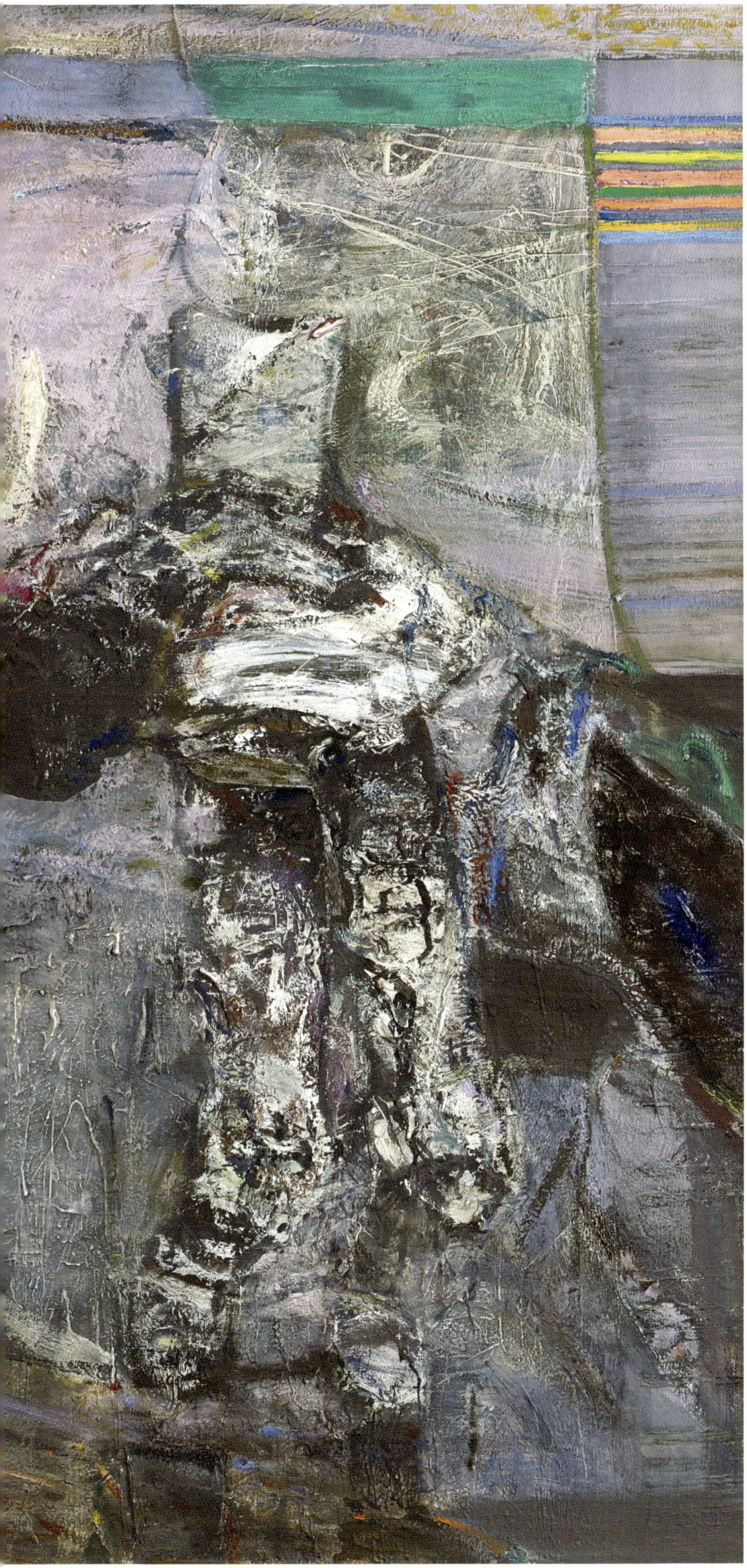

FIG. 4.5
Never Mind II
*c.*1966–67 / oil on canvas / 91 x 123 cm
private collection • courtesy of the Scottish Gallery

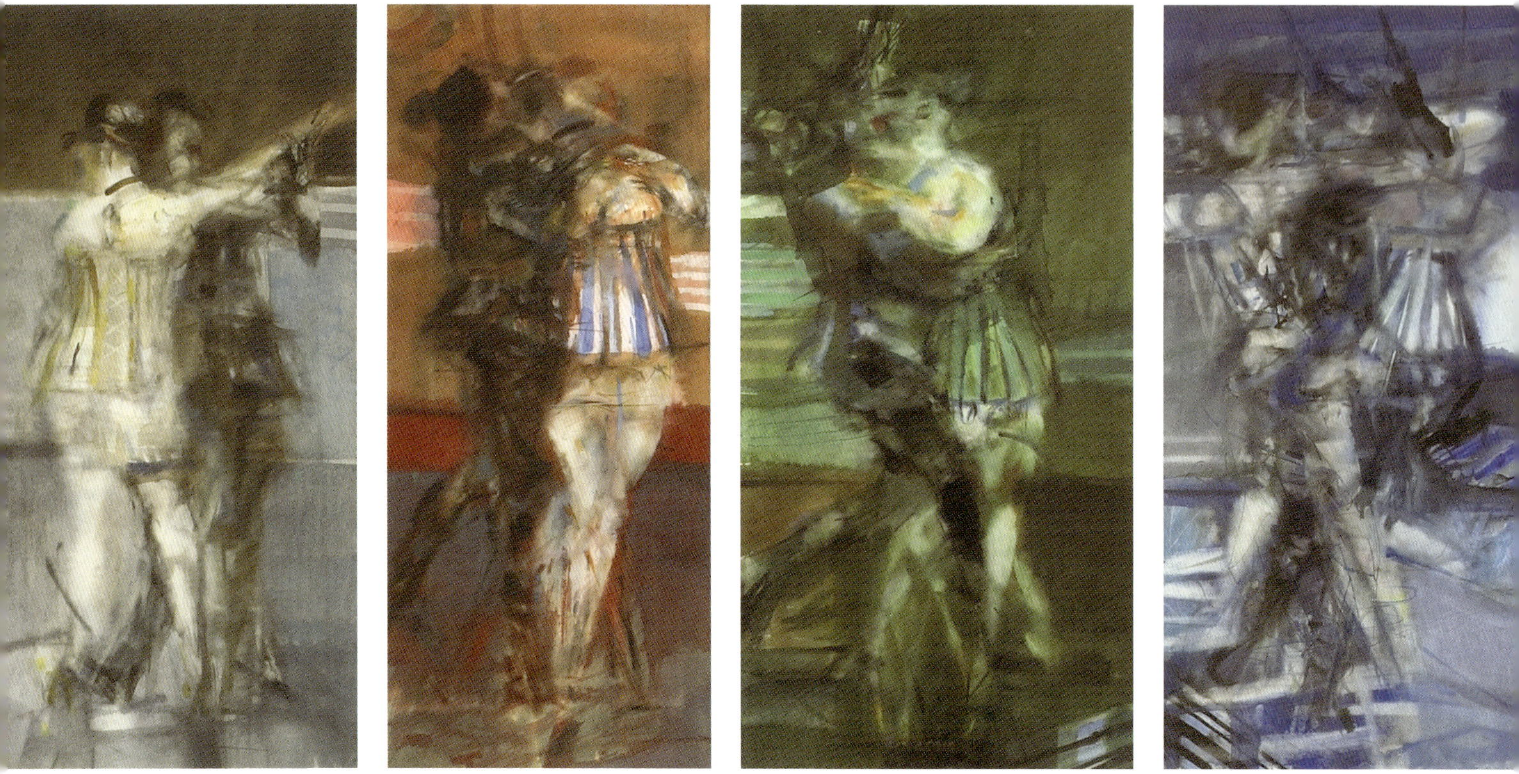

FIG. 4.6
On the Edge (polyptych)
1966 / watercolour on paper / each panel 68.5 cm high x 20–69.8 cm wide
City Art Centre, City of Edinburgh Museums & Galleries • photo: Antonia Reeve

academic; figurative and brutal, they depicted fear, sacrifice and death with themes matched to a careful choice and working of materials. *Never Mind* was a key painting which, as with *Nevermind II*, deals with the execution of a soldier in the rawest of terms. In both, a uniformed Napoleonic soldier observes a row of naked men awaiting their fate. The canvas was vertically divisioned to offer serialised imagery arranged across the work – this again bore the mark of cinematic influence. Douglas Hall, the keeper of the Scottish National Gallery of Modern Art, selected the works for the major 1965 show and contributed a short essay to its catalogue. Contextualising Robin's new art, Hall pointed out that while avant-garde painters in England and America had eschewed 'the manipulation of paint for decorative or expressive purposes', it remained a trait in Scottish art – though there were few, apart from Eardley and Philipson, who used expressionism to mirror human experience. These canvases were 'characteristically modern' in so far as forms were initially conceived abstractly and then gradually, though only partially, assumed meaning and representational form. Hall wrote of how Robin's new art developed from the cockfight paintings where the 'flying pigments' had matched the 'explosion of feathers' but that a new phase of work had now begun. He also pointed out that there are no heroes in this war art. In the first Crucifixion paintings – a highly ambitious subject to be carried through for some years – the 'aggressive paint[s] ... menace us with a threatening contagious dryness', which resulted from the new use of vinyl toluene in a number of canvases. Many of these works used mixed media with oil and vinyl toluene as their pigment-binding agents. Hall also pointed out that not all the new art was concerned with violence and pain:

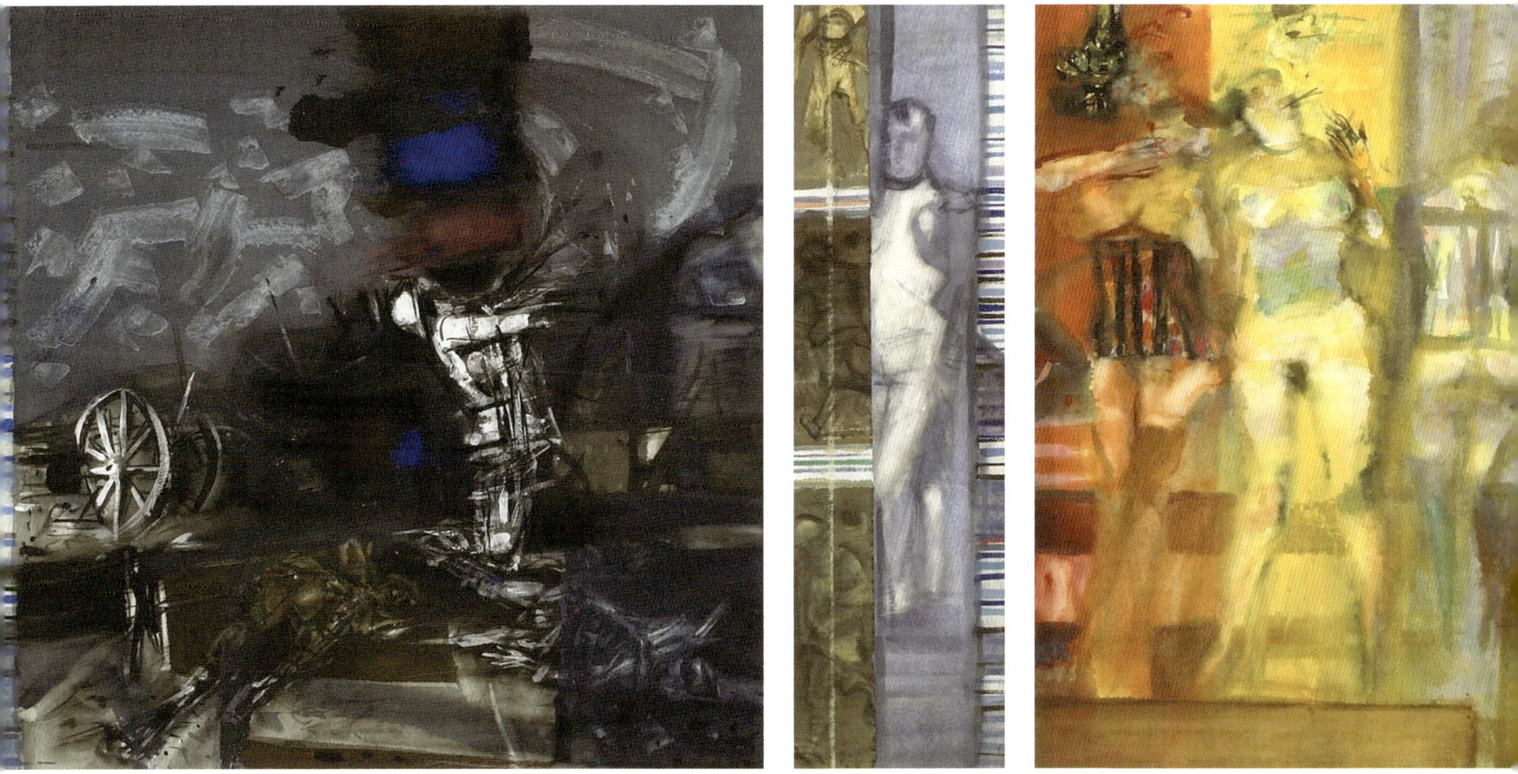

rather, the watercolours often had a quiet centre at their heart, and the ongoing series of cathedral interiors presented 'caverns of space' and 'zones of light'. Importantly, the watercolours included a number of female nudes; the odalisque or prostitute figure would continue to be a recurrent subject through the 1970s and into the 1980s. In 1966 a seven-panel watercolour polyptych *On the Edge* (colloquially referred to by Robin as 'the soldier and the floosy'), with its women, soldiers and a glimpsed Napoleon himself, would follow through the cinematic narrative in its dance of life and death [fig. 4.6].

During the show's planning, Robin viewed this landmark exhibition very much as work in progress, with further research needed to take it to a different level. Earlier in the year he had applied successfully for a Leverhulme Trust research grant, which enabled him to leave Edinburgh for a month following the opening of his show. He and Thora toured European museums, in particular seeking out altarpieces by Northern Renaissance artists. His recent major watercolour *Golgotha* had served as his own first multipanel contribution to the genre. It gained the Cargill Award on exhibition at the 1967 RGI exhibition and, following its purchase by Glasgow Art Gallery in the spring, he had summarised its meaning as reflecting 'the strife and anguish in the relationship of peoples in the world'.[5] This painting has winged side panels which, when closed, showed a traditional garden of delights and a descent into hell, while depictions of Adam and Eve (who had already appeared in his war-time mural twenty years previously) conveyed sorrow and shame but also hope. Predella panels include a cockerel and also an odalisque with a mirror, a figure of conceit which he independently reworked in both watercolour and oil on a number of occasions. War also featured, with two predellas here devoted to soldiers. The painting uses colour as metaphor, a golden light in the central panel indicative of the spirit of mankind 'in its highest aspirations' and figures presented in subdued hues in the side panels to be read as either 'the damned or the angelic host'.[6] In the left panel, the Garden of Gethsemane was painted in detail over a square of Japanese paper to provide a sense of spirituality. The right panel (which he regarded as the more important one) contained a kneeling, isolated figure 'in doubt and agony of spirit'.

The meaning of *Golgotha* and other works was left ambiguous, with the viewer asked to interpret the work as he or she wished, yet overall this work was all about representing aspects of humankind, a large subject of considerable ambition. The message was of choice but also of despair at man's seemingly endless inhumanity to his fellows. Indeed, as Robin himself confessed, the central panel – which included a Middle Eastern market – was begun as war was sparked in that part of the world. Its successors would be *Defenders of the Realm* [fig. 4.10], a major 1965 triptych plus five predella panels, and the 1966–67 oil and toluene triptych *Gethsemane*, which set out to deal specifically with 'the theme of man's agony and his victory over temptation' and was exhibited at the 1967 RSA annual show along with *On the Edge*. The latter was again both an essay in colour, panel by panel, and of temptation. Many of Robin's paintings in the coming decade would further explore the nature of humanity through specific incident.

To a great degree these paintings relied on a studied understanding of past European art, for which Robin had a huge respect. The 1965 Leverhulme research trip had been to Bruges to view a Jan Gossaert exhibition and to the Memling museum, then to Ghent for the van Eyck altarpiece, to Antwerp and The Hague (the Mauritshuis) and on to Amsterdam, Zurich and Venice. Zurich also importantly provided him with the chance to see works by de Staël and a summer exhibition of paintings by Rouault, whose later works brought 'a new and extreme richness to the properties of oil paint'.[7] At Colmar he sought out the celebrated Grünewald altarpiece in the Musée Unterlinden, with its nine images across twelve panels. The crucifixion at its centre struck him as an

> ... *intense drama created by the isolation of cruel representational fact against a dark spaceless background; the cruel insistent details of everyday fact in representational painting and the mystical sense of atmosphere with accompanying changes of scale, all giving a sense of the balance of the real and the supernatural in a work of great unity.*[8]

He would soon embark on his major series of crucifixion paintings, themselves stark and raw in their depiction of isolation and suffering [figs 4.8–4.10]. One of these, the *Crucifixion and Ascension* triptych of 1969 [fig. 4.15], is double-sided, with the front side panels including a rose window motif within a series of wide horizontal bands of colour and the reverse more figurative and, as with others of this time such as *Lament*, powerfully raw in its working of paint using the spatula and knife. The most ambitious of these would be *A Threnody for Our Time* [fig. 4.12], a major semi-abstract triptych on the theme of the Passion of

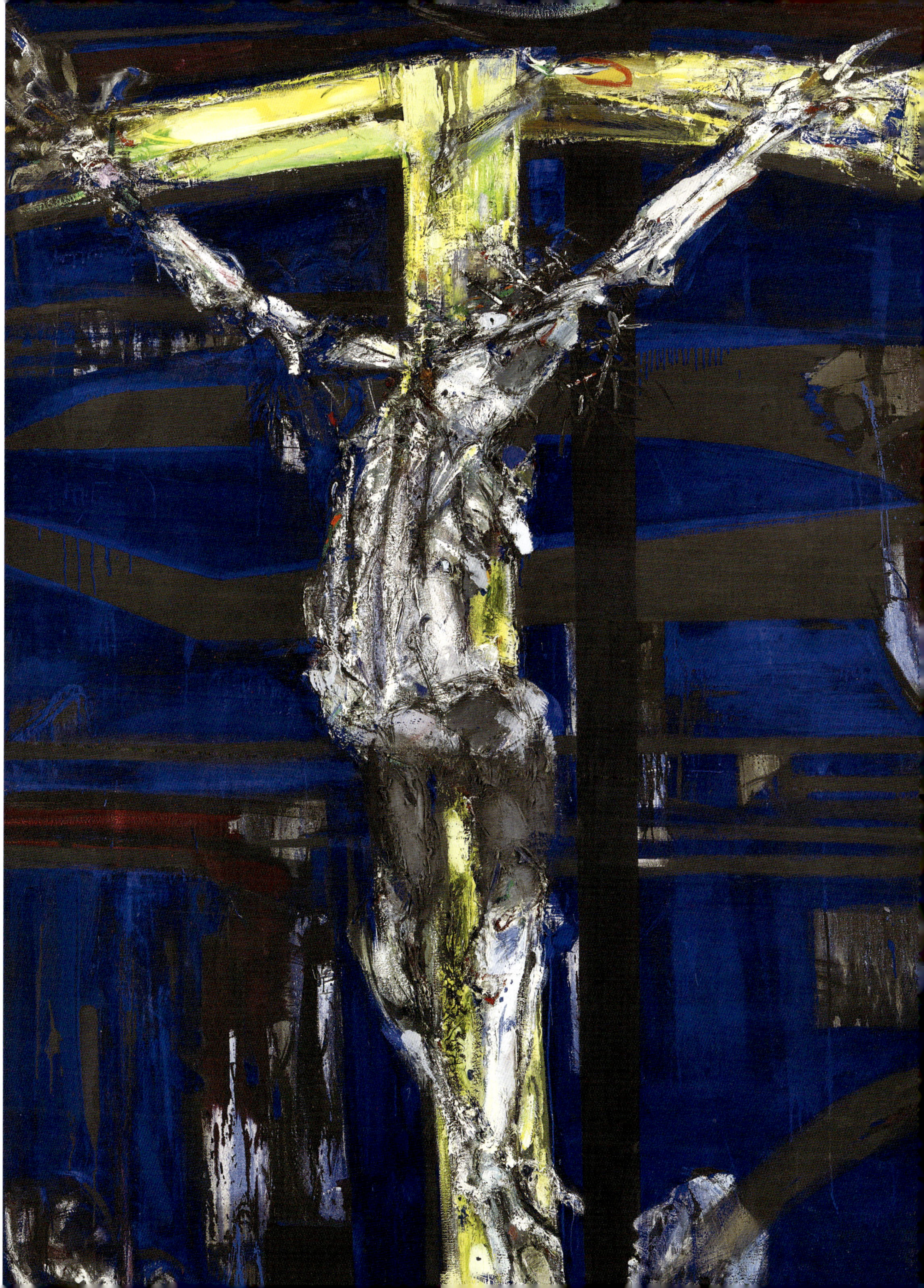

◂◂ FIG. 4.7
Crucifixion
1969–70 / oil and vinyl toluene on canvas / 214 x 152 cm
private collection • courtesy of the Scottish Gallery

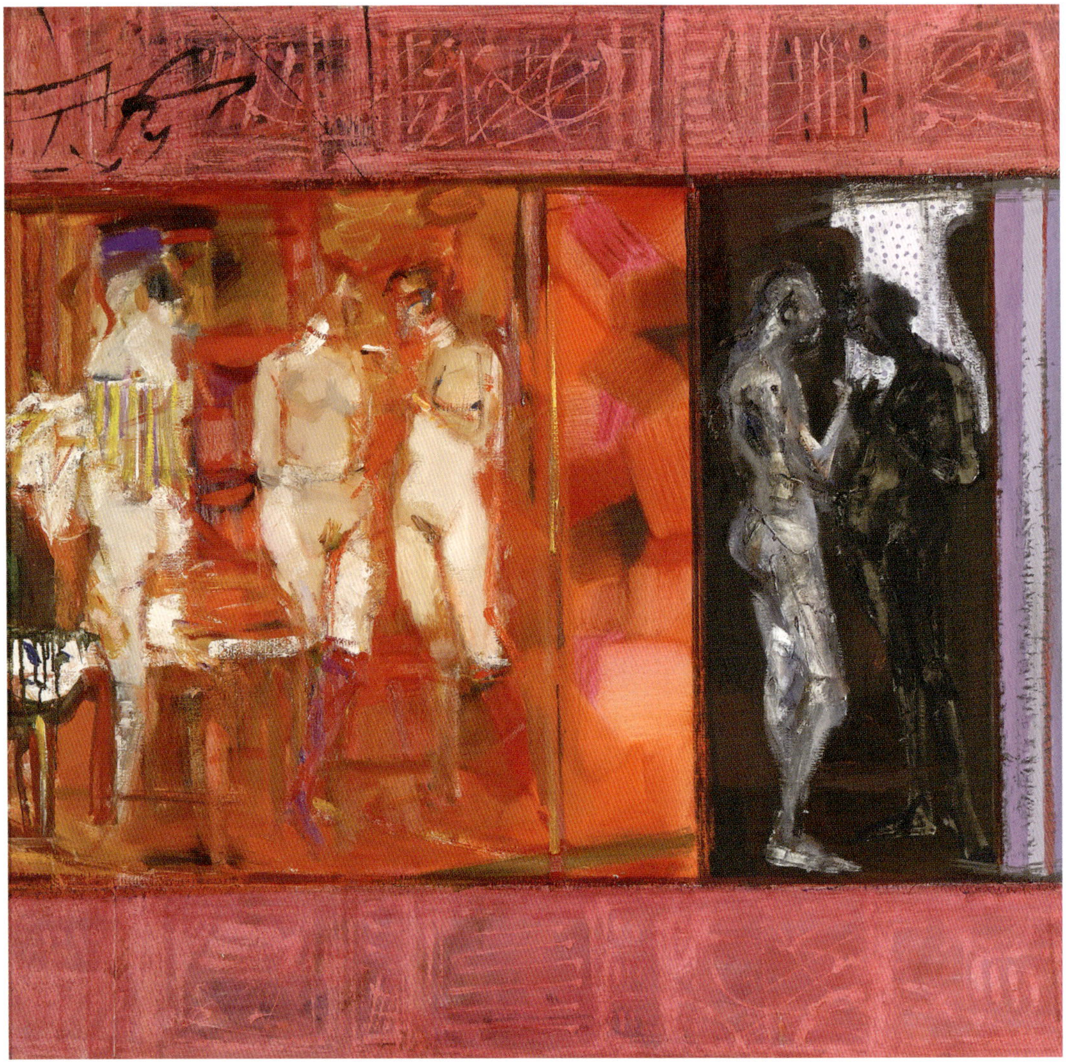

FIG. 4.8
Threnody in Red
1969 / oil on canvas / 100 x 100 cm
University of Aberdeen

▸ FIG. 4.9
Lament
1968 / oil on canvas / 213.8 x 160.1 cm
Royal Scottish Academy of Art & Architecture (Diploma Collection) • photo: Andy Phillipson

▸▸ FIG. 4.10
Defenders of the Realm (triptych plus predella panels)
1965 / oil and vinyl toluene on canvas
side panels 153 x 76.2 cm; central panel 153 x 153 cm; predella panels 30.5 cm high
private collection • photo: Antonia Reeve

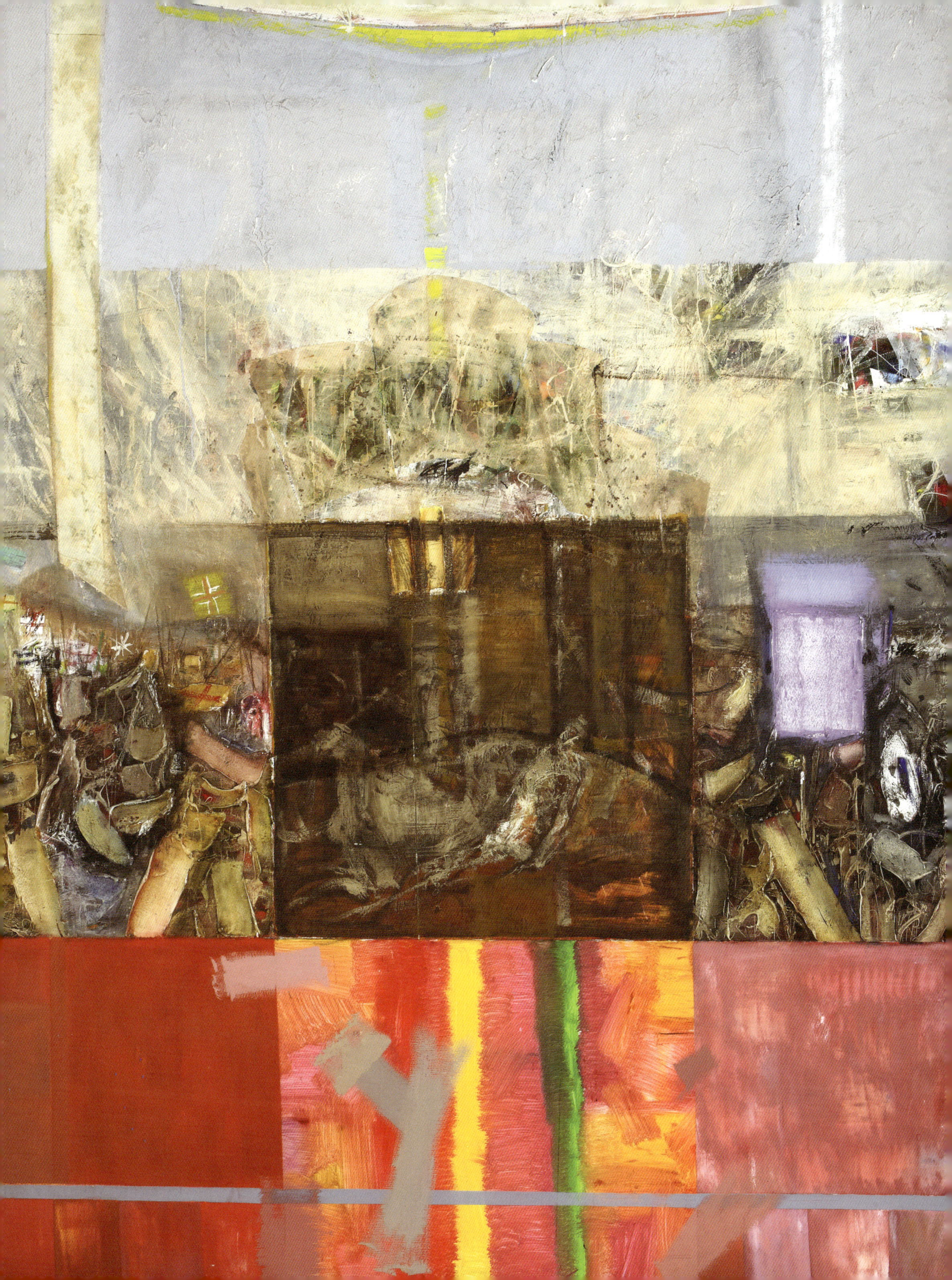

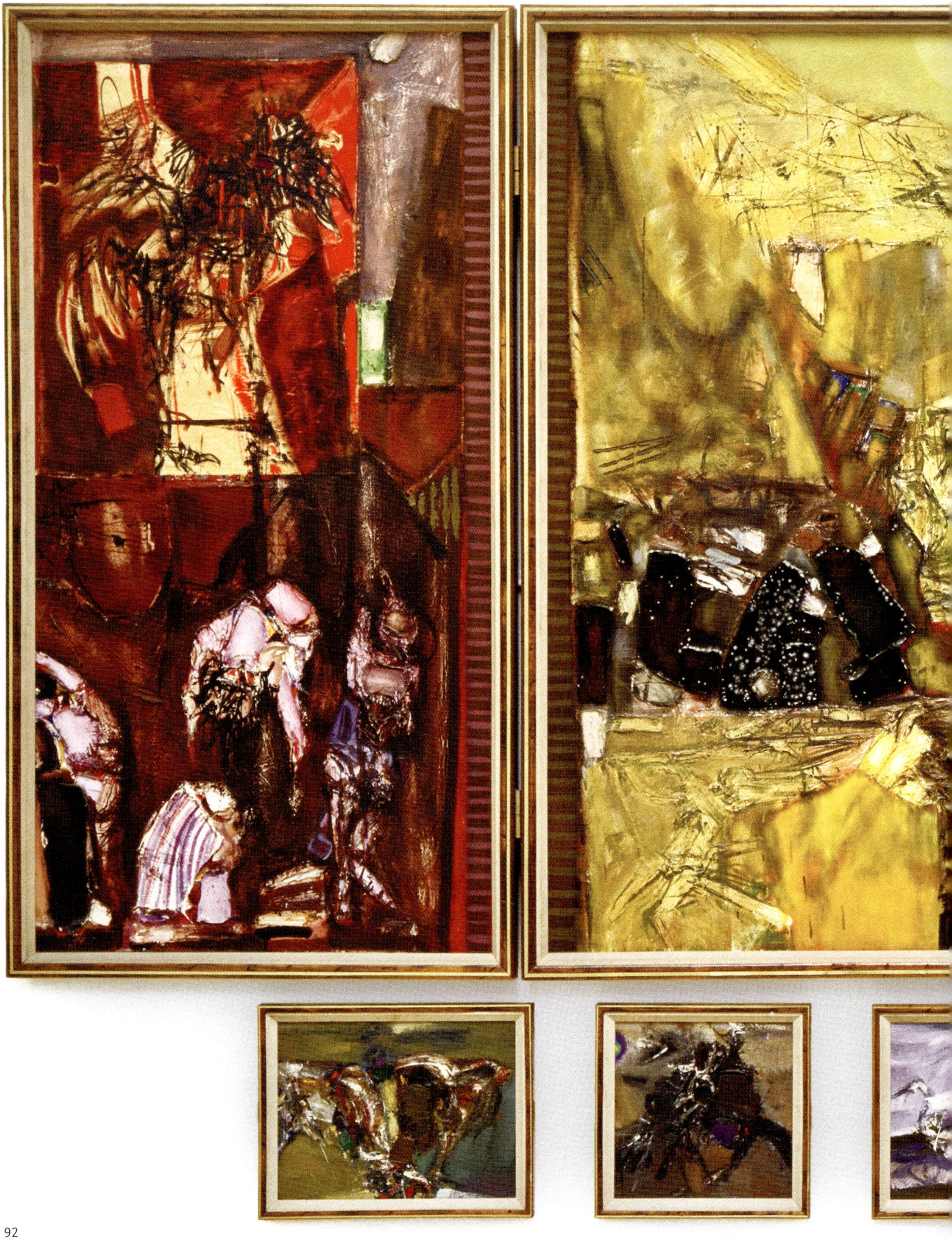

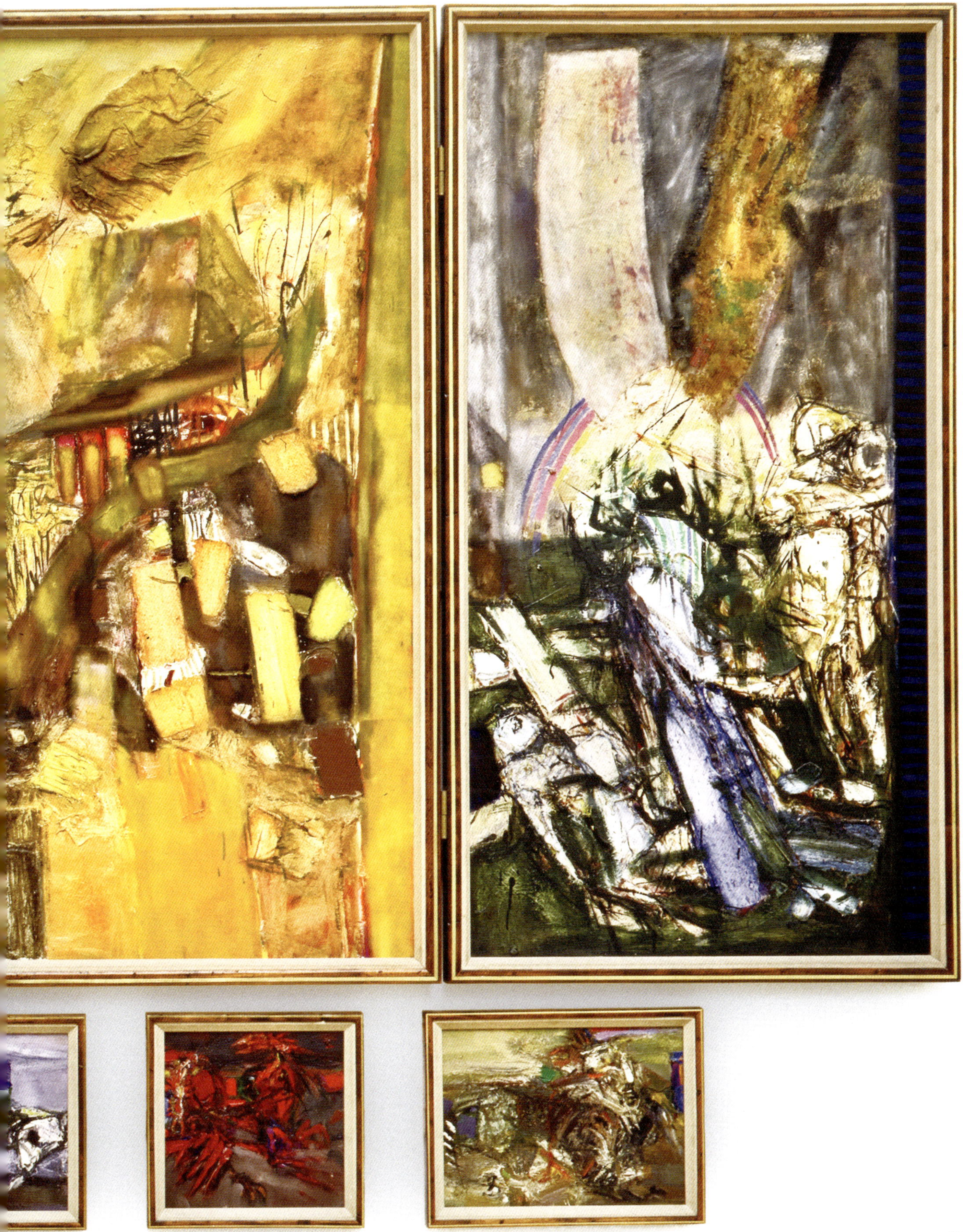

FIG. 4.11
Church Interior
1965 / oil and vinyl toluene and paper collage on canvas / 91.5 x 121.9 cm
National Galleries of Scotland • photo: Antonia Reeve

▸▸ FIG. 4.12
A Threnody for Our Time (triptych)
1970–71 / oil and vinyl toluene on canvas
side panels 274 x 142 cm;
central panel 274 x 228.5 cm
private collection • courtesy of the Scottish Gallery

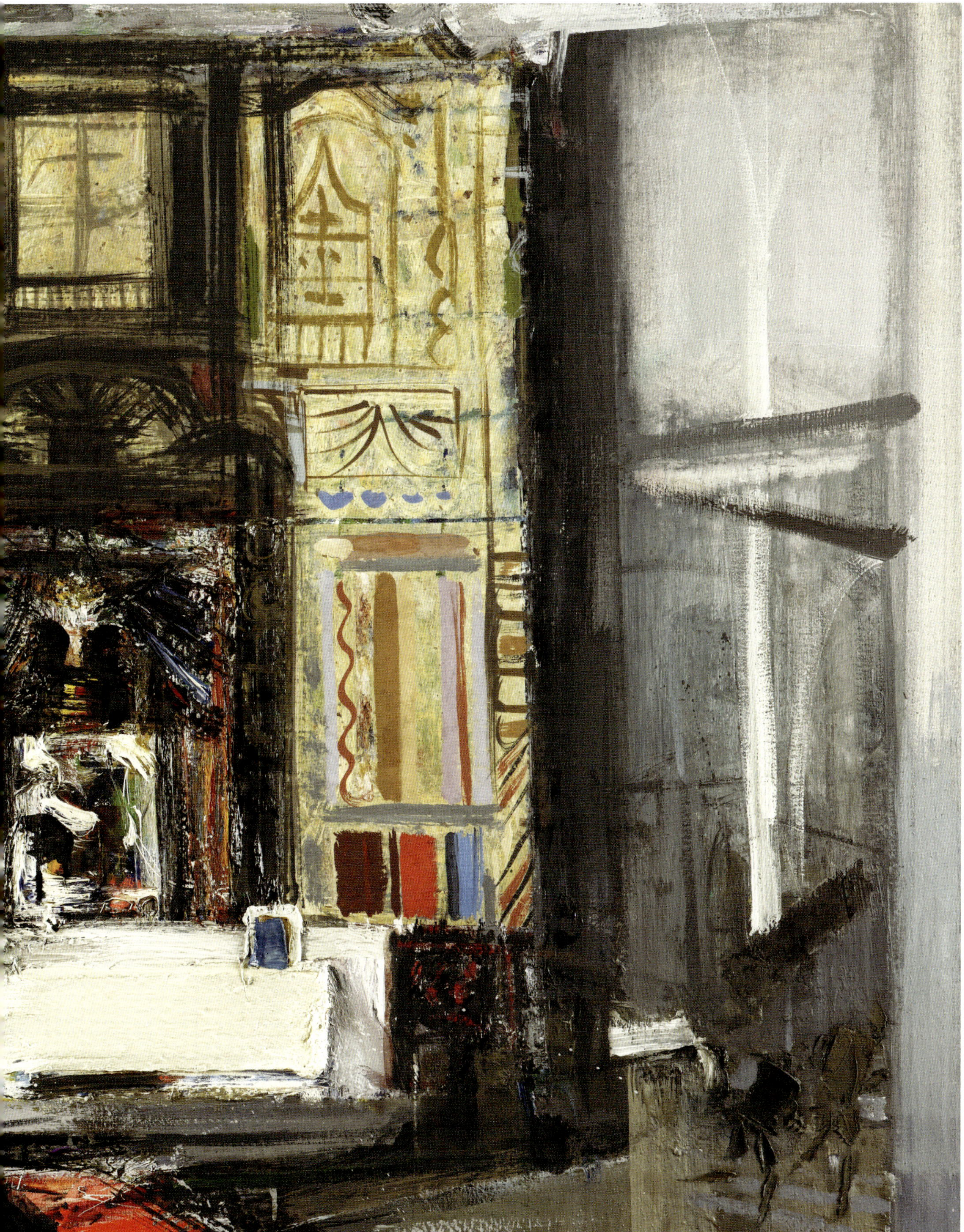

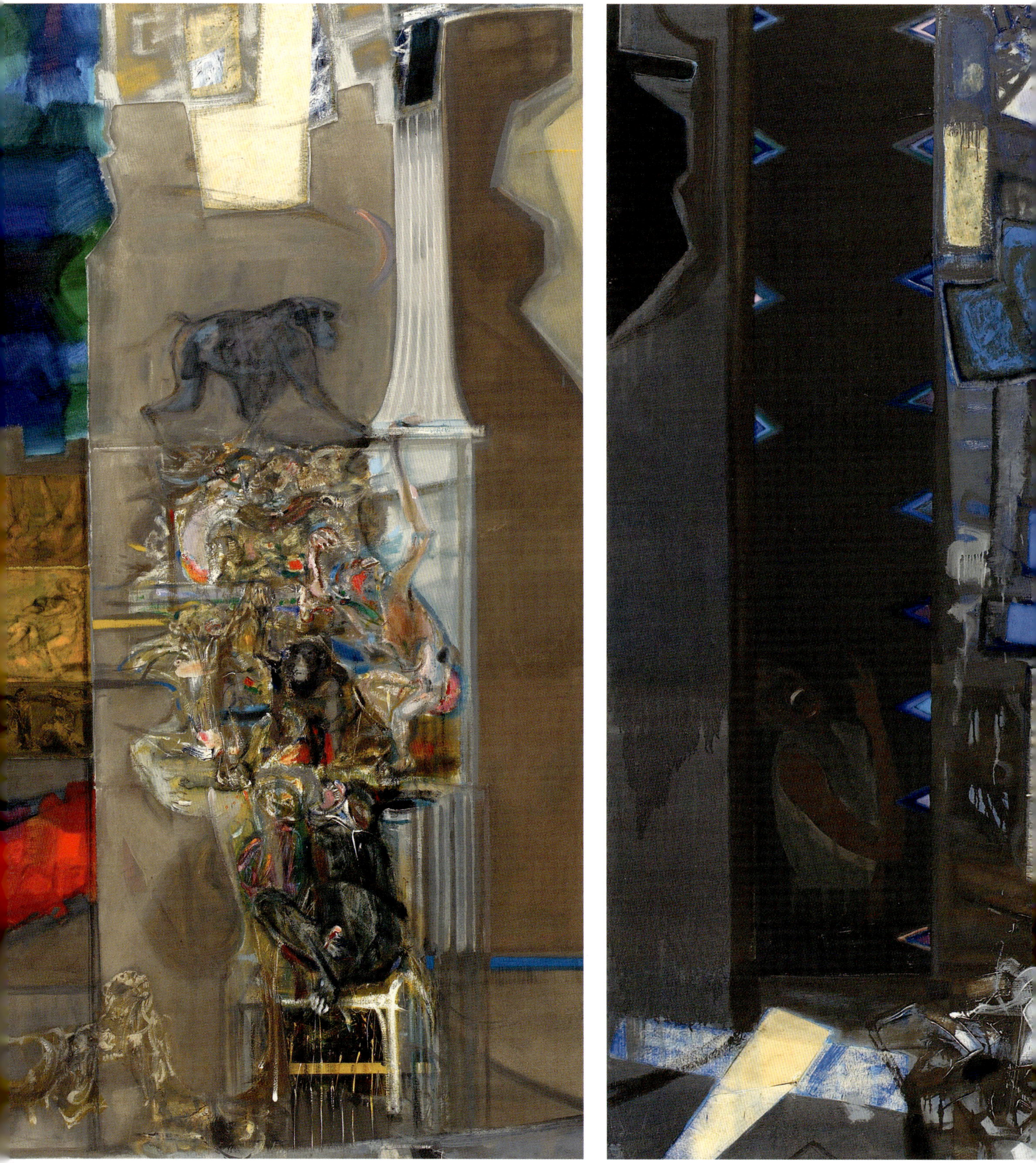

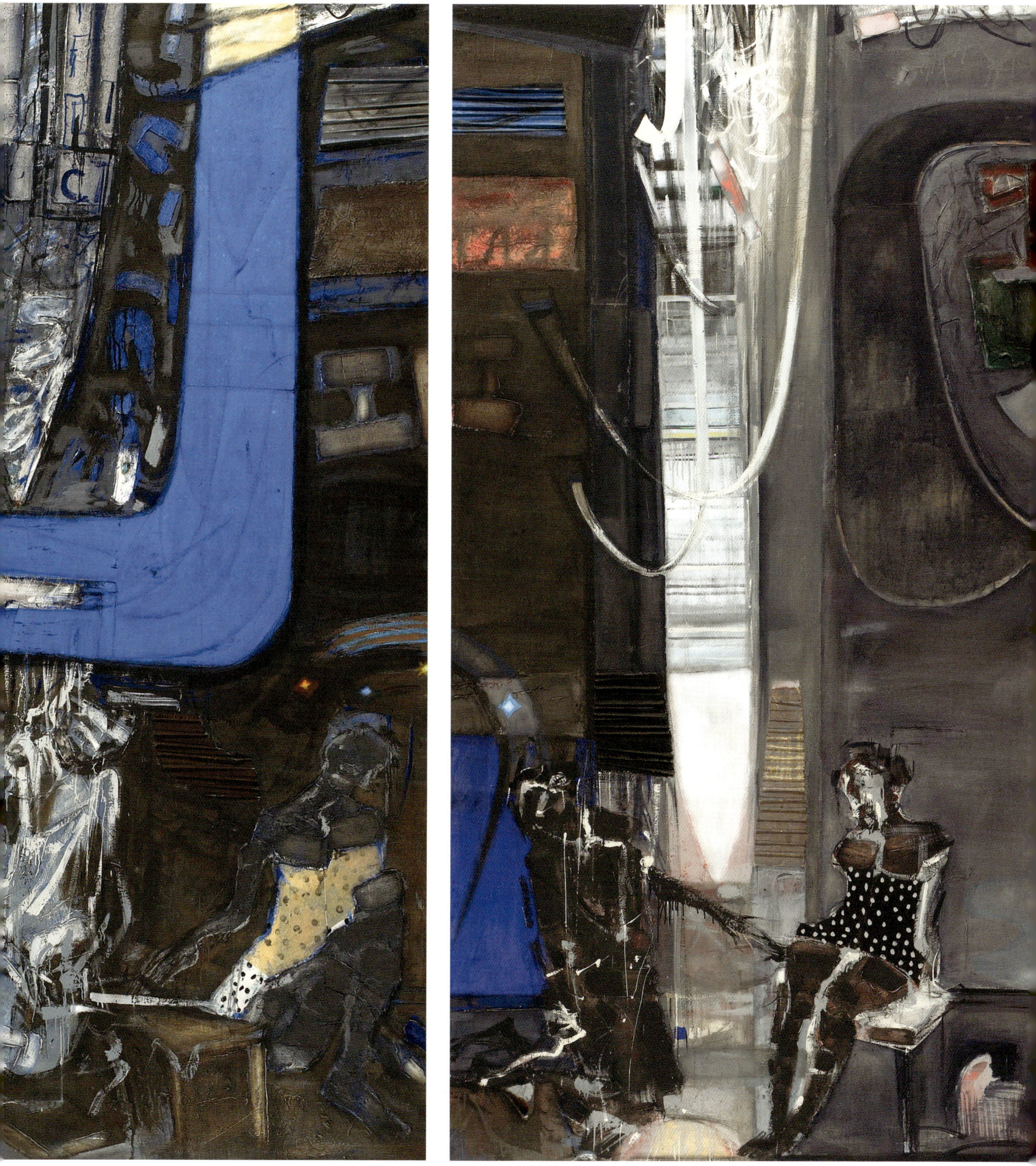

Christ, finally completed in 1971. It remains the most ambitious of his large-scale works and an individual response to past art and to Francis Bacon's *Three Studies for Figures at the Base of the Crucifixion* of 1962. Alongside these were further paintings of violence – some of his most brutal and thrilling cockfights [fig. 0.2].

Meanwhile, the year 1965 was not yet over in terms of exhibiting new work. Four paintings (*Golgotha, Stone the Crows, Burning in a Waste Land* and *Execution*) were included by Bill Buchanan in the exhibition of 'Contemporary Scottish Painting' prepared by the Arts Council Scottish Committee for the IBM Gallery in New York. The show, selected by Buchanan, ran through November and December, and included work by Eardley, Neil Dallas Brown (1938–2003), Henderson Blyth, Ian Mackenzie Smith (born 1935), John Houston and David Donaldson. The year thus finished on a high note, but not everything had been positive. The year had also seen Robin's friend Robbie Scott Hay die unexpectedly. One of the last paintings of Robin's he bought is *Church Interior* [fig. 4.11], an essay in light, space and surface presented through mixed media. Reid & Taylor's company designer John Packer took over as managing director, with T.R. Robertson now the designer. Under Packer's direction, this unique Borders gallery broadened its scope, loosening ties with the Edinburgh painters, though Robin remained in touch off and on through much of the 1960s, suggesting exhibitions.[9] Exhibitions already planned were honoured: in December MacTaggart opened an Anne Redpath memorial show, and a second would be held in 1967. Much of the Scott Hay collection of Scottish art – forty-three works in all – was given to the Scottish National Gallery of Modern Art in 1967, and in that year a memorial exhibition of Scott Hay's own landscape watercolours was shown in The Factory (renamed the Scott Hay Gallery), with a generous catalogue introduction by Robin. The connection between Robbie Scott Hay and the College was wider than simply the personal contributions made at Langholm by Robin and Jimmy Cumming, as his central Edinburgh flat in Cannon Street Lane was used by (and later became the property of) the College for its academic visitors.

The College of the mid-1960s was a place of increasing opportunities amidst the maintenance of tried and tested traditions. In November 1965 Robin wrote a paper arguing for an independent School of mural art 'to preserve traditional methods of mural decoration' outside of D&P and Design and Crafts. This could incorporate aspects of stage design, given the nationwide interest in a national theatre. Although this idea came to nothing, he applied himself personally to this form of public art and, in 1966, was commissioned by architects Spence, Glover and Ferguson to paint an eight-panel mural, *Flight*, for the 'buffet' (refectory) of their new Glasgow airport terminal at Abbotsinch [figs 4.13–4.14]. These beautiful panels, painted in the studio in oil on panel, come close to abstraction but represent speed, air and a landscape fleetingly viewed from above. They remained *in situ* for ten years, when all were dismantled and given to Glasgow museums. The installation was also part of Robin's ever-present interest in colour, which continued with his membership of the UK's Colour Group. Colour was a subject being debated across different sections of the College at this time, with talks organised by the Group being held at Lauriston Place. The College records show that between at least 1966 and 1968 Robin was in touch with Dr Romuald Lakowski of the University's psychology department, who was secretary of the Group's Scottish Section and actively contributed to its discussions.[10]

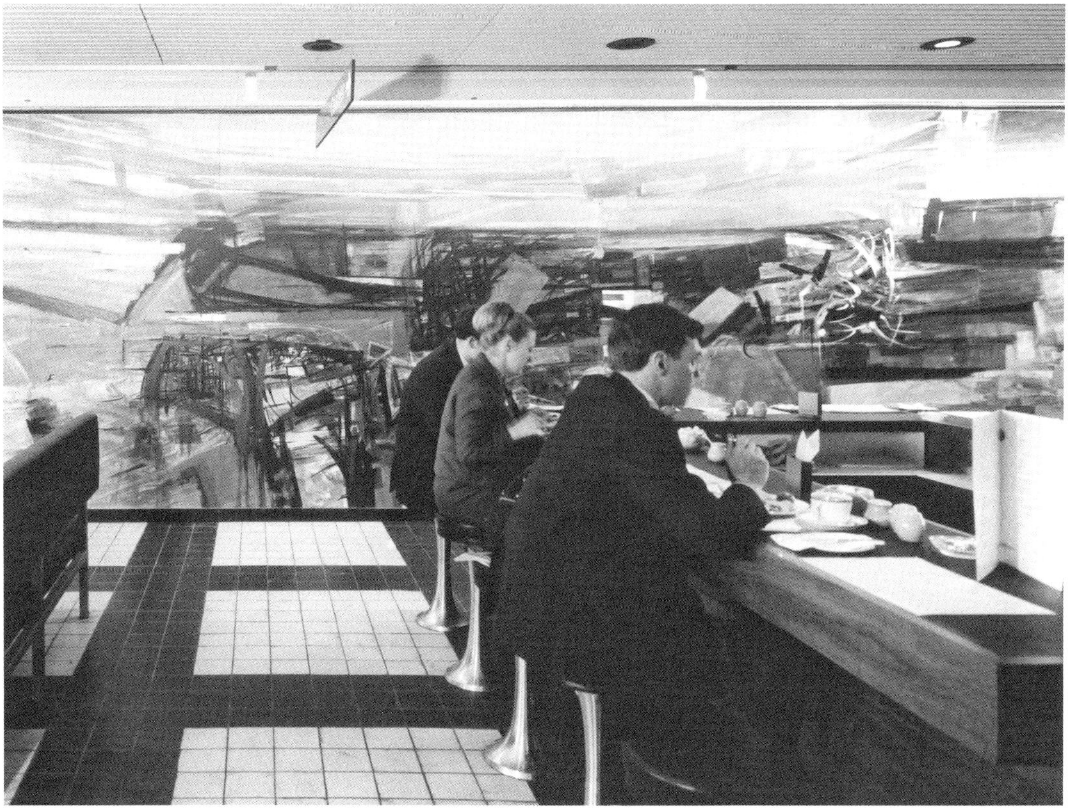

FIG. 4.13
Flight in the refectory at Glasgow airport, *c.*1966

▸▸ FIG. 4.14
Flight (panels 4 and 7)
1966 / oil on panel / each panel 255.5 x 146.5 cm
side panels 153 x 76.2 cm; central panel 153 x 153 cm; predella panels 30.5 cm high

By this date the majority of Robin's many extramural commitments deliberately aimed to expand College activities and modernise its position within the cultural landscape. In 1966 he was approached by the modernist architect Peter Womersley (1923–1993), asking for art for the entrance hall of the new hospital in Haddington, East Lothian – to be placed on a 'brick wall painted in donkey brown' with a khaki green floor, a 'bullrush' circular carpet and chairs in a pinkish flame and light grey colour. Some younger members of his D&P staff, such as Bob Callender, were recruited to assist.[11] The College by this date had also become regularly visible in the city during the Festival exhibitions held in the Scotsman Steps – a staircase passageway leading from the North Bridge entrance of the *Scotsman* newspaper building down to Market Street. Robin encouraged its development and worked with *The Scotsman*'s editor, Alastair Dunnett (1908–1998), to recruit students for its hanging committee. The students themselves were already contributing to such *al fresco* art exhibitions off their own bat. For the 1963 Festival, two leading College students, John Bellany (1942–2013) and Sandy Moffat (born 1943), had displayed their paintings with others on railings by the Castle Terrace car park[12] and in 1964 and 1965 they famously staged their own joint exhibition on those next to the RSA, carrying their paintings daily from the backroom of Milne's Bar in Hanover Street.[13]

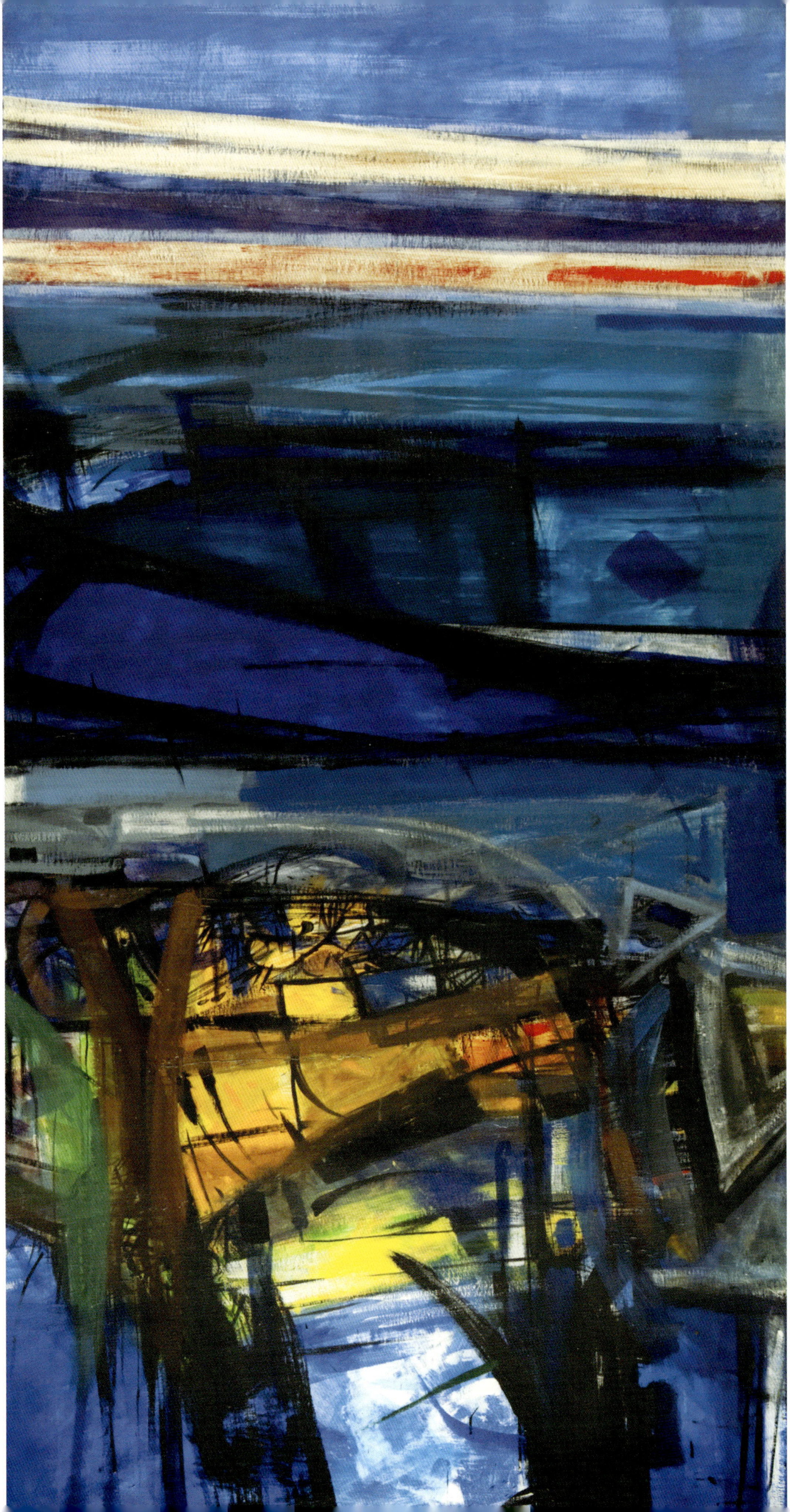

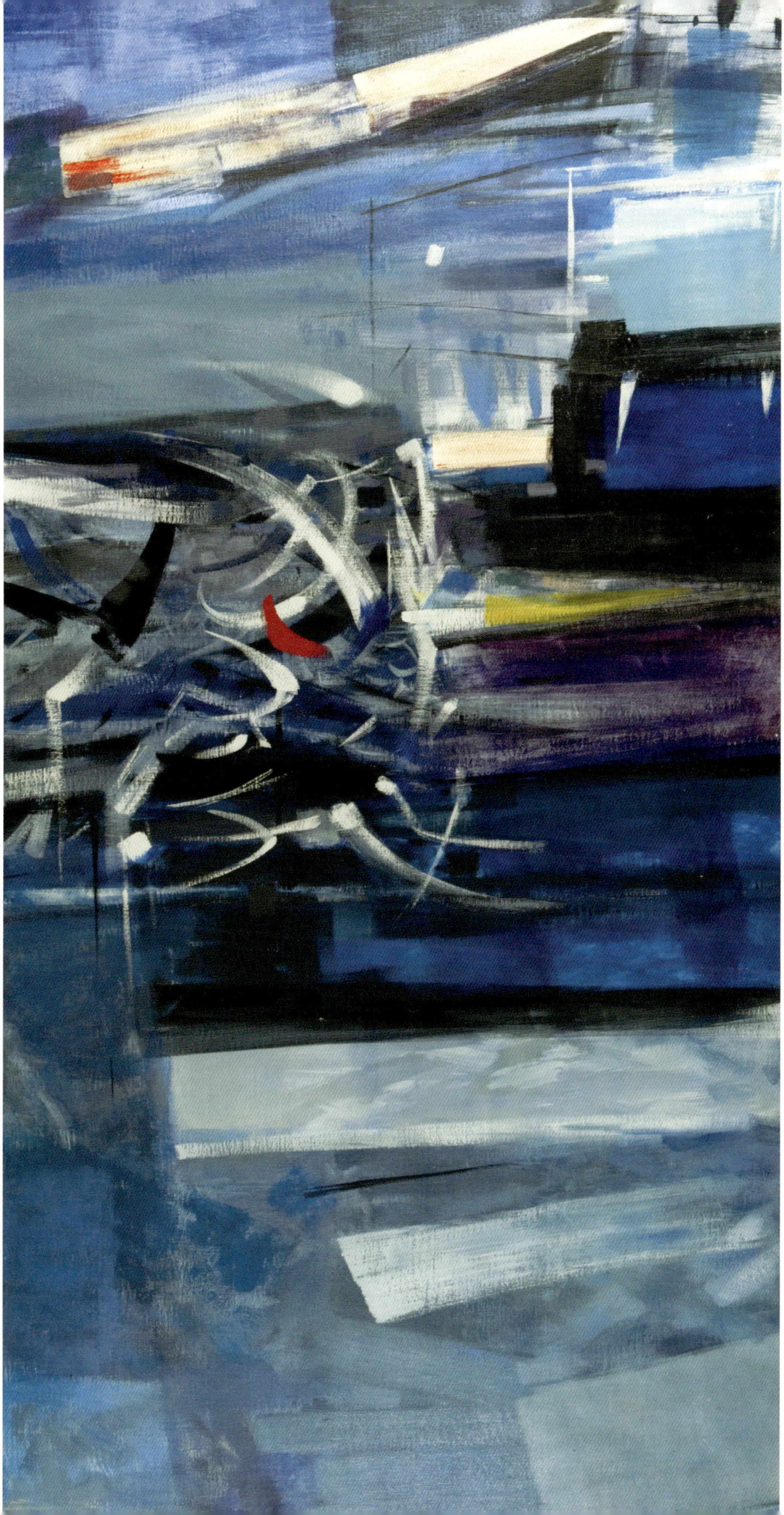

Providing the right balance of opportunities for art students includes bringing in outside voices. Robin was always keen for both staff and students to be exposed to as much art at first hand as possible. As part of their course, mid-1960s seminars for third-year D&P students were taught in the National Gallery on the Mound where they were led – and assessed – by Colin Thompson. Films on French art were borrowed from the local French Institute for screening at the College. In addition, travel money was found: in early 1967, as the new College principal Stanley Wright was settling in, Robin negotiated funds for over forty students to visit Paris to see the Picasso show and London to see 'Young Contemporaries at the Tate'. Edinburgh students had shown in London for several years. John Bellany told his biographer John McEwen of how, as president of the College's student sketch club in his final year, he had organised the smuggling of student paintings on a train to London; caught red-handed in the act by the station master at Waverley, the students were saved by Robin's arguing for them and the paintings were then transported free of charge to London.[14] In addition, Robin occasionally arranged for student work to be displayed in commercial galleries, and in this regard built up a working relationship with Marjorie Parr, a contemporary art dealer in Chelsea. It was, however, rare for a former student to have a one-person show in the College, and the exception here was Bellany. In late 1967 it was agreed that his new paintings should have a showing in the sculpture court, the College's principal exhibition space. Bellany turned down the offer of a teaching contract but gave Robin a painting which, much later, he was astonished to find had pride of place in the Philipson home.

Equally significant for the student experience were the exchanges between staff in Edinburgh and other art colleges throughout the late 1960s and early 1970s. Some came as assessors and examiners, others simply to share ideas in the studios or give a talk in the College's first-floor lecture room. Robin had always wanted to invite artists to Edinburgh, and indeed the visits of Australian painters Sidney Nolan and Arthur Boyd were memorable for both staff and students. In the mid-1960s, the Royal College of Art tutor with whom Robin was most often in touch was Carel Weight, and the two discussed potential new Edinburgh tutors who might be drawn from both D&P and the cream of RCA students. The artists who visited as assessors – and they usually visited twice in an academic year – were regularly encouraged also to spend time in the Postgraduate School. It would be unfair to give the full credit only to Robin for the long and impressive list of artist visitors, as many were suggested by colleagues, but in retrospect it seems only proper to acknowledge his backing for them. He certainly was anxious for students to be exposed to as many ideas and approaches as possible. Both Weight and Peter Blake gave talks to the students in March 1968, and that September the artists shortlisted for external assessors in D&P for 1968–69 included Weight, Robert Medley, Kenneth Rowntree, Richard Hamilton (1922–2011) and Tom Hudson. Michael Rothenstein (1908–1993) worked with the School of Printmaking students in October and readily planned a second visit while Joe Tilson (born 1928) came in January 1969. In April lectures were given by Ceri Richards (1903–1971) and Hamilton. Plans for studio teaching visits in the new session were aired that month, and the list of suggested artists is impressive – Bridget Riley, Eduardo Paolozzi, Richard Smith, Tilson, Leonard Rosoman, R.B. Kitaj, William Scott, Richards and Roger de Grey, among others. The range of British artists involved with the College would carry on through the coming decades: one examiner in D&P in the early 1970s was Howard Hodgkin (1932–2017).

Robin also served *ex officio* on the Board of Hospitalfield, the extraordinary Arbroath house and art collection which hosted summer residencies for the Scottish art schools. In these years he was also supporting, where possible, the Demarco Gallery which had opened at 8 Melville Crescent in 1966, following the art space programmed by its director Richard Demarco at the Traverse Theatre since 1963 and its own gallery in James Court from the following year. The Gallery in its new and former guise was showing a mix of mainly American and British professional artists, some of whom were Robin's colleagues or former students. Robin himself had work in the Gallery's inaugural show at Melville Crescent in August 1966 – a huge show involving fifty-three artists from Britain, America and Australia – and was included in a show organised by Demarco in Warsaw in May 1967. A relationship had quickly developed where visitors to the Demarco Gallery were often encouraged to visit the College – this was how Nolan had spoken at the College in 1966. The flow of artists between organisations was part of the culture of the late 1960s and early 1970s. However, the most innovative connection between the Demarco Gallery and the College would happen in August 1970 when 'Strategy: Get Arts' was presented in association with the Kunsthalle in Düsseldorf. This show of cutting-edge German art included an installation by Joseph Beuys.[15] Students, mostly from D&P, were more than willingly dragooned by Robin to help with installations when the famous brought their art to the students' own studios.

Against this swell in promoting fresh ideas, the need for modernising the College curriculum felt ever more necessary. Staff committees debated the future, and memos and letters flew back and forth before and after committee meetings. Between 1969 and 1971 especially, staff voiced their opinions regarding proposed changes. For example, in September 1969 Derek Clarke declared his strong objections to Robin's proposal for life painting – once so important to the latter's own teaching – to be dropped from third-year classes. The provision of classes in drawing and mural painting became a hot issue in 1970–71, with Robin favouring an inter-School approach. This did not please Tony Hatwell, head of Sculpture, who in January 1971 demanded that his School should offer its own, dedicated, classes in drawing. As late as 1978, 'the figure' was 'regularly provided as the main subject of study' in painting – traditional ways lasted a long time.[16] Timetabling issues often prevented any one section or School from winning the day. Robin supported retaining the diploma classes much as they were but advocated an overall slimming down of subjects. Interestingly, 'advanced anatomy' remained a third-year subject until 1972.

Gradually, the way forward in terms of updating graduate qualifications became clearer. An associateship (not supported by Robin) was proposed at one stage but eventually an honours degree ratified by Heriot-Watt University replaced the old diploma in the early 1970s. This change was the result of pressure on the College as a government-funded Scottish Central Institution, and was agreed in response to reports written by civil servants and professional educators. In 1978 Robin wrote frankly to Kim Kempshall of his despair at recent ways in art education: 'it is an extraordinary world, this world of art, where people who no longer do it themselves decide they have to set up advice departments to tell other people how to do it.'[17]

The College records are littered with letters received from societies and art groups requesting talks. Not all applicants were offered Robin's time, but he was always particularly keen on the provision of art for hospitals, such as the Royal Edinburgh at Craighouse, where leading Scottish psychiatrist Professor Morris Carstairs asked for paintings in the spring of 1969. In the late 1960s Robin also joined the selection committee of the new Pernod Scottish Art Competition, organised by the public relations company Lonsdale Information Ltd and sponsored by the liqueur company Pernod Fils. This offered awards to young painters in an annual exhibition held initially in the English Speaking Union gallery in Atholl Crescent before transferring to the City Art Centre, until that building (on Regent Road) closed in 1976. The judges included David Baxandall from the National Galleries; Demarco; Ian Mackenzie Smith, artist and director of Aberdeen Art Gallery; Robert ('Otto') Scott Irvine (1906–1988), head of art at George Watson's College; and Robin. Personal interests are also recorded, including Robin's support for the Edinburgh Biafran student appeal in late 1968. There seemed little time to take up Ronald 'Bingo' Mavor's idea of a National Art Circuit, part of a University Arts Trust being established by the Arts Council of Great Britain.

Nonetheless, alongside all of this, College responsibilities and an increasing involvement with different committees such as the Hospitalfield board – and not least the Royal Commission, which held monthly meetings in Edinburgh with site visits required around the country – Robin somehow found time to have a private life and to paint. Photographs of his College studio in the late 1960s and early 1970s show him resting, dwarfed by a forest of easels with each one supporting a large canvas in progress, or he is captured hard at work on his studio platform [fig. 4.15]. His ambition never faltered. Two exhibitions were planned for 1968, a solo one with Roland, Browse and Delbanco and a group one at the Demarco Gallery. Another was mapped out for the Loomshop Gallery in Lower Largo the following year. The pressures were considerable, and were not helped when in May 1968 he ended up in hospital for a gall bladder operation.

On his recovery there was again a real sense of a new beginning, and discussions were soon underway for a number of major shows for 1970 and 1971. In 1969 he bought the former schoolhouse at Killimster in Caithness as a studio for Thora. She was pleased to have a working studio in her native Caithness, and it became a holiday home for both of them from where they could visit Thora's mother, who moved back north from Edinburgh. It was furnished with some rugs from Bill Gillies's College studio, given on his retirement. The same year he was appointed to the Council of the Edinburgh International Festival and, not least, accepted the position of Secretary of the Royal Scottish Academy, the result of recognition of his work through the decade as head of D&P and his well-established status as a painter. Working for the next four years alongside architect William Kininmonth as president, sculptor Hew Lorimer as treasurer and Denis Peploe as librarian, he had now become a working Council member of the most elite art establishment in Scotland.

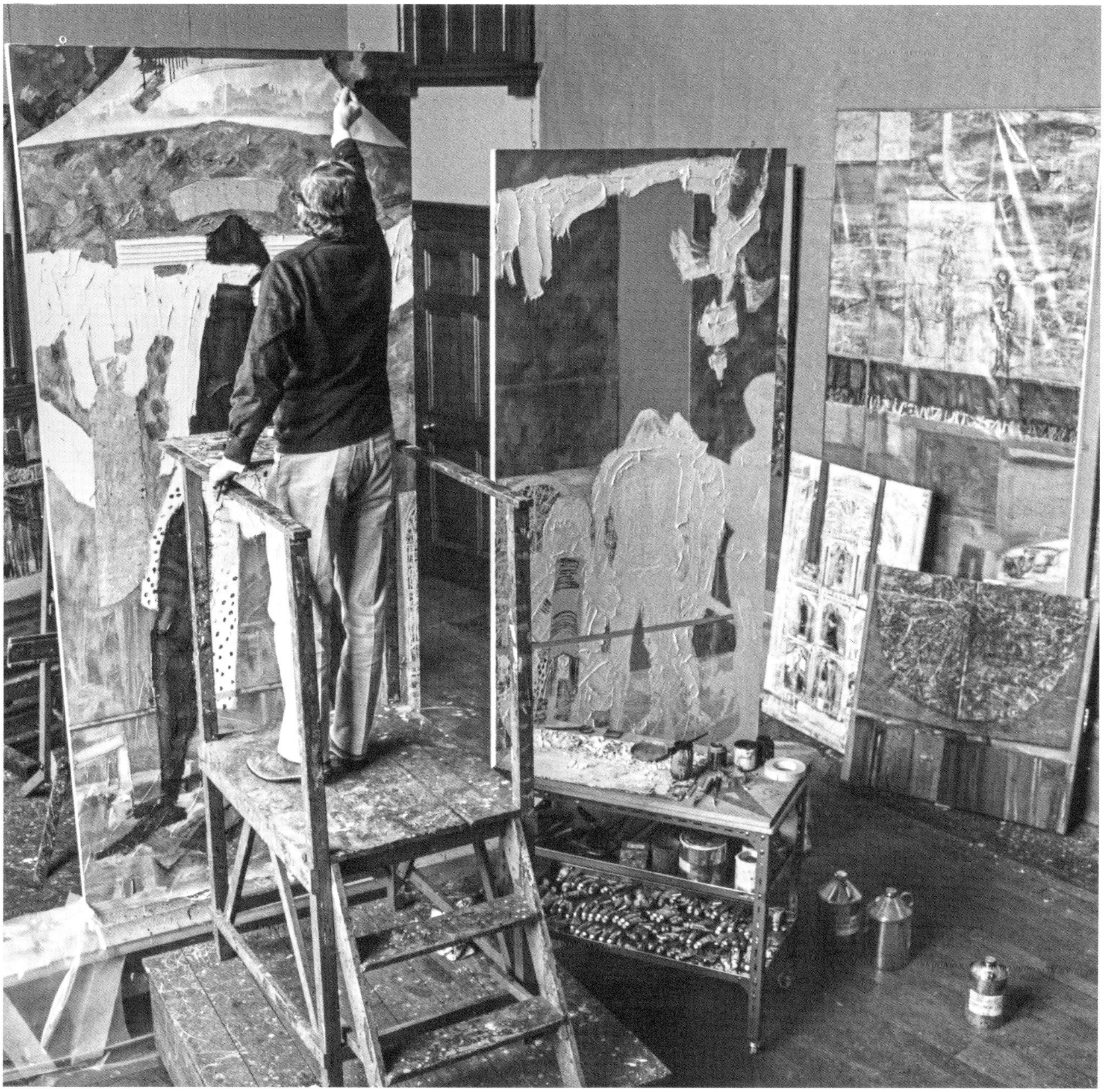

FIG. 4.15
Robin working on the *Crucifixion and Ascension* triptych, 1969
private collection

5 'THE MAGICIAN OF THE BRUSH'

The year 1970 would be memorable. Two major exhibitions were scheduled to be held in the spring, plus a one-man show of new work was also planned for the Scottish Gallery at Festival time. By this date Robin had become ever more deeply involved in the Scottish arts scene, and was an active contributor to many organisations beyond the College or the RSA. In March he spoke twice at dinners in the North British Hotel, including the BBC's retirement dinner for his friend George Bruce. Both men had been involved for the last three years in the Lamp of Lothian Collegiate Trust, established by the Duchess of Hamilton in the East Lothian county town of Haddington. Its core ecumenical aim, of restoring derelict buildings in the south of the town for community use, was augmented by a public programme of temporary exhibitions, musical performances and poetry readings. Robin had been asked by the actor Tom Fleming (1927–2010) to be a founder member and readily agreed. The executive committee included the cellist Joan Dickson, university administrator and author David Dorward, George Bruce and Fleming, along with the actress Lennox Milne, who was responsible for much of the committee's early paperwork.

With his Langholm experience so recent, the idea of a community arts centre held much attraction for Robin. He advised on all the exhibitions for the Lamp of Lothian's annual festivals, including mixed shows, paintings by Bill Gillies or his own work. In Fleming's obituary of Robin, he would be said to have given 'generously of his time and of his paintings to further the work of the Trust', and judged to be 'a superb master-craftsman of uncanny skill ... [who] encouraged the most lowly talents of amateur painters and schoolchildren, commending them to throw caution to the wind and be adventurous!'[1] He would surely have been in his element in such surroundings, and those words rightly acknowledge and emphasise the encouragement he is known to have given to many people throughout his life, whether amateurs, students or fellow professional artists. His working span of arts organisations was extraordinarily wide.

The range of cooperation and sharing of expertise across the arts in Scotland in the early 1970s is worth mentioning. At this period Scottish painting was enjoying a confidence at home which was in part rooted in the quality of art coming out of the art schools. The optimism of the 1960s still filled the air, with curators and others keen to show the best being produced by young artists. As the University of Stirling's MacRobert Arts Centre prepared to open in late September 1971, the

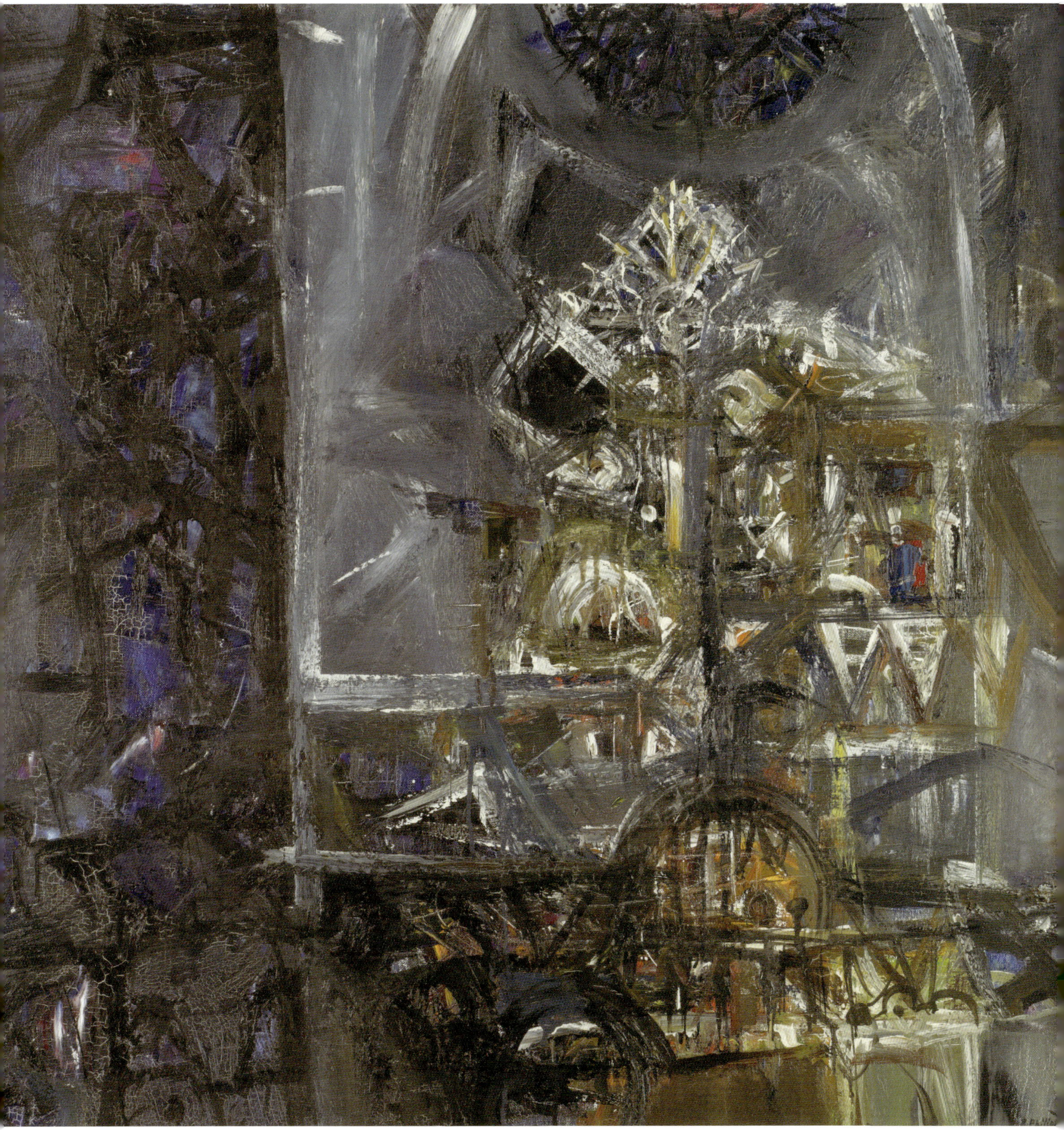

FIG. 5.1
Blue Cathedral
*c.*1972 / oil on canvas / 90.5 x 90.5 cm

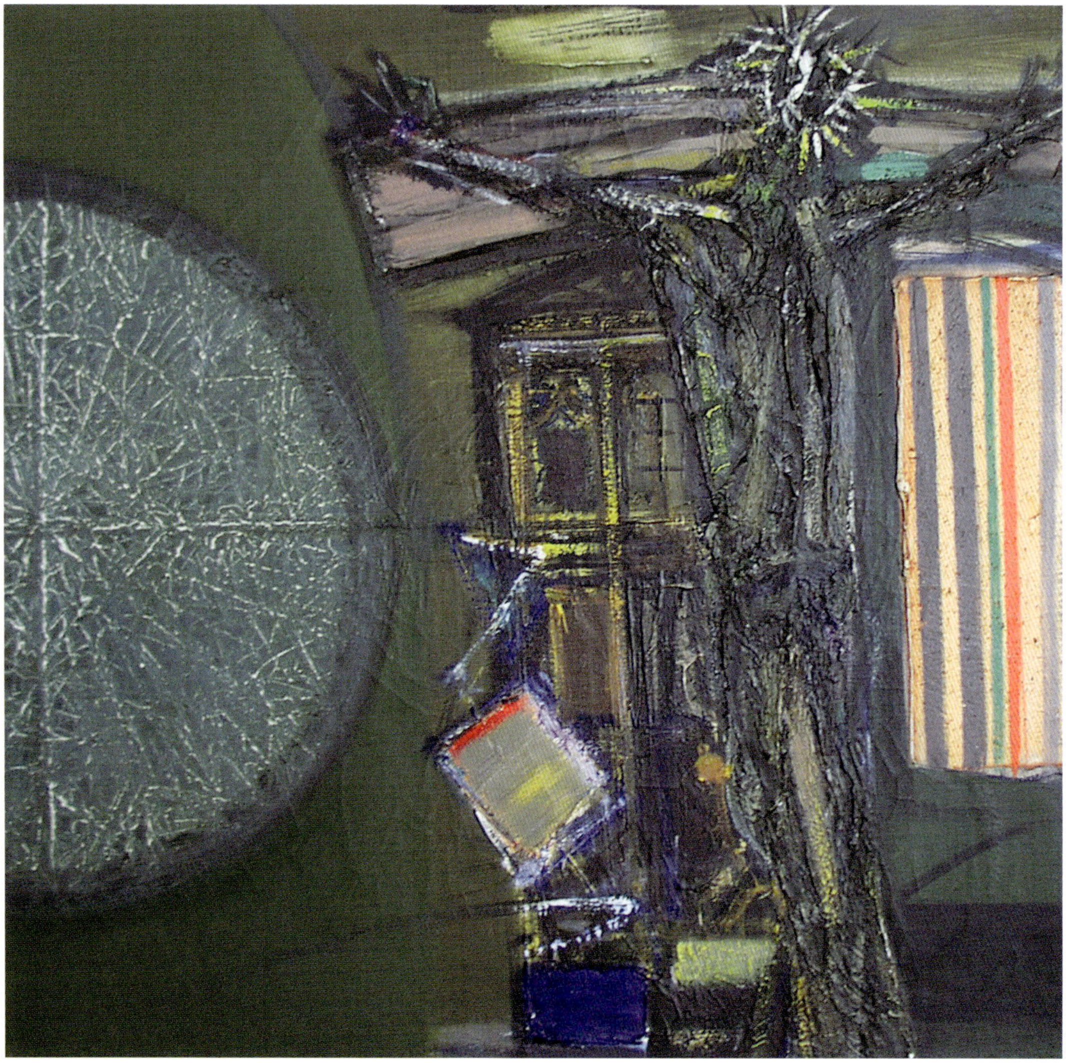

FIG. 5.2
Rose Window and Crucifixion
*c.*1973 / oil on canvas / 55 x 55 cm
private collection • courtesy of the Scottish Gallery

heads of painting at the art schools (Robin, Henderson Blyth, David Donaldson and Alberto Morrocco [1917–1998]) were invited to select a student exhibition. This complemented the annual Pernod Scottish art competition, and yet another proposal, in November 1970, from the Law Society of Scotland for a student art competition to celebrate its anniversary with entries invited from the College and Glasgow School of Art. As with the Pernod, prizes were to be awarded, but this time it was open across all subjects: entries included sculpture, tapestry, ceramics and stained glass as well as painting, and the prize was won by a painter, James McGlade (born 1948). However, the extremely limited entry of thirteen pieces – with a surprising total lack of entries from Glasgow – resulted in this being a one-off show.

The build-up to the opening of the first shows of 1970 put pressure on Robin. He replied to the Ash Barn Gallery in Petersfield, Hampshire, that his available works were with Roland, Browse and Delbanco, and he was also dubious about whether he would have anything for the Pitlochry Festival Theatre's summer season – that would have to wait for 1971. In March he wrote to a friend, the sculptor Norman Forrest (1898–1972), of 'the chore of life' and that he was beginning to feel that the job of RSA Secretary was proving an additional burden. The exhibition 'Cockfight Rosewindow' opened on 4 April at the new gallery at 19 Charlotte Square run by the Scottish Arts Council before touring Scotland and the north of England.[2] By this date Robin's output was prolific and his dealers both north and south of the border helped track down the ninety-four works, which mostly came from private hands. In the catalogue, Bill Buchanan took the opportunity to give a broad assessment of Robin's art, mentioning the exotic figures (kings, odalisques, matadors, magicians and jesters) who regularly peopled his paintings. His animals were chosen for their association with both fierce sexuality and a sense of nobility – rams, horses, bulls and, above all, the cockerels. The artist enjoyed pairing images to energise his art: cockfights were works which looked at what he called 'cruel beauty' and they provided an almost perfect vehicle for the releasing of a deep tension. Had there been more space, Buchanan might also have provided some contextual comparisons, especially to the art of Michael Ayrton, known to Robin not only as a sculptor but of course also as a Harley Brothers printmaker. Others provided a limited assessment, with the show reviewed in *The Scotsman* by Edward Gage, who placed him in the company of Delacroix in his sense of the exotic and delight in 'sensuous pigment and coruscations of colour'.

In his review, Gage also covered the Philipson exhibition which had simultaneously opened at the Music Pavilion in Pittencrieff Park, Dunfermline, as part of the Carnegie Festival of Music and Drama. There, the larger recent academic paintings were displayed and admired for their literary or didactic themes. Gage referred to the paintings as dealing with the worlds of the spirit and the flesh, of presenting complex images of martyrdom and also some new reflections on racial co-existence. Douglas Hall again supplied the catalogue essay, in which he emphasised how the works on display showed an awareness of current developments in art though Robin trod a personal path, ignoring the tendency to be reductive in art and instead had been 'compelled to pour out his professional skill with increased lavishness'. Hall found in the pictures a desire to convey a feeling of strangeness, as found in ancient art, an otherness or what has been called 'a sacred fear', which was also an aim in Kokoschka's art. Hall looked to the success of the watercolours on show, where 'colour was used as an aspect of space.' In the church interiors and rose window watercolours 'a floating plane of colour' was 'established at a distance from the eye'. He credited this to 'a response to the colour field paintings of the 1960s', which in part may have been the case though these recent pieces were intuitive and more personal in their creation.

At this point Robin was exploring several different series of images. Those more readily accessible and better known were long established – the paintings of cockerels and rose windows. Others, such as the series of crucifixions, were powerful in their own right, and one, as Terence Mullaly wrote in *The Daily Telegraph*, were 'deeply impressive'. But Mullaly considered that the subjects were at odds with their scale: large canvases might be in fashion but here uncertainties in design and composition were sometimes visible. Nonetheless, he regarded Robin as a 'magician of the brush ... in his hands oil paint is a thing of delight, colour appeals directly to the senses, and before his work there is an almost tangible sense of well-being.' He found nothing but success in the newest work, a 'preoccupation with figures of a white boy and a black girl' seen in some tiny watercolours and some medium-sized oils of church interiors. Later in the year, Mullaly would call Robin's Festival show at the Scottish Gallery 'one of the most satisfying one-man shows to be held in the British Isles in recent years'.[3]

Of these two spring shows the one seen in Dunfermline, although smaller, was the more important. The exhibition spanned a range of ideas, some long established and others fresh and new. The first concerned Robin's lasting interest in the whole concept of threnody, a lamentation on the death of someone. His paintings continued to deal with the experience of pain, desolation and his despair at the futility of war. As noted, the art of Grünewald had influenced a series of large figurative single canvases and polyptychs as Robin sought to illustrate man's inhumanity to man. Alongside the Crucifixion paintings there were *The Way to Eternity, On the Edge, Never Mind* [fig. 4.4], *Defenders of the Realm* [fig. 4.10], *Golgotha, Threnody – Meeting* and *Threnody for Our Time,* all dating from the years 1964 to 1971. Robin knew that titles were important, writing for the catalogue of his 1989 retrospective that 'a large complex work has several strands of meaning running through it – the images and the paint and colour used to define them interacting with the ideas they evoke. To correspond with this,the name needs to stir a train of thought by its sound as much as its sense.' But he kept his titles short and often reapplied them to later works, sometimes numbering a series as they came off the easel. Often he did not specifically identify or detail the layers of meaning in a painting.

The concept of the multi-panelled devotional altarpiece dominated many of these ambitious works, exposing a religiosity and gravitas which impressed as much as (and was realised through) the emphasis on materiality. A number had been or were soon bought by institutions – *Stone the Crows* by the Arts Council's Scottish Committee (it is now with the Royal Scottish Academy), *The Way to Eternity* by Scottish Television, the vast *Defenders of the Realm* by the building construction firm Cruden, and *Never Mind* by Glasgow University. The Carnegie Trust in Dunfermline purchased *Threnody – Meeting* in September.

The second theme represented in the Dunfermline retrospective and later at the Scottish Gallery illustrated the positive end of the emotional spectrum. Savagery was replaced in places by love and tenderness. At this stage these paintings were not large canvases but small works, some on paper, in which strength was achieved by colour and a clear narrative. George Bruce was later credited for their collective name 'Humankind', and the title was applied from this early date to works which illustrated a powerful narrative of emotional contrast. As the show in Dunfermline demonstrated, Robin was beginning to explore interracial relationships and prejudice. The first oil paintings properly labelled *Humankind* were made in 1970, probably following the exhibition, and would be followed by many others through the decade. In 1971 some sixteen oils with this title (carefully numbered I to XVI) were included in his show with Roland, Browse and Delbanco, mixed with subjects such as *The Screens* and *Monkey,* some paintings of interiors and so on. He also treated the subject in pastel. In the late 1950s he had discussed the use of this 'medium capable of a rich luminosity' with Joan Eardley, who had recommended

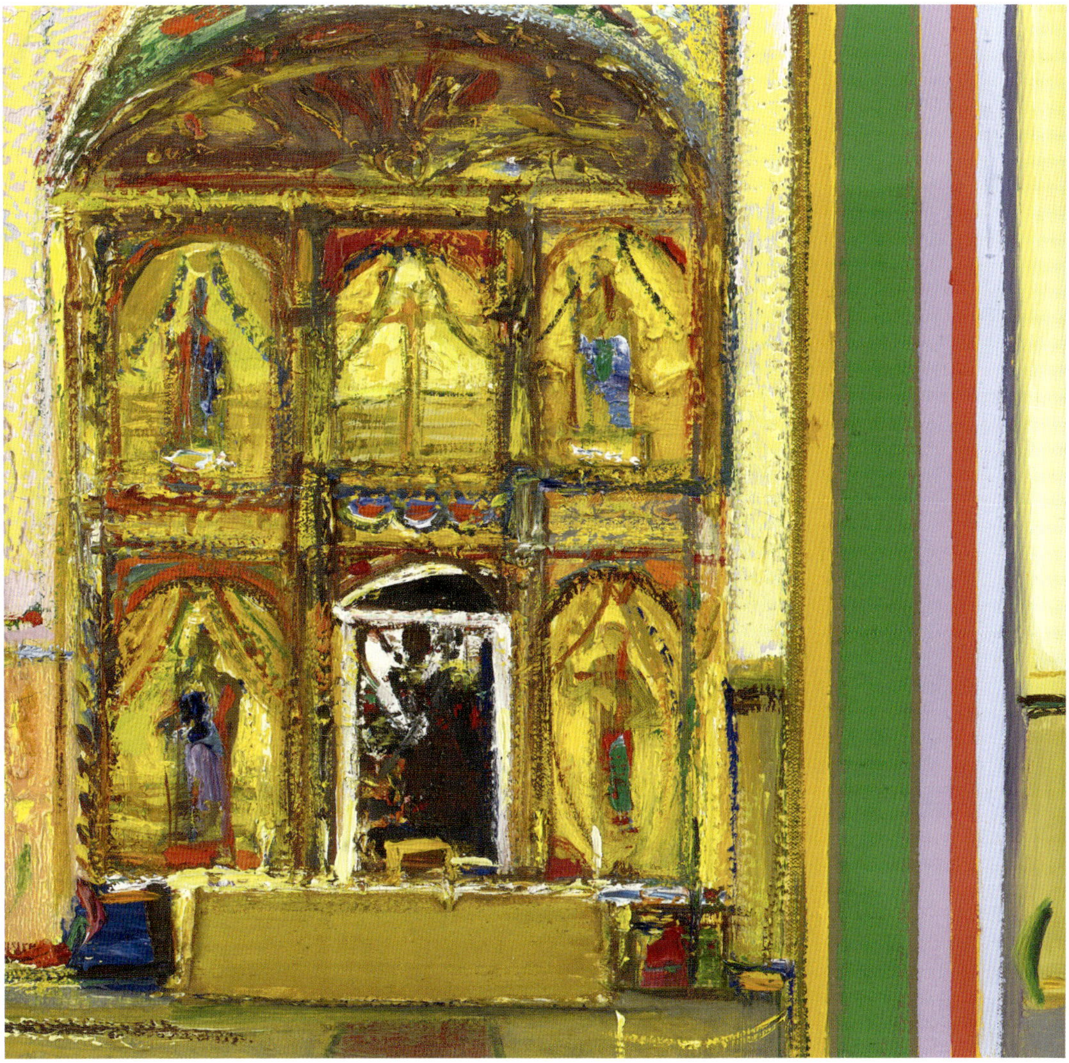

FIG. 5.3
Mexican Altar
1971 / oil on canvas / 30 x 30 cm
private collection • courtesy of the Scottish Gallery

the use of quality coloured sandpaper as a suitable base. Robin adopted this, using only 'the finest sandpapers' in a variety of colours from France which he rubbed face to face 'to get the tooth in condition'[4] prior to working on it. It is a medium which would produce some of his most beautifully sensuous, even exquisite, pieces.

As the exhibitions of 1970 demonstrated, Robin was very much true to his own ideas and was not influenced by what was being produced elsewhere in Britain. That is not to say he did not admire the work of other painters: he commented on how Francis Bacon could produce the most wonderful skin tones. In 1971 he participated in a mixed show in the United States, a welcome return of his art to a country which had fascinated him. The Maine State Commission, in association with the Scottish Arts Council, organised a show of 'Twelve Scottish Painters' at the DeCordova Museum in Lincoln in May. *The Boston Globe* was quick to interview the Maine Council director, who pointed out that the Scots were outside the ever-changing 'international style'. Their works invited contemplation rather than excitement. Robin's paint attack in his paintings was considered comparable to that of

Rauschenberg, while what was called his 'eerie' painting, *The Stoning*, was found to hold similarities to Bacon.[5] Robin may have been flattered to an extent but probably also relieved that the character of Scottish painting was deemed not to follow any style but was at heart individual.

Although the Law Society's exhibition had disappointed, Harry Jefferson Barnes remained in regular touch with Robin, and in October 1971 he again pursued the idea of a tapestry. This time Dovecot Studios had been approached by the directors of the Bank of Scotland, who were interested in commissioning a large piece for the main banking hall in their Glasgow main office for both visual and acoustic reasons. It was a 'rather daunting American type banking hall created about 1936'. A tapestry would have to be roughly 7 or 8 metres wide. Initially the bank had considered a heraldic design (for which Dovecot had been known twenty years earlier), but Jefferson Barnes had persuaded them that a modern art piece would be preferable. Robin's was the only name which had won unanimous approval from the Board. He considered the idea seriously and with enthusiasm, visiting Lord Polwarth, the chairman of the Board, at home. However, he confessed that he had 'seriously run out of energy' and had had to spend a few days in hospital. He would be looking to apply for a sabbatical year and 'if successful, will look first at the great tapestries in France, then forget them and then begin to design one for myself'.[6]

As ever, there had been extramural talks to be given by Robin that autumn including one on 'New Directions in Scottish Painting' as part of a series of public lectures on 'The State of the Arts in Scotland' for Heriot-Watt University. And there had been little let-up in the production of paintings, watercolours and pastels. In December he gathered together a show of paintings by Scottish artists, including Thora and himself, for the Lamp of Lothian Collegiate Centre. Further exhibitions had taken place through 1971 – a one-man show with Roland, Browse and Delbanco, a small one with Cyril Gerber's Compass Gallery in Glasgow, plus the promised contribution to Pitlochry Festival Theatre's summer show; work had also been sent to a group show in Canada. The London exhibition had presented a variety of paintings including sixteen small works on the theme of Humankind, some already seen in Dunfermline. The series had been well received, following its first exposure in Scotland the previous year, and would develop through the decade.

Robin's brief illness in late 1971 was undoubtedly triggered by overwork, and in particular by College demands, which included producing a required proposal for restructuring the D&P courses and methods of assessment. In February 1972 he presented an application for a year's sabbatical from the start of the autumn term. In it, he proposed to develop his own work in France, partly to consider ideas for the bank's tapestry, then to proceed to visit art schools in Germany, the Netherlands and America – although excluding the United States as he was already aware of their courses. Among the lists of his recent achievements he mentioned his recent election (October 1971) to the Scottish Advisory Panel of the British Council. He confessed he was genuinely lacking in energy and that the sabbatical would serve to reinvigorate him. In other correspondence he expressed his concern at the undoubted pressure his absence would place on colleagues. The sabbatical was

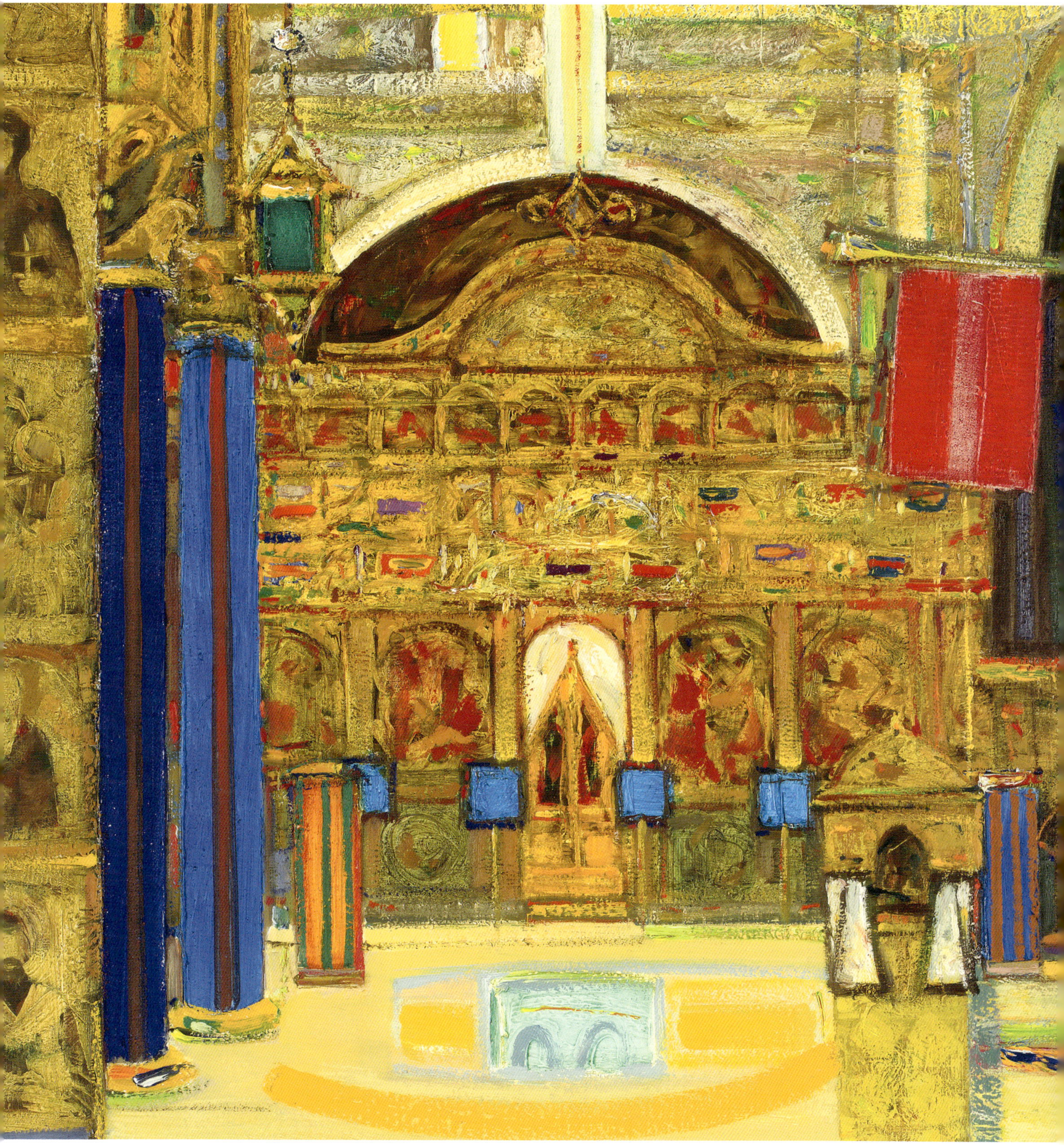

FIG. 5.4
Byzantine Interior
*c.*1974 / oil on canvas / 74 x 74 cm
private collection • photo: courtesy of Lyon & Turnbull Auctioneers

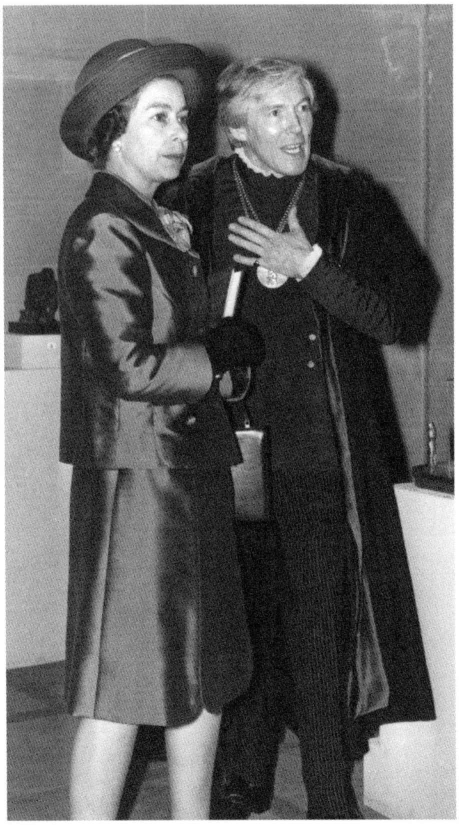

FIG. 5.5
Her Majesty The Queen with Robin, as President of the RSA, during the royal visit to the RSA Annual Exhibition on 11 July 1973
Royal Scottish Academy of Art and Architecture archives

approved in late May, and it was then agreed that David Michie (recently promoted to a D&P senior lecturer along with Bill Baillie, Derek Clarke and Jimmy Cumming) would shoulder the headship and accordingly be paid a responsibility allowance.

By July, the travel plans had been amended. Robin hoped now to visit France but then move on to Greece and thereafter Ethiopia. Writing to Lillian Browse as he busily completed paintings for his next London show, he noted that

> *... my mind is really open but these are places which intrigue me. I have never been to Greece and I am rather fascinated by the photographs which I have seen of the monolithic churches in Lalibela – Mariam – etc. In any case it will be good to be away from the College and its many problems and I would like to at least give myself some opportunity of gleaning new ideas. Thora will come out to spend some time when I find a place which will interest her.*[7]

When he drove off for France in September, he took as a travelling companion Diana Mary Pollock (born 1945), who had recently been hired as secretary to College principal Stanley Wright. Diana and Robin had first met fleetingly at the Demarco Gallery in Melville Crescent, and in November 1971, when working for the Edinburgh company Anglo-Continental Travel, she had advised on a student trip to Paris to see a Francis Bacon retrospective. Within days of Robin's departure Thora received a phone call: he had been taken seriously ill while crossing the Channel and had been admitted to the Hôpital St Claire in Boulogne. He was operated on for colonic cancer. Thora joined Diana at the hospital and arranged for Robin to convalesce at the Hôtel de Lorraine, where they were joined by David Michie and Bill Baillie, keen to visit their friend, and by Christopher, his sister Phyllis's schoolboy son, who was sent over ostensibly to practise his French. It turned out to be a jolly time for the visitors, with entertainment and laughter all round in the hospital plus visits for some to the local market, where the tall Michie could be spotted at a distance in his Scottish tartan 'tammy'. Robin was hospitalised for over two months. After the first month he was encouraged by the medical staff to draw – and each day he recorded the flowers and cards which had been sent [fig. 5.6]. He left hospital on 4 December, spending the next week reacclimatising himself locally to the outside world. Recovery took time, and he never made it to Greece or, at this stage, to Africa.

Back in Edinburgh, the rest of the winter remained a period of convalescence. He painted watercolours for a couple of months, and only returned fulltime to College work the following summer. Meanwhile, at the RSA changes were afoot. On 14 March 1973, Robin was elected its incoming President (PRSA), a position he would fulfil for the next ten years [fig. 5.5]. He took a particular pride in the appointment, and it was one which would have gladdened Bill Gillies before his sudden death the following month. It was an unpaid post (other Academy office bearers receive an honorarium) but an appointment of great distinction and respect – his would be an official voice for Scotland's artists. The architect Esme Gordon (1910–1993) took over from him as Secretary and Jimmy Cumming was elected Treasurer. The new Council, his 'crew' as he called them, would consist of friends and supportive colleagues – John Houston, Elizabeth Blackadder, David Michie, Ann Henderson (1921–1976), David Donaldson from Glasgow School of Art and William Littlejohn (1929–2006) from Gray's School of Art in Aberdeen. Through the coming decade Robin would play a full part in the RSA, and it was a role he thoroughly enjoyed. He developed the RSA activities, revitalising the long-established RSA School of Painting Competition from all four Scottish art schools into one of its most important annual exhibitions. In 1976 he gained his Council's approval not to charge a commission on student work to encourage purchases. The same year saw the introduction of fourteen bright exhibition banners hung between the pillars on the main north and south entrances – a feature which persists to this day.

Exhibitions were, and are, regarded as a particularly important public face of the Academy. The quality and range of Festival shows on the whole remained strong, despite the difficult financial climate of the 1970s. His friendship with Colin Thompson helped steer some shows into reality, allowing diplomatic relationships with collectors such as Armand Hammer to be established: 'Four Centuries of Masterpieces' were displayed in 1978, to be followed by 'Daumier' in 1981 and 'Leonardo' in 1982. The type of academic exhibitions seen through the 1950s and 1960s was now highly expensive to mount, so collectors had to be courted to provide (and financially support) loans. Other exhibitions were varied – a show of Bonnard drawings was seen in 1979 and the following year one to celebrate seventy years of tapestries woven at Dovecot Studios was brought forward two years to fill a gap. Some exhibitions made a financial loss – the 1976 show to celebrate the 150th anniversary of the Academy, for example – but others such as Ceri Richards in 1975 and a show of Eardley's Catterline paintings in 1977 (shown alongside 'The Modern Spirit: American Painting 1908–35') brought in a profit. It can be said with fairness that all the Festival exhibitions – the highlight of each year apart from the annual exhibition – bore Robin's mark. They displayed art which he personally considered worthy of an international showing and he usually had his Council

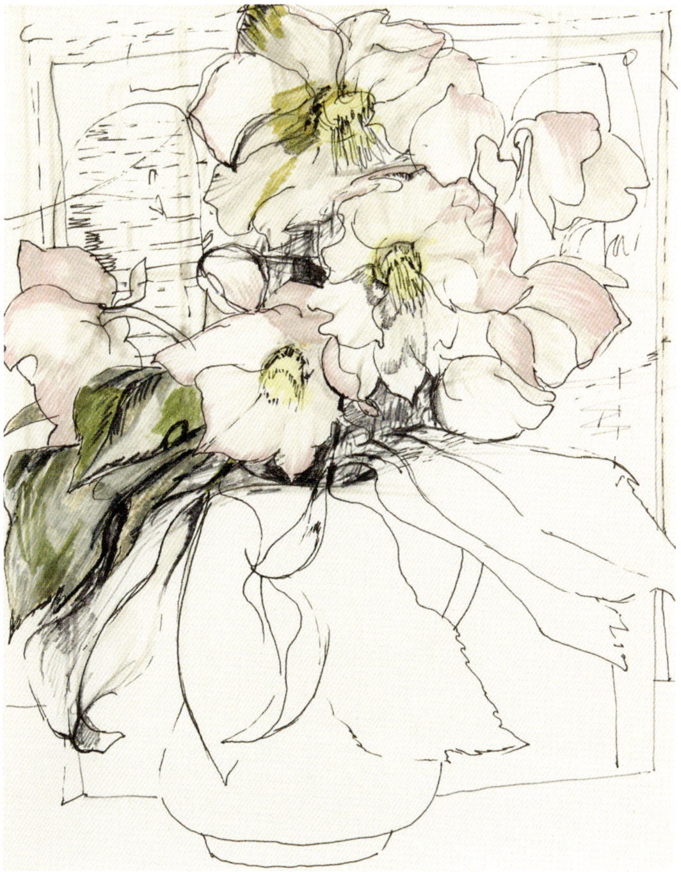

FIG. 5.6
Christmas Roses
1972 / ink and wash on paper / 25.5 x 20 cm
private collection • photo: courtesy of Lyon & Turnbull Auctioneers

with him. The period as PRSA covered the year of the Queen's Silver Jubilee, 1977. The records of the RSA detail his strong but unsuccessful advocacy of marking it officially. Equally, they record his persuasion in providing Academy financial support for national collections such as the Tate Gallery and the Scottish National Portrait Gallery in their bids to save paintings for the nation.

The day job of being head of D&P meanwhile continued apace. Following his illness he was back in post by June 1973, supplying Peter Blake with information for the latter's summer fortnight at Hospitalfield, an appointment fixed on Robin's recommendation. He was happiest progressing opportunities for staff and students and generally disliked professional educators and their dull committees. In August 1974 he was invited to serve on a new Art and Design committee – an amalgamation of the Council for National Academic Awards and the National Council for Diplomas in Art and Design. He declined to join Jefferson Barnes, F.H.K. Henrion, S.C. Mason, Colin Melbourne and Ian Simpson: his time was all too precious, especially following his recent illness; and he pointed out in his letter of apology that it was already much taken up with the Royal Fine Art Commission and his work for the British Council. On the other hand he was delighted to add his name to exhibition committees of honour, for example to be made a patron of the Pennsylvania Academy of the Fine Arts exhibition 'Masterpieces of American Painting' in 1975.

Among settled plans for 1974 were two exhibitions outside Edinburgh. In the spring of 1974 Moray Arts Club showed twenty-two of Robin's paintings in Elgin to mark the 750th anniversary of its cathedral. Naturally, many were of cathedral interiors and in a real sense the selection was a paean to that building. Although a relatively small show, a number of works were very familiar from earlier exhibitions. Private collectors who loaned pieces included Margie Scott Hay, Sir William Kininmonth, Michael Laird, Sir Thomas Risk and Anthony Wheeler, while the Scottish National Gallery of Modern Art lent several Scott Hay collection pictures, Scottish Television *The Way to Eternity* and the Universities of Stirling and Edinburgh *The Martyr* and *Entrance to the Cathedral*. Only three (crucifixion) paintings came from the artist. Robin asked Elder Dickson to contribute the short catalogue introduction in which he wrote that the paintings used the language of the poet, 'symbolic, allusive and infinitely flexible', not the 'clear knowledge of the rational intellect'. Although dealing freely in abstractions, the external world had not been rejected but reshaped in accord with 'his inner world of fantasy and intuitive vision', and 'darker areas of consciousness' were identified. However, Elder Dickson viewed Robin's approach as being of his time and generation – realistic words from an old friend and former colleague now somewhat at odds with contemporary art.

A little later, George Bruce offered to write the catalogue essay for a retrospective of thirty-nine paintings held in August at the Lamp of Lothian Centre. He concentrated on an analysis of *Stone the Crows*, rooting it, as all since have done, in Robin's response to Losey's film. Bruce also celebrated the mature recent paintings of Gothic and Byzantine church interiors, with the latter using a favourite Indian yellow augmented decorously by bars of reds, blues, greens and blacks [figs 5.1–5.4 and 5.7], and a number of paintings of 'ladies of pleasure' (by now an established theme) – including one in which the composition was divided by

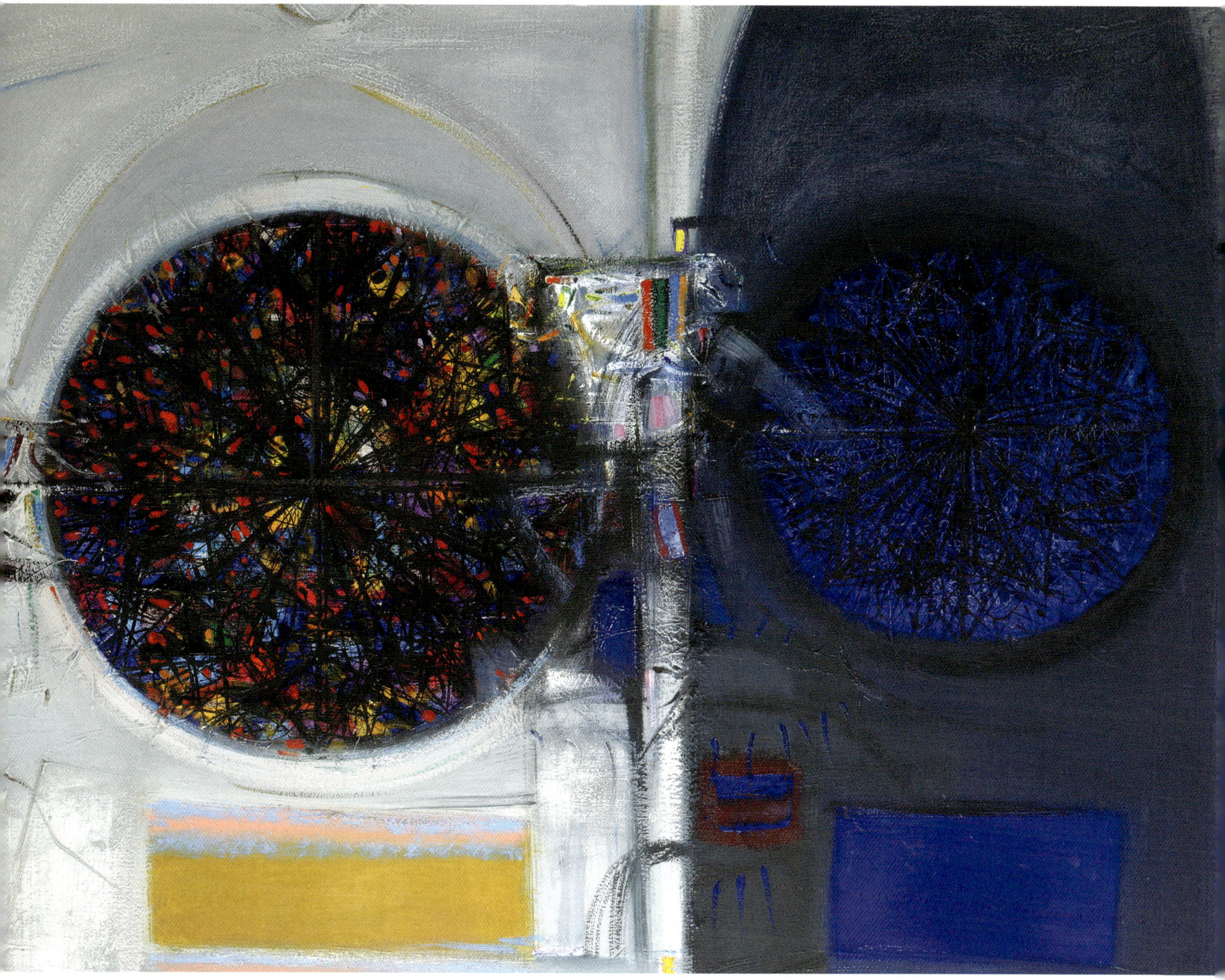

FIG. 5.7
Cool Interior: A Remembrance
*c.*1968 / oil on canvas / 90 x 120 cm
University of Stirling

'a flat grey ovoid', a negative space which concentrated power in the figures either side. Across the picture plane, the demi-mondaines displayed the rawness of their trade and also a sense of elegance. In addition, he announced the developing subject of 'Humankind' in which mankind was placed alongside 'the natural free movement of the animal creation'. Boy and girl, white against black or vice versa, were placed together 'with great delicacy' and always in spaces enclosed by straight lines in contrast to the freedom of animals such as a zebra. It was gently noted that feelings of tension and desolation filled such paintings.

Robin was again unwell in the autumn of 1974 and was offered a term's sabbatical, which he declined on grounds of depleting the staffing of D&P. By this date his marriage had been under pressure for some time and Thora and he were divorced in 1975. He must have remained disappointed that his sabbatical travels had not turned out the way he had wished. In particular, he regretted he had not been able to visit Africa: tokens of its colours and animals had been entering his art for several years. As already noted, the idea of anti-apartheid had also begun to appear in his painting, although at this stage only in relatively small-scale work. He had first joined the Glasgow Anti-apartheid Movement in 1970, lending his name to its cause alongside those of many other distinguished figures – Sir Compton Mackenzie, Stanley Baxter, Lord Macleod, C.H. Waddington, Lord Ritchie-Calder, Tam Dalyell, Rt. Hon Jo Grimond, and Naomi Mitchison – and that December he attended a meeting in the Usher Hall regarding arms to South Africa addressed by Denis Healey, Peter Hain and Lawrence Daly. But an opportunity now came along which would allow him to visit Africa and have the experience of a lifetime. His connections with the Edinburgh branch of the English Speaking Union and its gallery in Atholl Crescent (advising on exhibitions when and where he could, setting up the Pernod competitions, attending receptions for visitors) and his friendship via Robbie Scott Hay with William Thyne led to his being encouraged to submit a personal application for a William Thyne Scholarship in the spring of 1975. That autumn the RSA Council noted that its President had been awarded the 1976 Scholarship. It was an award made to 'those distinguished in their own fields to foster relations and so permits the holder to spend a period of two months in a country of his choosing, selected from the Commonwealth or USA. With all the fascination it holds for him, Robin Philipson had selected South Africa for a visit in the autumn of 1976'.

Although few sketches and no diaries have survived, Robin's months in Africa surely allowed him time to explore cities and visit townships. Later on, in October 1979, he was invited by art dealer Michael Le Marchant of the Bruton Gallery in Bruton, Somerset, to participate in a Georgetown mixed exhibition he was preparing – an invitation he declined due to lack of time. However, he did establish a relationship with the Everard Read Gallery in Johannesburg, where his painting was shown in September 1980. His time in Kenya and South Africa greatly enriched, and contributed to a stabilisation of, Robin's art for the next decade and in fact for the rest of his life, granting it a sense of resolution which had been hitherto absent. Public recognition also doubtless contributed to a new calm and confidence. Before he left Scotland the year had already proved to be a remarkable one. Robin's election as PRSA provided him with authority and stature, and he received the honour of a knighthood 'for services to the arts' in 1976. As president he had been elected, *ex officio*, an Associate of the Royal Academy in London, and subsequently would be made a full Academician in 1981; as PRSA he was also given honorary membership of the Royal Hibernian Academy in 1974. The year 1976 also showered him with other awards – he was made Commandeur de l'Ordre Nationale du Mérite de la République Française and received an honorary doctorate from the University of Stirling – Aberdeen would follow suit in 1978 and Heriot-Watt in 1985.

Not least, in 1976 he accepted an invitation to join the Board of the National Museum of Antiquities of Scotland. In that year, too, his home world changed when on 28 August he married Diana Pollock at Mertoun Parish Kirk in the Scottish Borders. And further recognition of his art came with the publication of the first monograph, as opposed to catalogue essays or articles, on his art. Edinburgh University Press, led by Archie Turnbull, issued a series of pocket-sized hardbacks in a short series of six under the overall title *Modern Scottish Painters*. The first was on Anne Redpath by George Bruce, with the second on Gillies by Elder Dickson. MacTaggart was penned by H. Harvey Wood, Maxwell by David McClure and Eardley by Bill Buchanan. The last of the six, on Robin, was written by his old friend, the broadcaster and poet Maurice Lindsay, and it offered a poetic account based primarily on recent interviews. On its cover Lindsay stated that 'the President of the RSA is a creator of powerful images, a narrator who is deeply concerned with the human dilemma and whose unmistakable personal style has remained consistent since he first made an impact with his terrifyingly beautiful studies of fighting cocks.'

For the Festival, the Scottish Gallery celebrated Robin's knighthood with a one-man show: this would be his eighth such exhibition with his Edinburgh dealer. It was intended to be principally of 'watercolour painting and the character and behaviour that are inherent in water, how it influences the shapes and forms in the works themselves, and the fascination and magic it holds for the artist'. But Robin remained equally drawn to material issues and meaningful imagery, which seemed to fight for supremacy in his mind, for his own commentary in the catalogue on his recent painting continued with words which chimed with Lindsay's. The paintings dealt with the

> *dilemma that exists between Black and White and this recurring counter-point is punctuated by powerful comments on the truth of the good and bad nature of man and beast. There is also a curious atmosphere built of hints and whispered communication not just confined to the figure images, but working on the contrasting areas, the harmonies and discords that make up the work. This extended theme is exciting and vigorous and remains free for individual interpretation.*[8]

He wished a response to his art to be personal, as private and individual as his own was to the art of the past and to contemporary work. He pursued core themes which had been there for much of his career, with the experience of New Mexico thirteen years earlier still informing richly worked views of interiors. Paintings were decorative, in the best sense of the term, using a range of media and colour. But within some were to be found confrontations, an uneasy meeting of figures.

In some respects Robin never changed his agenda, wishing always to explore the boundaries of representation through those of his materials. In 1977, a year in which a retrospective had been presented at the University of Stirling, he returned to the idea of mural painting. *Summer* [fig. 5.8], a semi-abstract golden savannah, had been commissioned by Dundee College of Education two years earlier with funding secured from the Edwin Austin Abbey Memorial Trust. With so much else happening, the project had been forced onto a back burner. When completed, the single panel painting was placed in the library of a new modernist building in Park Place. It followed a succession of paintings for academic buildings which had started in 1963 with the commission for the entrance hall of Napier Technical College. Stirling University gave him a one-man exhibition in May–June 1977, and Robin donated his oil *Cool Interior* [fig. 5.7] in memory of its first principal, Tom Cottrell (1923–1973). The number of paintings in British public collections now numbered over fifty and were being seen regularly in permanent displays and mixed loan shows. He was by now, if not exactly an elder statesman, at least a key Scottish establishment figure.

▸ FIG. 5.8
Summer
1977 / oil on board / 410 x 323 cm
University of Dundee Museum Services

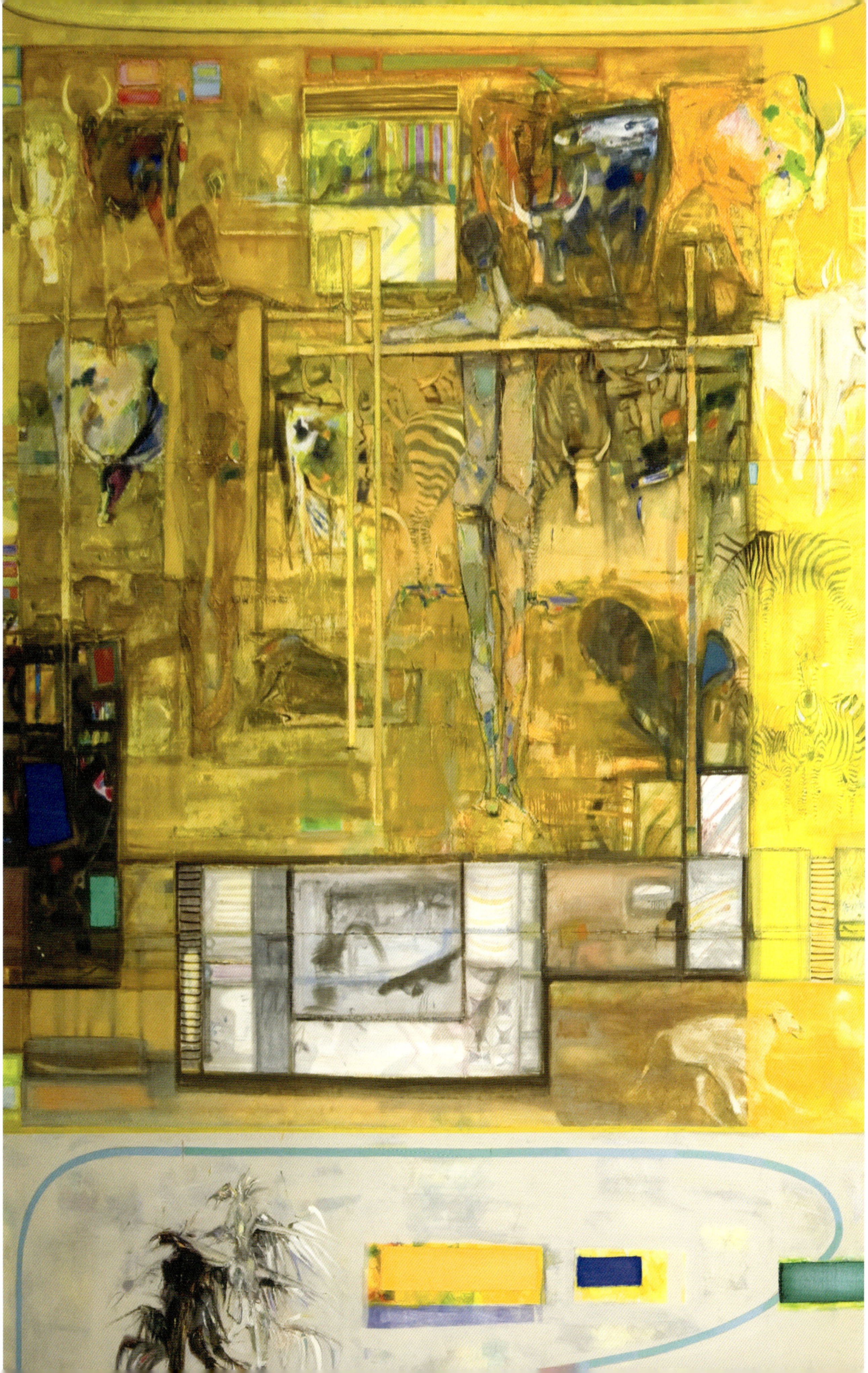

6 GARDENS OF DELIGHT

For years, Robin had been a stalwart of the major Scottish exhibitions: not only was his art to be expected in the large mixed shows in Edinburgh and Glasgow but also in a range of small commercial galleries. Increasingly now, he worked through a series of related, often small, works which explored a subject from various angles. In August 1978, four of his Women Observed series were collected for stock from Roland, Browse and Delbanco by the Leonie Jonleigh Studio, Guildford, while in Scotland the Loomshop Gallery in Lower Largo exhibited thirty-three paintings – a satisfyingly broad range including not only several in the same series but also two from a short series, The Eternal, three Cockfight studies, a Mexican Altar painting and no fewer than six still lifes. The last were some of the most beautiful and satisfying paintings of this period in terms of colour and compositional balance. Pieces of quiet, steady painting, they were relatively small in scale and attractive to the domestic market and very different from the large 'academic' works where Robin sought to present grand ideas. In the following decade an important dealership would be the Bruton Gallery run by Michael and Sandra Le Marchant, with several one-man shows in addition to the gallery holding some works in stock. Bruton's stable of artists included Michael Ayrton and now Robin.

Awards continued to come Robin's way in these years. He had been nominated in 1977 for the Sir William Y. Darling Bequest for Good Citizenship in recognition of his contribution to the Fine Arts in the city and to mark the 150th anniversary in 1976 of the RSA. In 1978 he was elected a Fellow of the Royal Society of Edinburgh, Scotland's national academy, in recognition of his standing and contribution to the visual arts. Almost immediately he was asked to give a public lecture, which he agreed, with some hesitation, to deliver the next year. He chose to speak about the importance of colour to an artist, and his rough notes contain quotes from Chevreul and Itten, analysing their contributions to the development of painting. The talk was illustrated by slides including a still life of apples and oranges by Paul Cézanne, Jan van Eyck's *The Virgin and Child with Chancellor Rollin* ('a symphony of contrasts, colour, shading, form, proportion and texture') and Renoir's *Moulin de la Galette*. The refined nature of such work was echoed in many of his own still lifes of this period, which are classical in the sense of a fine Cézanne – a mature, studied reflection on the world about him [fig. 6.1].

Beyond such contributions Robin's presence in the city took many forms and illustrates the range of his social circle at the time. One of his friends was François

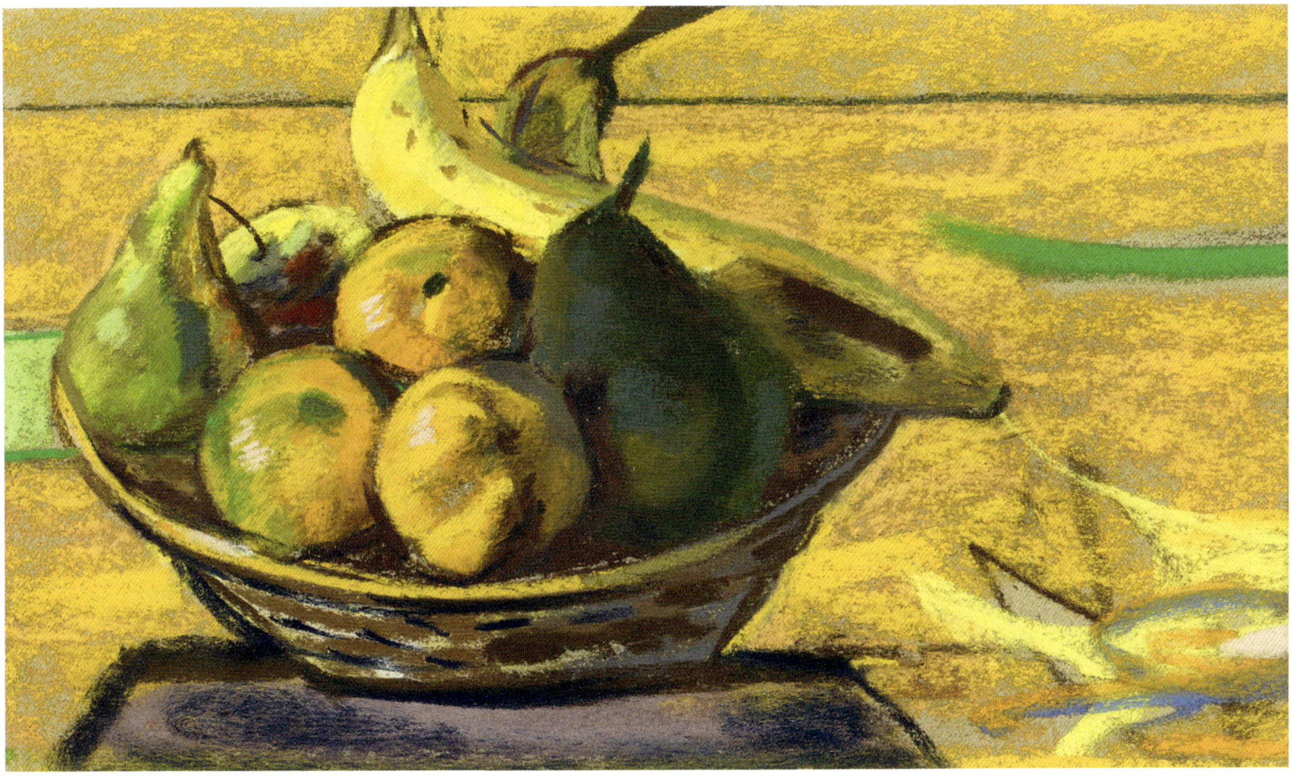

FIG. 6.1
Fruit
*c.*1980 / pastel on paper / 23 x 37 cm
private collection • courtesy of the Scottish Gallery

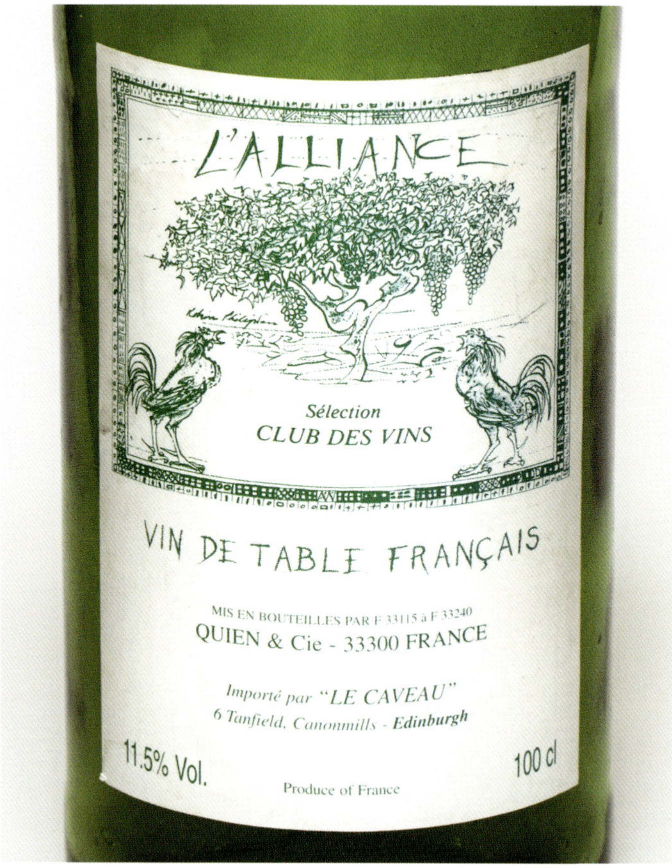

FIG. 6.2
Wine label designed for L'Alliance, 1979
private collection • photo: Antonia Reeve

Aliane, proprietor of Le Caveau, a French restaurant in Merchant Street off Candlemaker Row. Aliane was famed as a wine importer, with his office based at Tanfield in the Canonmills district of the city. His wines were offered under the label 'L'Alliance', which was both a reflection of the 'Auld Alliance', the historic friendship between the countries of Scotland and France, and a neat word-play on his name. Le Caveau itself became famous as the first wine bar to open in the city, with top-quality wines and cuisine as standard. It was located relatively near the College and soon after opening quickly became a favourite place to entertain visitors. In late 1979 Robin, very much in the spirit of French artists, designed wine labels for Le Caveau in return for a case of wine [fig. 6.2]. His graphic design incorporated a vine weighed down by grapes and two cockerels, printed in a bright green and possibly by a leading local firm, Waddie. Other gummed labels for more general domestic use were also printed with a cockerel design.

These were also years heavily spent on committee work. His membership of the Royal Fine Art Commission continued until January 1980. During his last few meetings, the Commission considered ideas for a mural for a ground-floor space in a former fruit warehouse in Market Street owned by the city and then being transformed by its architects to serve as the second City Art Centre. For this café space Robin was keen to hold a student competition, but with no money then on offer and opposition from city councillors the idea collapsed. In the end funding was found for a competition for established artists and William Crosbie (1915–1999) appointed to produce a 1950s-style scheme which reflected the history of the city. But Robin was also giving time to charity work on top of everything else. He donated paintings in aid of a range of causes and was in demand as an exhibition selector. He judged the 1980 Edinburgh Festival Fringe poster competition, a neat complement to his official Festival designing over twenty years earlier, and in late 1981 he willingly helped me to select 'Artists Unlimited' at the City Art Centre. One of his later honorary positions was as Keeper of the College Portraits at the Royal College of Surgeons of Edinburgh, where he advised on the curation of their collection. Such interests continued through the rest of his life.

Meanwhile, at the College Robin was developing the idea of artist residencies. He was in touch with Philip Wright, the art director at the Scottish Arts Council, anxious to share resources where possible. In November 1975 Robin had spent time in Yugoslavia, and, although it took five years to come to fruition, the

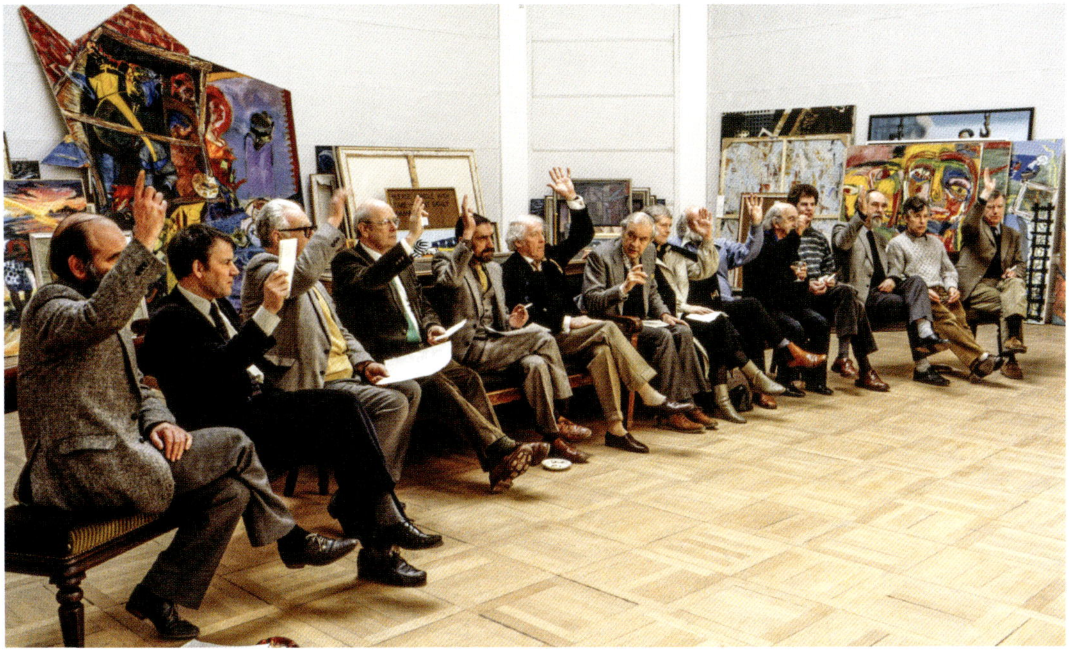

FIG. 6.3
The 1986 RSA exhibition selection committee at work with (third to seventh from the left) Esme Gordon, Bill Baillie, David McClure, Robin and PRSA Sir Anthony Wheeler, and (third from the right) David Michie
private collection • photo: Antonia Reeve

Council was able to offer the College £1,500 to bring Professor Marko Kramanovio to Edinburgh as artist-in-residence for three months in the spring of 1981. It was almost Robin's last contribution to the College, from which he retired in the summer of 1982. The following year it was all change in his extramural life as although he had resigned from the Fine Art Commission and now demitted office as PRSA he was appointed an honorary member of the Royal Incorporation of Architects in Scotland. While no longer shouldering presidential duties, he continued to play his part as an Academician, and always enjoyed serving on the RSA's annual exhibition selection panel [fig. 6.3]. But despite lessening his load, he remained in demand as a committee man, and, like all who retire, he took on duties which particularly appealed to his private nature, such as joining the trust administering the Scottish National Orchestra Endowment Fund.

Life was now shifting into a new gear both at home and in the studio. Although having never previously considered himself a family man, he and Diana adopted a son, Jasper George (born 1981), and then a daughter, Rebecca Mary (born 1984), from America, and family life soon became an essential and joyful part of his week. In 1987 a son, Anthony John, was born to Diana and Robin [fig. 6.4]. Everyday routines changed forever, and the simple pleasure of having children around the house was a new experience. When Jasper was a toddler, his father was quoted as saying that 'there is a particular sense of urgency to get up at weekends: Jasper makes sure of that. We now spend a long time over breakfast and there's the sheer delight of seeing a little face each morning.'[1] The simultaneous excitement and newfound contentment of these years triggered a new phase in his art: confident, relaxed, he painted in a way which remained exploratory but was less troubled by the needs of academic ambition. Henceforth a serenity is to be found at times in his painting.

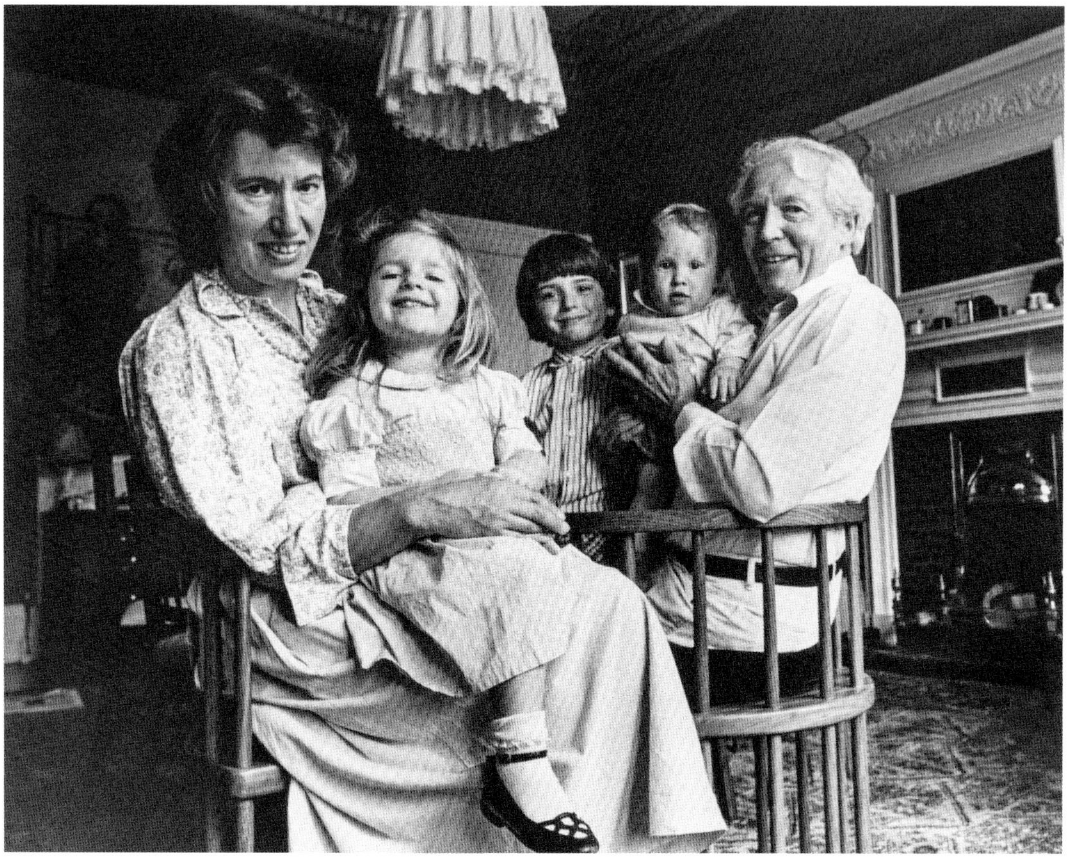

FIG. 6.4
Diana, Rebecca, Jasper, Anthony and Robin at home, 1988
private collection

Having at last more time to devote to his painting, Robin's output increased, with the results soon seen in exhibitions at home and abroad. He sent five works to a show of 'Six Leading Contemporary Scottish Painters' which the Graham Gallery on New York's Madison Avenue presented in December 1982 and January 1983 in association with the American-Scottish Foundation Inc. Robin knew his market and sent five works which included two landscape 'meadows' pieces and two interiors. By now he seemed content with perfecting colour, contributing to the 'Edinburgh School' of MacTaggart, Redpath *et al.* at their most decorative. But going in that direction, and without the tensions of College administration, released fresh ideas, and new challenges as well. A major solo show of oils, pastels and watercolours with the Scottish Gallery was presented at the 1983 Festival and it was a triumph [fig. 6.5]. Terence Mullaly wrote in *The Daily Telegraph*[2] that Robin now had the chance to re-explore his own achievement and that the first impression of the new work was 'one of voluptuous delight'.

At the show's centrepiece was a large triptych of three women, *Presentation*, which, as Mary Rose Beaumont wrote in the catalogue, represented women not as the Three Graces but fallen women or three aspects of Eve 'who contains the seeds of damnation'. As many as eleven pastel studies for it were also exhibited. The edginess of many depictions of nude women had been a trait of Robin's art since the mid-1960s, becoming more visible in the Women Observed series (and its counterpart, Men Observed) of the 1970s [figs 6.6, 6.7, 6.8]. Gender

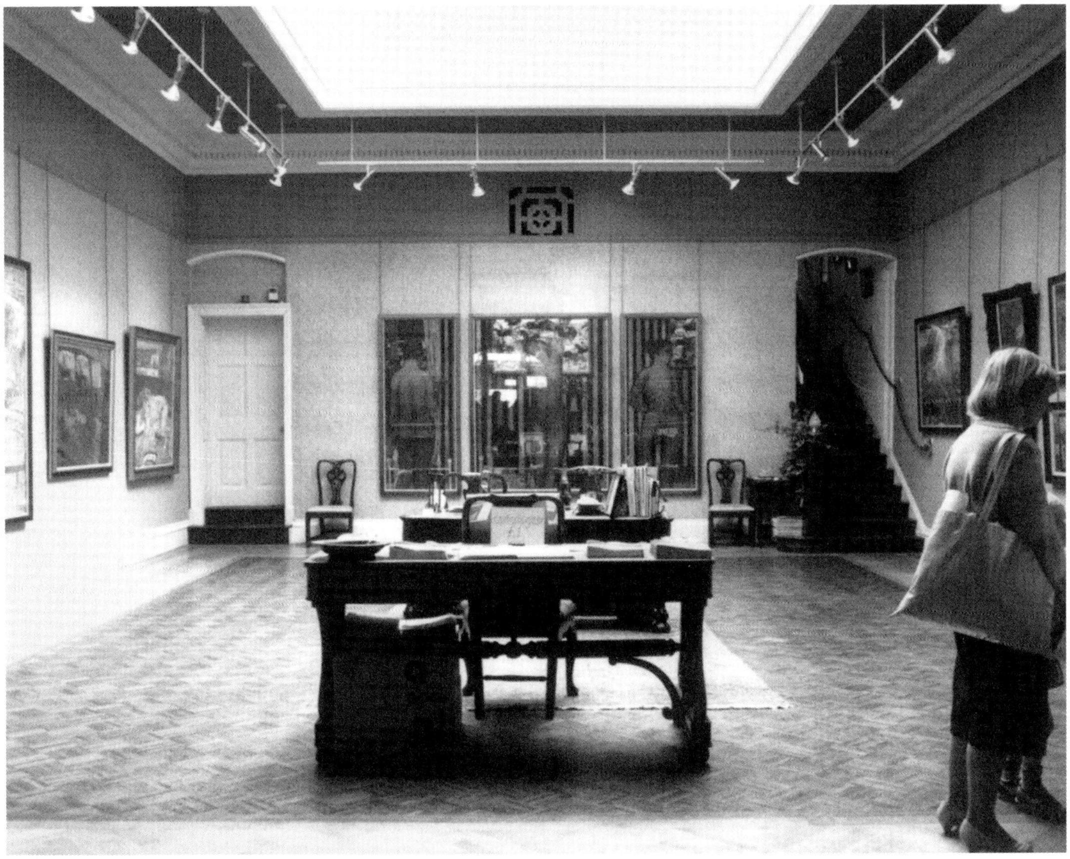

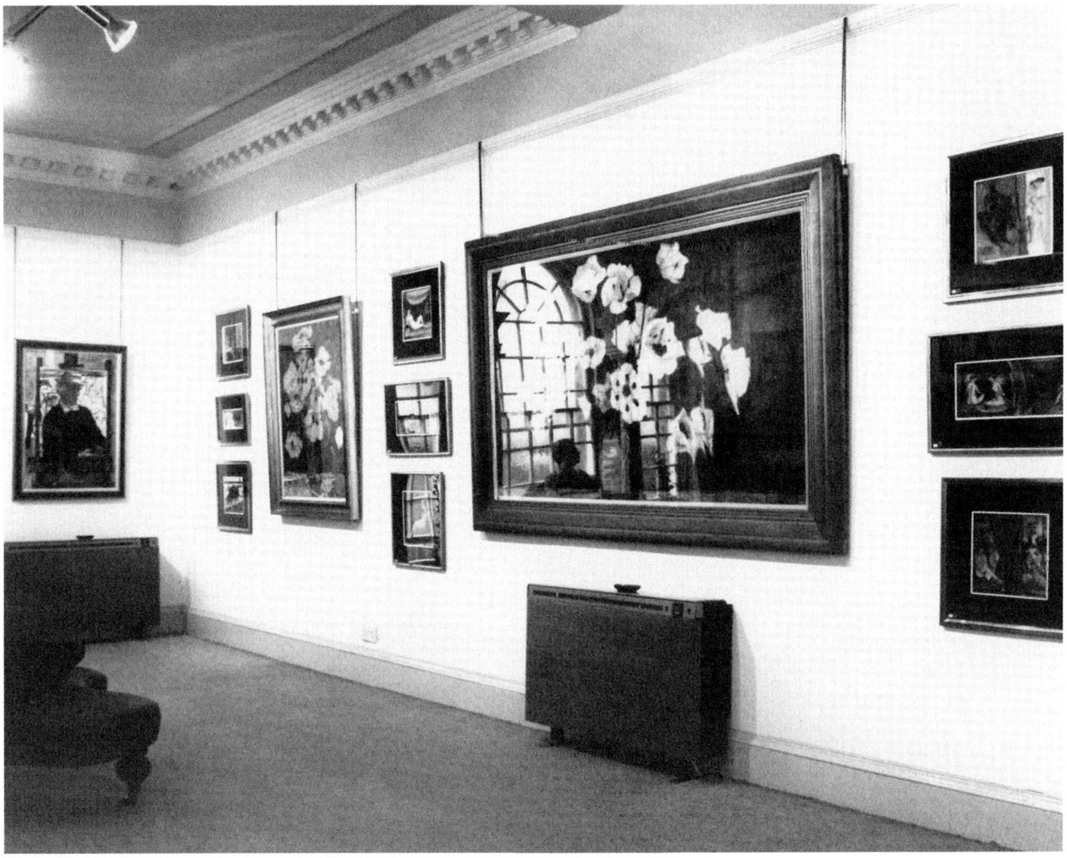

FIG. 6.5
Views of the Robin Philipson exhibition at the Scottish Gallery, 26 Castle Street, August 1983
courtesy of the Scottish Gallery

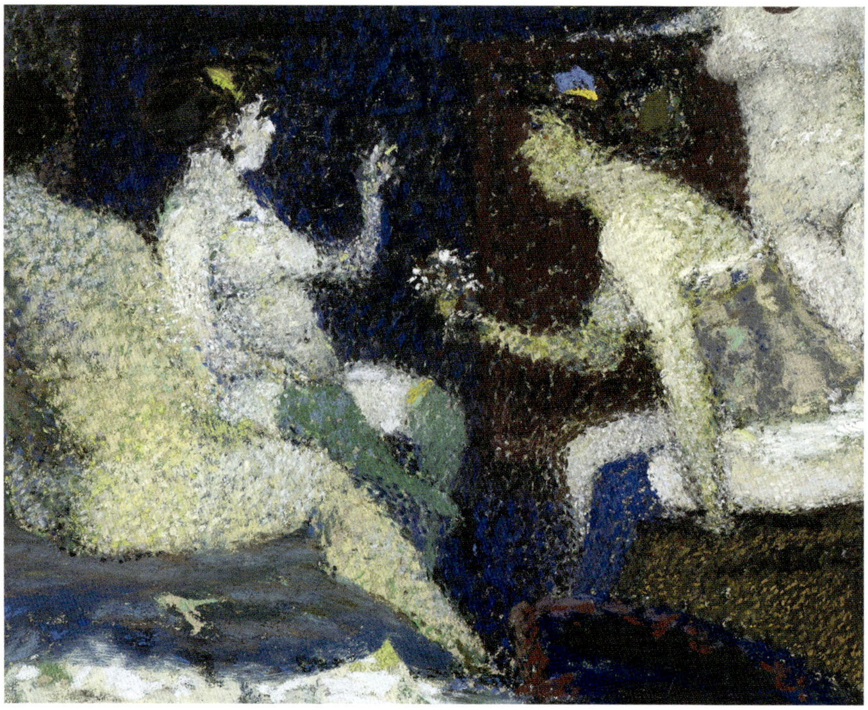

FIG. 6.6
Companions XVI
1983 / pastel on sandpaper / 22.5 x 28 cm
courtesy of the Scottish Gallery

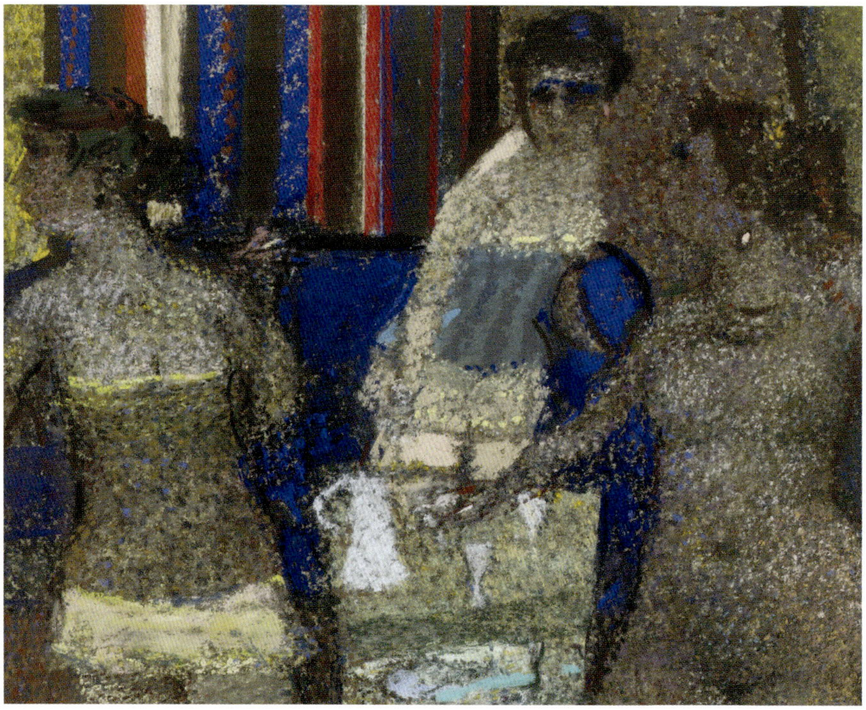

FIG. 6.7
Companions III
1983 / pastel on sandpaper / 22 x 28 cm
private collection · courtesy of the Scottish Gallery

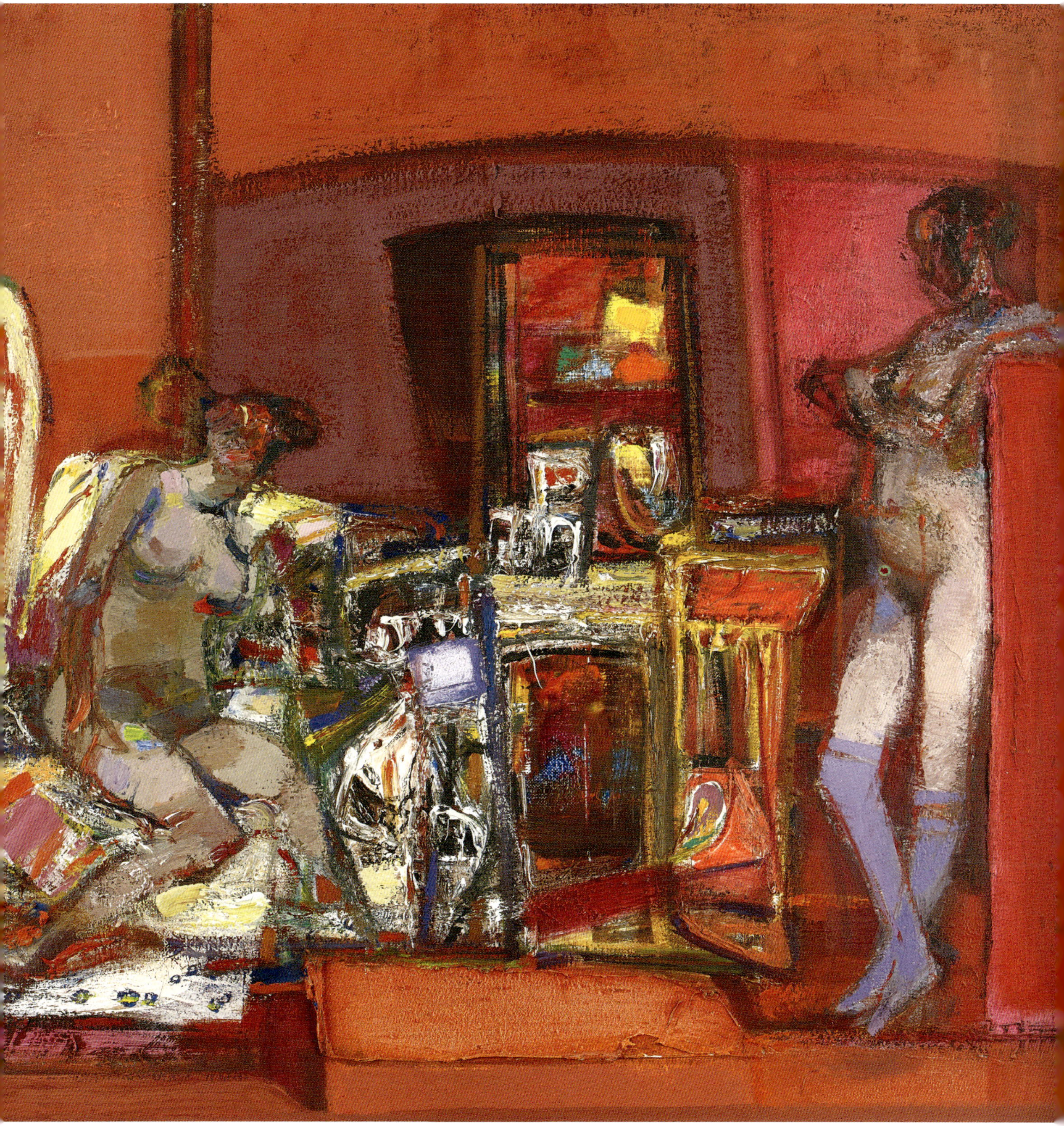

FIG. 6.8
Women Observed
*c.*1979 / oil on canvas / 66 x 66 cm
private collection • courtesy of the Scottish Gallery

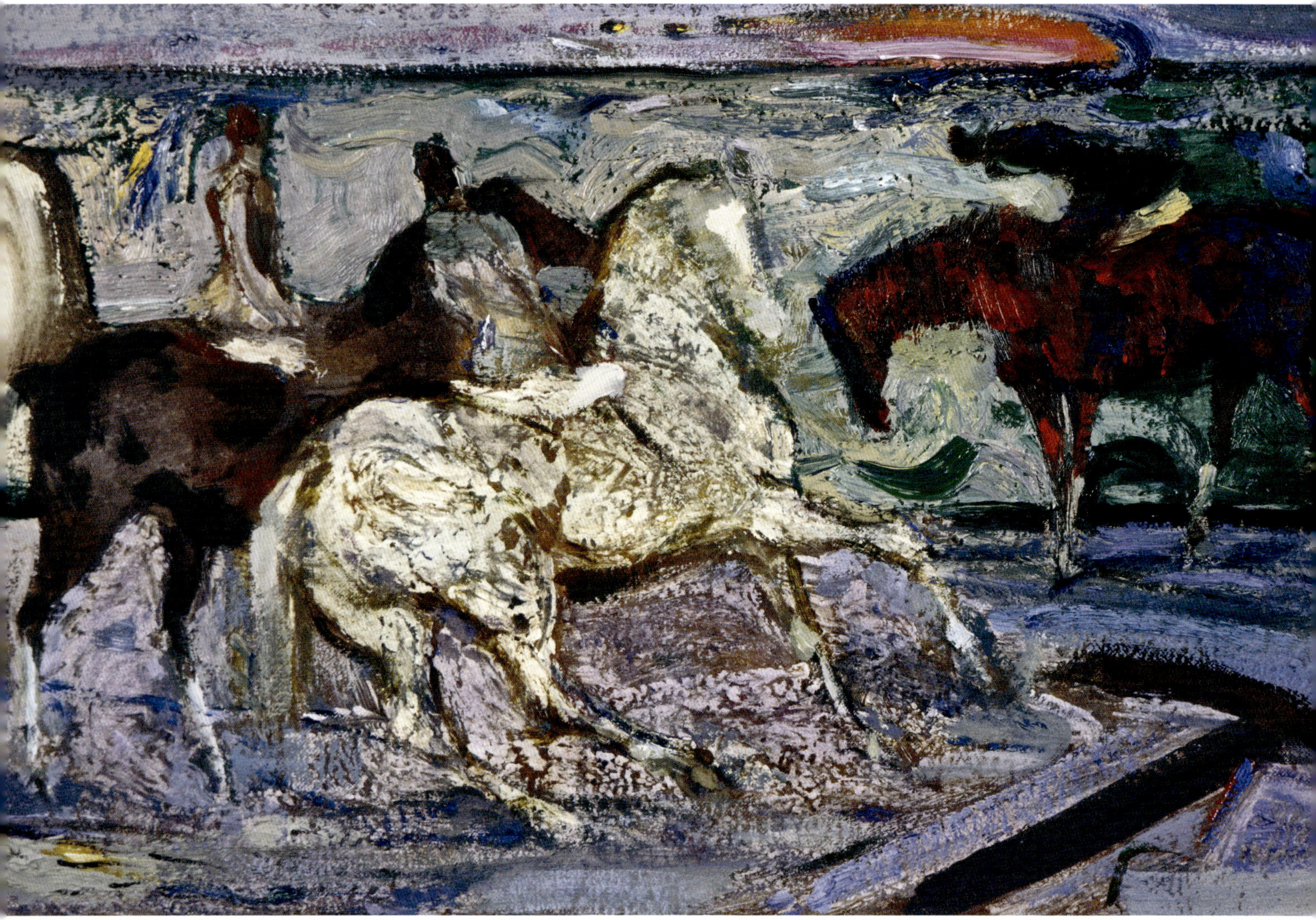

FIG. 6.9
Horsemen
*c.*1982 / oil on canvas / 30 x 45 cm
private collection • photo: Antonia Reeve

and sexuality, the rawness of the primitive in both mankind and the animal kingdom, were subjects which he worked and reworked with devotion. Horses and riders are also regular subjects from this period [fig. 6.9]. Battles were fought within nature: men on horseback appeared across the foot of a large canvas, *The Covering Sea*, the main subject being a giant wave about to engulf the riders. Mullaly called this an extraordinary painting, while Beaumont upped the description to refer to it as 'a roughed-up Hokusai'. Horsemen, a subject which had attracted him since the late 1950s, came into their own in some works, as did wild, snarling dogs, the memory of some encounters in India during the war [fig. 6.10]. These were executed in thick impasto and as light against a flat dark background. A series of paintings devoted to nearly all these subjects filled his studio from the late 1970s onwards, their canvases layered with many applications of paint.

The tension or energy within such subjects contrasted with others in the show which displayed a calmer simplicity, combining skilfully and thoughtfully the romantic with the classical. On an end wall upstairs was a self-portrait in a jaunty straw hat. This was a painting within a painting, an illustration of a canvas on an easel, and an idea gleaned from knowledge of past artists; he also used the idea for a series of still-life and cockerel paintings of the early to mid-1980s, and these give a glimpse of his studio at the time [figs 6.11, 6.12]. On the adjacent walls of the exhibition [fig. 6.5, bottom] a new subject was introduced – jugs or bowls filled

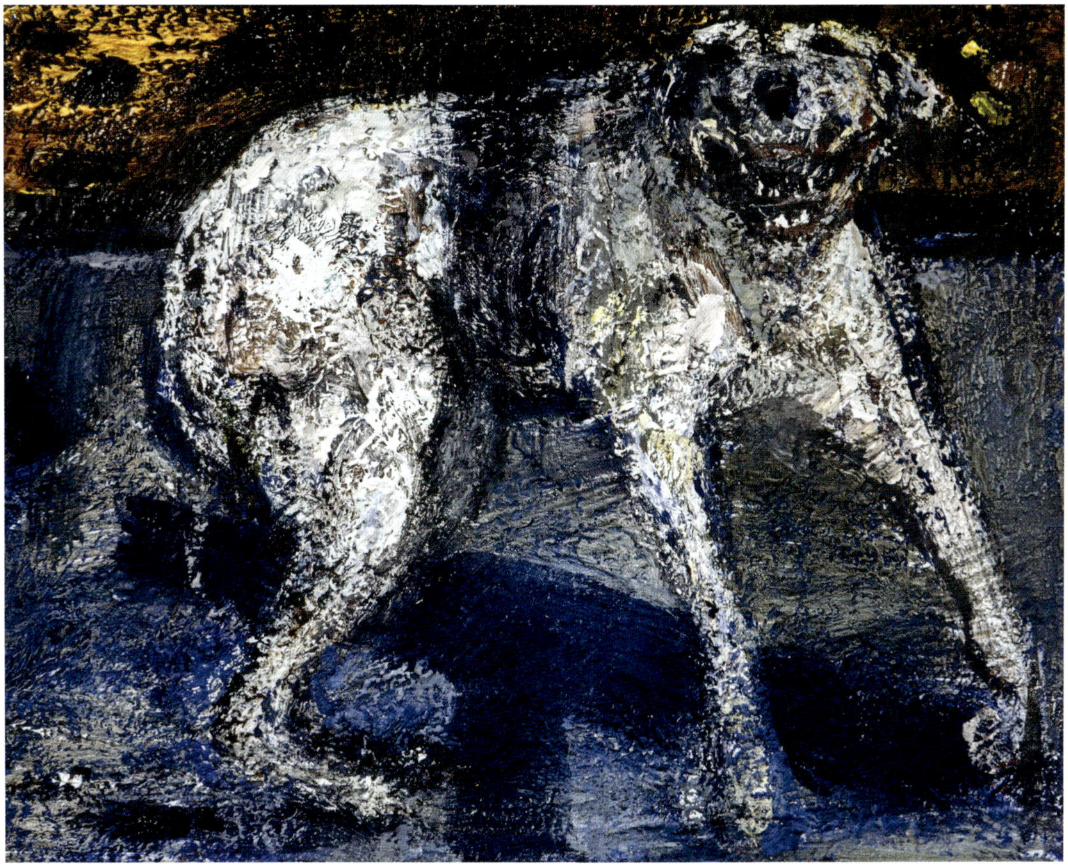

FIG. 6.10
Dog
*c.*1982 / oil on canvas / 24 x 36 cm
private collection · photo: Antonia Reeve

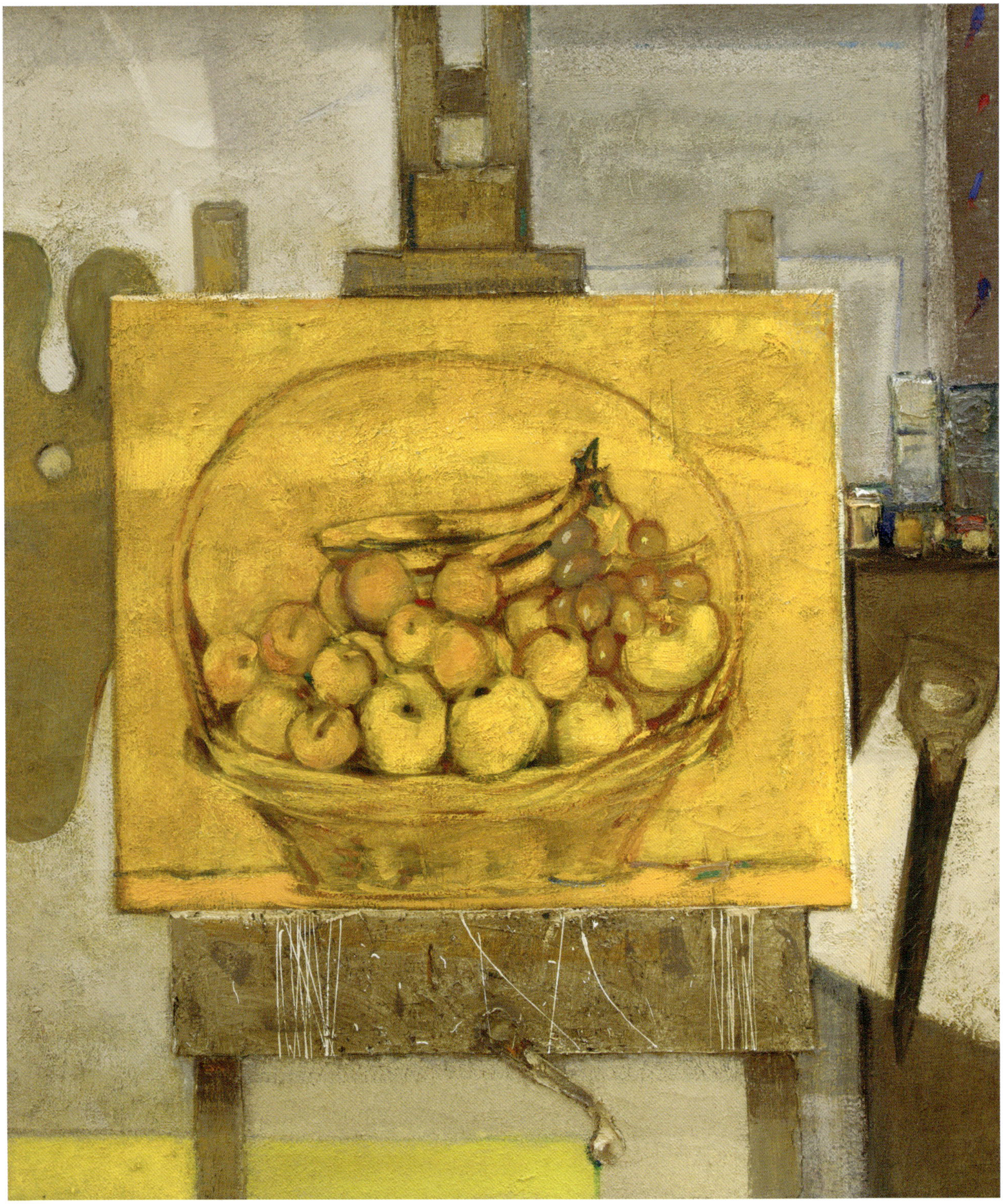

FIG. 6.11
Fruit
1984 / oil on canvas / 91 x 76.5 cm
private collection · courtesy of the Scottish Gallery

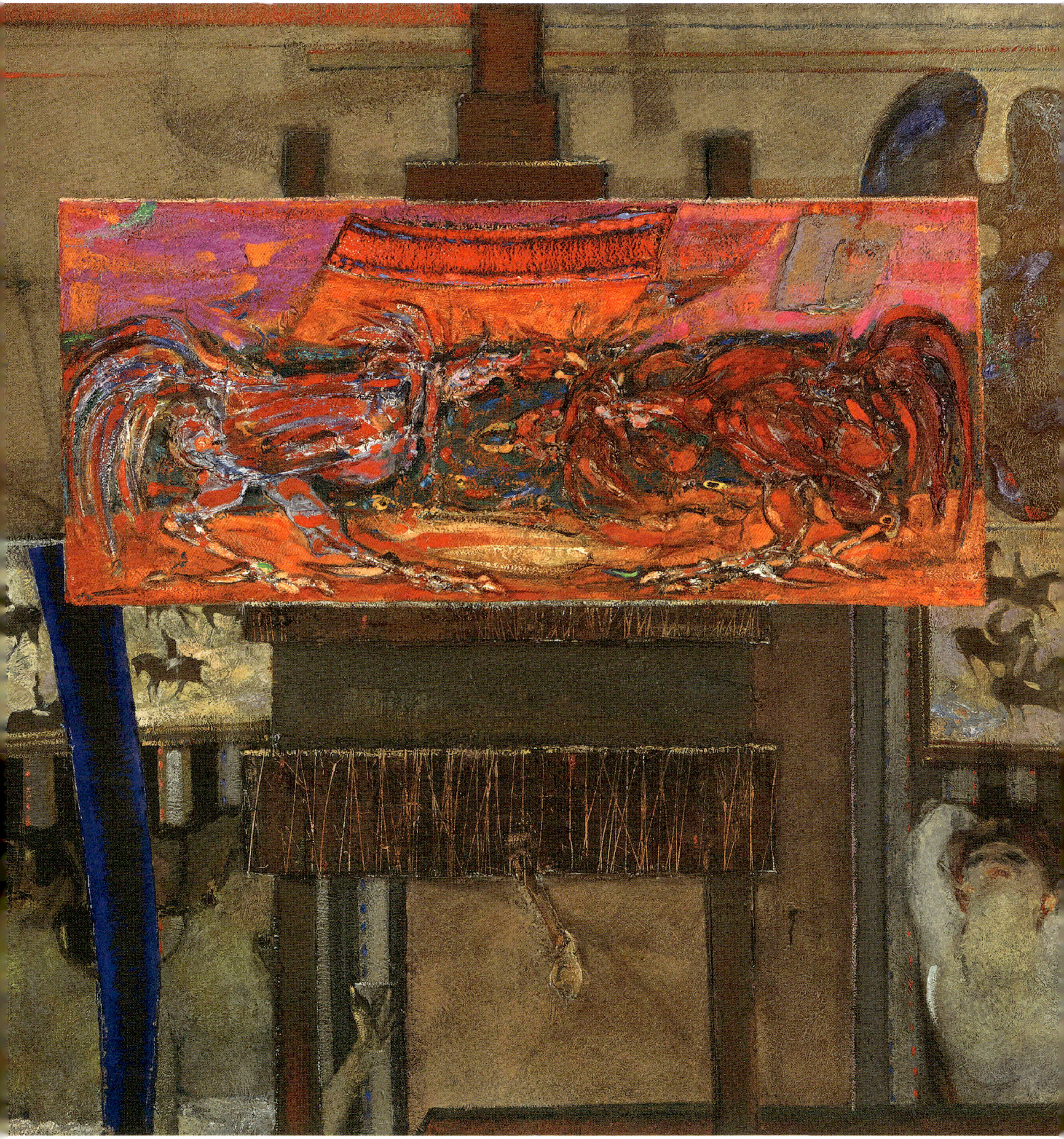

FIG. 6.12
Cockfight
*c.*1980 / oil on canvas / 122 x 122 cm
courtesy of Duncan R. Miller Fine Arts, London

with full-blown poppies, painted against different coloured backgrounds such as pale blue, a rich Mediterranean blue, Indian red and yellow. Beaumont rightly called the poppy flowers 'as fragile as crushed paper'. They were experimental works, distinct from but also related to the poppies long beloved of European artists such as Nolde. Robin the gardener grew them in the Crawfurd Road garden and studied them closely. Here he was returning to his early method of building up many layers of underpainting before applying a glaze of colour on top.

> *What attracted me to poppies was their splendour – the sheer power and yet the delicacy of their colour – the cold and warm reds and very subtle translucent lights. I began by modelling their form in whites and a range of neutral colours. When this 'white' stage was quite dry, the strong colours were created by laying thin glazes of pale translucent paint over the top, sometimes up to ten or more one on top of the other. Some of the blacks are built up in the same way over a bed of very rich blue or crimson.*[3]

As he also remarked, this careful construction meant that colour had to be worked out well in advance, with forms precisely determined, and it was a major move away from the intuitive, expressionist way of thinking and working still to be seen in the Dog series. Jack Firth later wrote of the challenge of painting red poppies:

> *... red is supposed to be an aggressive colour but the red of poppies is sensuous and soft, like brushed velvet, and has an opulence which defeats most painters. It needs patience and craftsmanship; forcing the intensity of the colour with the raw pigment can produce a surface like leather. Robin's poppies are more akin to flesh.*[4]

He also mentioned Robin's trick of reviving a vase of poppies with a dose of neat lemonade to allow a further day's painting. Subsequent paintings continued to concentrate on the fragility of these blossoms, and all offer a sense of the temporal values of nature [figs 0.1, 6.13].

However, not everyone was enthralled by the latest work on show, and some considered the new work unadventurous and 'safe'. Andrew Brown, the director of the 369 Gallery in the High Street (and a College Fine Art graduate), submitted an article with the punning title 'Eardley Promise' to the Scottish edition of the *Radio Times* ahead of the transmission of a film on that artist. Here he launched an attack on Robin who, Brown said, after showing early promise had buried himself in the art politics of the College and the RSA.[5] His painting was the art of the establishment, safe and unadventurous, and Brown attacked what he saw as the Gallery's 'bourgeois smugness'. It naturally fuelled a response from the Scottish Gallery director, William Jackson, and a private letter demanding an apology was sent to the BBC's Scottish editor by George Bruce.

The 1983 show had led directly to a major one with the Bruton Gallery in late 1985 in which there was the same range of subjects. Writing in the *Arts Review*, artist and critic Felix McCullough called the show 'a fascinating amalgam of new departures and thematic terminations'.[6] As McCullough pointed out, some paintings marked 'man's descent into darkness and despair', while others were resplendent in vibrant colour, capturing the essence of life at its finest. Poppies

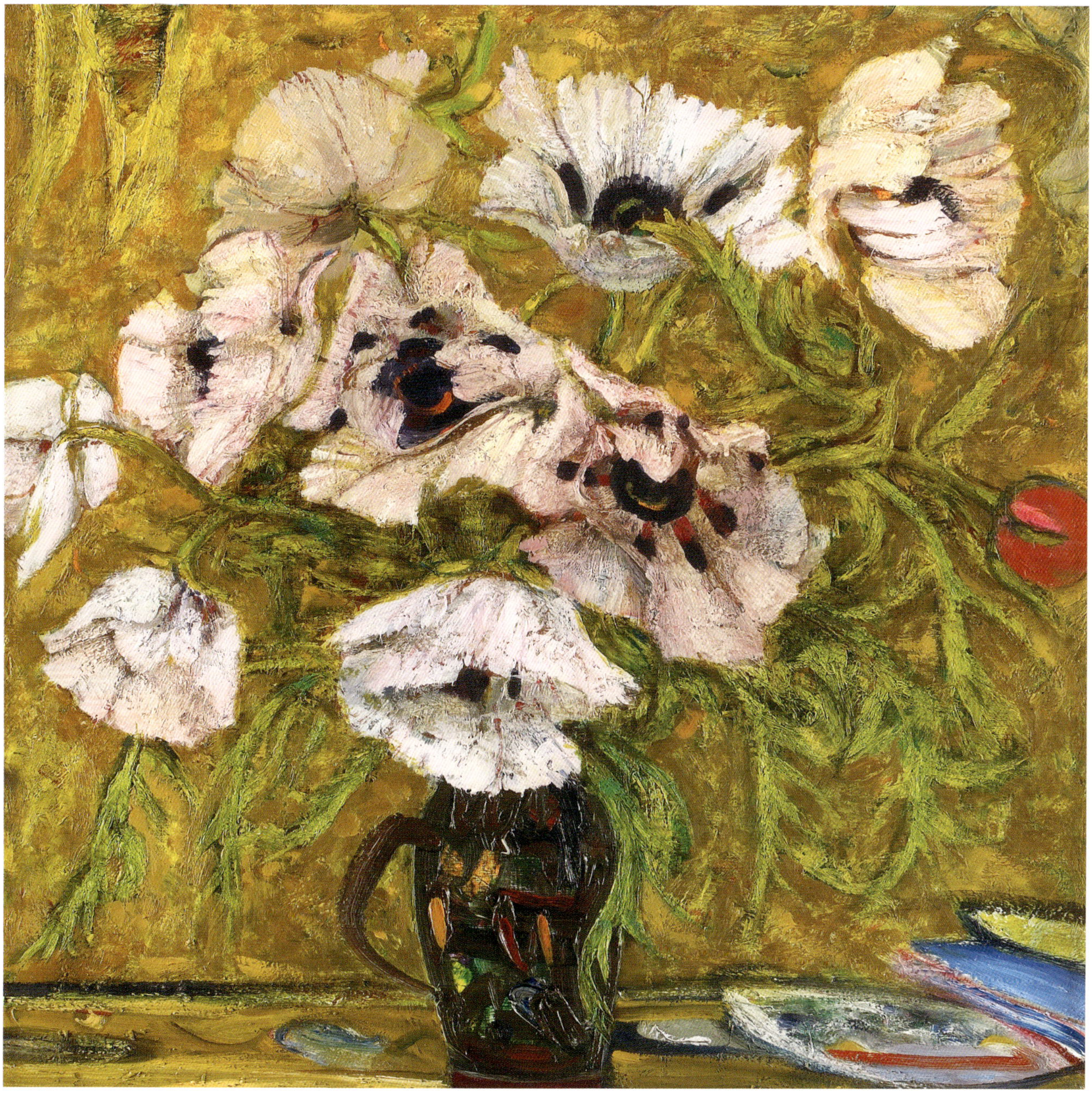

FIG. 6.13
Poppies on a Yellow Ground
*c.*1988–89 / oil on canvas / 76 x 76 cm
private collection • photo: courtesy of Lyon & Turnbull Auctioneers

were seen as the ephemeral made monumental. Robin was an artist who painted dangerously, creatively, producing exercises in painterly reconciliation of the diverse through mixed media. Not all poppy studies were in oil: some matched their fragility in the delicacy of watercolour.

The decade was an extraordinarily prolific one, with paintings, pastels and watercolours on view and well received by the press. Continuing also to contribute to mixed shows such as that of Scottish painting at the Oriel Gallery in Mostyn, Wales, and the annual society exhibitions presented in Edinburgh, Glasgow and London, he had solo selling exhibitions with Roland, Browse and Delbanco through the late 1970s and 1980s (1977, 1981, 1985 and 1988). The Knightsbridge Gallery, working with that dealer, included him in a mixed show entitled 'Three Scottish Painters' (Bill Baillie, Jack Knox and Robin), mounted at the Wichita Art Association in Kansas City in September 1984. In 1987 the Fine Art Society, with galleries in Glasgow and Edinburgh as well as London, hit on the idea of mounting a double show with David Donaldson to celebrate their turning seventy. The RSA lent Donaldson's recent portrait of Robin seated in front of one of his *Dog* series, and the catalogue had an introduction by George Bruce. This show was again a mix of the sensational – animal carcases, a subject which Rembrandt and Soutine had worked, but also the powerfully lyrical. It included two triptychs, *The Trap* and *Ho! Ho! The Hobby Horse*. The latter combined the horror of animal carcases (ever the researcher, he had visited the Edinburgh abattoir at Gorgie in preparation) wearing eighteenth-century-styled dressing-up coats and set against a merry-go-round of nudes and shadowy figures who also occupy the two wing panels. Indicative of the physicality of life, these were also powerful exercises in colour – clear blues and fuchsia pinks contrasting with flesh and grey blues. Some related paintings were also presented as a series – *Merry-go-round*, *Arena* and a series of small oils called *Adam and Eve*, which used angrily worked paint on primed leather to emphasise the flesh of temporal existence. They were displayed in a Lamp of Lothian show in 1987 with some taken for stock by the Bruton Gallery.

Robin's ever-present devotion to the values of materials and to technical investigation and trials also resurfaced in the mid-1980s in a different field when Dovecot Studios directly approached him with the idea of a tapestry. Now his longstanding interest in tapestry would finally be realised. Dovecot by now had returned into the ownership of the Bute family, and in 1984 the Marquess of Bute and managing director James More had fixed on the idea of a 'Scottish collection' of tapestries to be woven in collaboration with modern Scottish painters. Other painters to be involved into the early '90s included Elizabeth Blackadder, William Littlejohn, Alberto Morrocco, John Bellany, John Houston, Derek Roberts (born 1947) and Adrian Wiszniewski (born 1958). This time a new design was not requested: instead, Robin was asked if a 35-mm colour slide of a recent painting might form the basis for a collaborative new work. One painting in the Humankind series was selected and the tapestry [fig. 6.15], on its completion in 1988, would share this title.

The weavers – Harry Wright, his son Johnny, Shirley Gatt and David Cochrane – worked closely and enjoyably with Robin on translating an image of his oil into a two-metre tapestry [fig. 6.14]. He regularly visited the studio to engage with the weavers, discuss problems and debate ideas. It must have taken him back to his

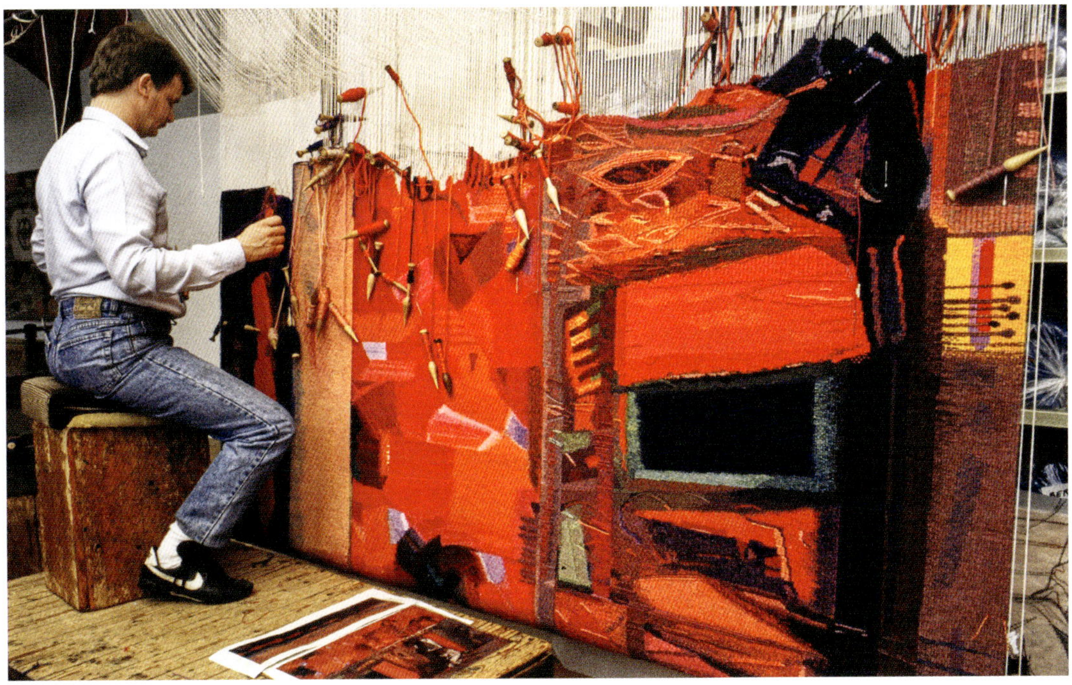

FIG. 6.14
Johnny Wright weaving *Humankind* at Dovecot Studios, 1988
photo: Antonia Reeve

times at Reid & Taylor. The tapestry is extraordinarily rich, its colour and textures taking on a life quite independent of its source. It was a totally new work of art in which, to quote Robin, 'a swift brushstroke had to be translated into the medium of tapestry on its bed of time. A heavy loaded spatula, pressing down a great slab on the painted surface had to grow on its own terms.'[7] Making it was a journey and adventure for all concerned. Robin sent James More a note to be used in the publicity brochure which summed up the equality of the partnership:

> *... a dialogue ensued that I found completely captivating and it's this kind of interpretation that reinforces the notion that a new piece of creativity is on its way, and that is something that one cannot underline too strongly.*
>
> *I think it would be impertinent of me to say that I learned something from the master weavers. I believe we would settle for the notion that we both learned from each other as we built a completely independent and completely new work of art.*[8]

Other tapestries soon followed. *Poppies on a Blue Ground* [figs 6.16, 6.17] and *Meadows*, ones which worked particularly well in terms of texture and palette, were woven in 1989 with the latter duplicated in 1992; and two smaller tapestries on the subject of *The Judgement of Paris* and *Fruit and Fish* were produced in 1991. Family life by this point in the late '80s was at the centre of Robin's world, with three youngsters making demands on much of his time. Although he had always had a home studio, he now found less peace to work there, and kind friends offered him the use of a space in their Glenorchy Terrace flat as a studio. This was less than a kilometre from home in Crawfurd Road and it granted him the freedom to work. It was here that many of the lustrous paintings of poppies would be produced over the next four or five years.

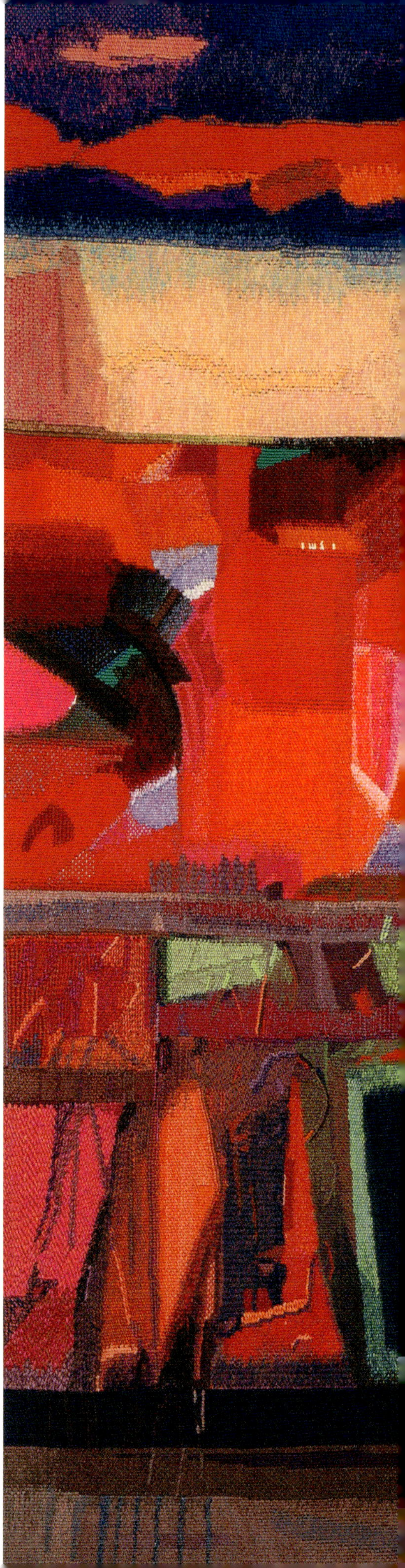

FIG. 6.15
Humankind
1988 / cotton warp, wool / 213.5 x 213.5 cm
woven by Dovecot Studios • © CSG CIC Glasgow Museums and Libraries Collections

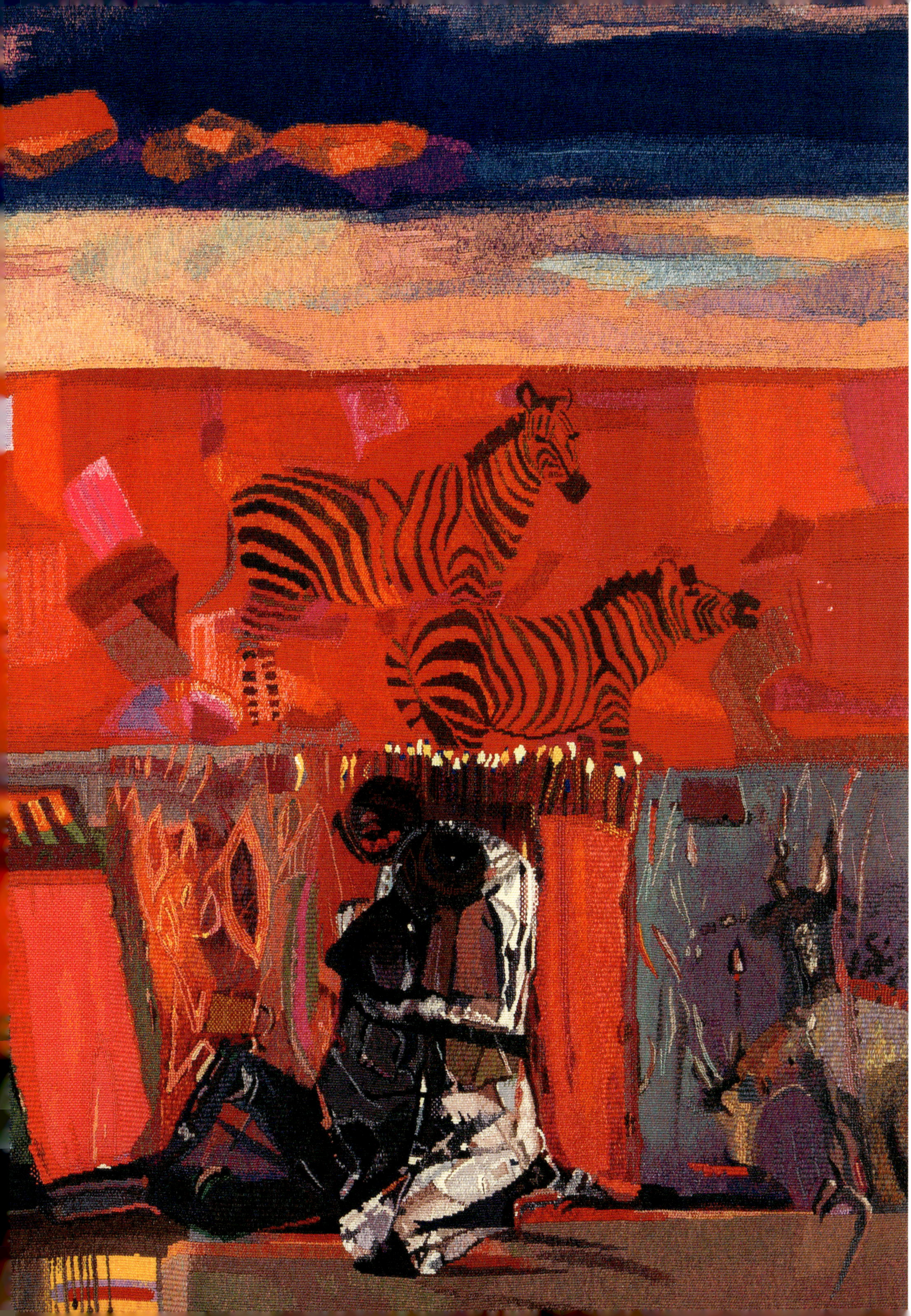

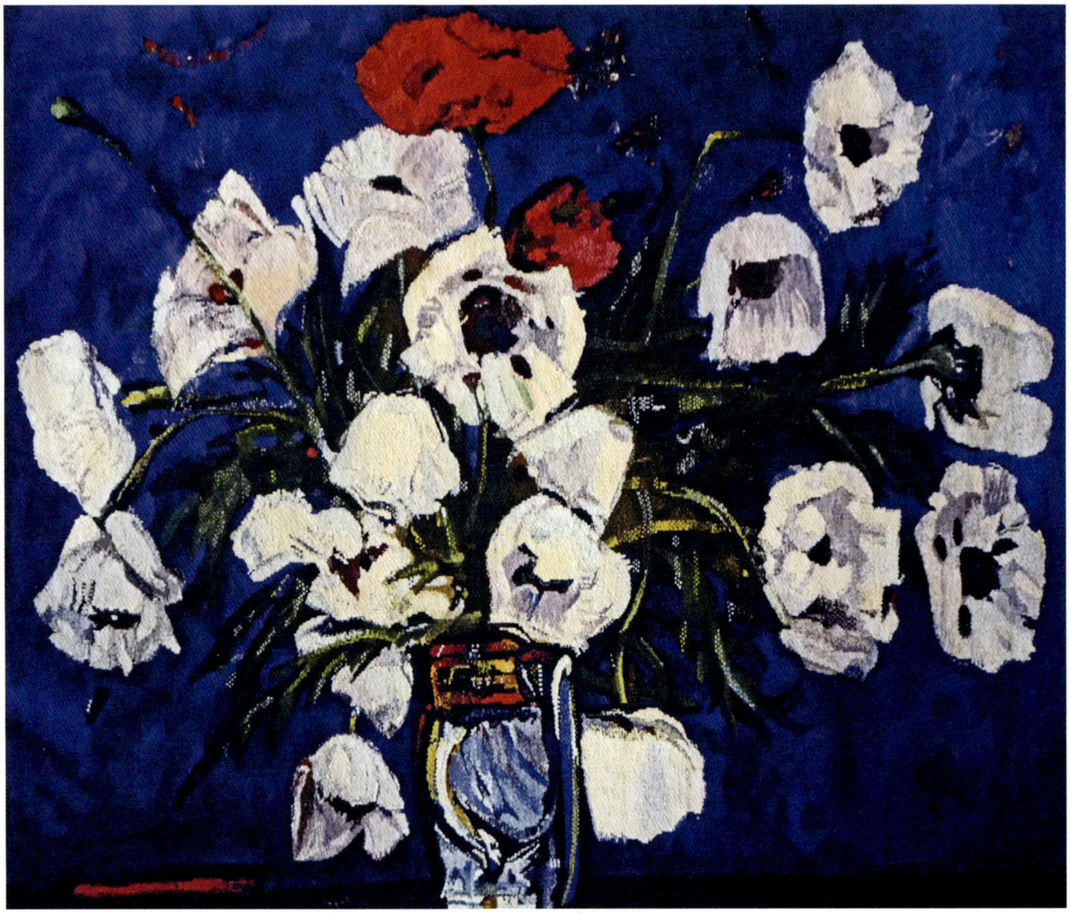

FIG. 6.16
Poppies on a Blue Ground
1989 / cotton warp, wool / 122 x 147 cm
The Edinburgh Tapestry Company Archive at Mount Stuart Trust • photo: the author

As the *Humankind* tapestry was being warped on the loom, a second, relatively small, one-man exhibition opened at the Bruton Gallery. Called 'The Secret Garden', it developed a theme used for a single painting Robin had recently donated to charity in aid of the Glasgow Garden Festival of 1988. The result brought together many ideas from across his career, from rose windows to zebras and cattle, women, fighting cocks and fish. It seemed that Robin was taking stock of his life, taking note of his core interests and achievements. A one-man show in the Scottish Arts Club during the 1988 Festival brought together more than thirty loans from members, many of whom had purchased their Philipsons from the Scottish Gallery over the years. Out of both of these shows came the idea of a major retrospective at the College for the 1989 Festival. Robin called on Colin Thompson to help curate it and to locate many other works which had sold and even changed hands over the years. Together they decided it should be a thematic display to celebrate the ideas behind his career and demonstrate the variety of technical approaches. The craft gallerist Ann Hartree, then employed as the College's exhibitions director, arranged the loans and a catalogue was produced with an introduction by art historian and dealer Roger Billcliffe. In all, 162 paintings plus the two large recent Dovecot tapestries (*Humankind* and *Meadows*) were included. Publicity was good, and what would turn out to be some of Robin's last interviews were published. It would be the last time during his lifetime that Robin's work over a forty-year period would

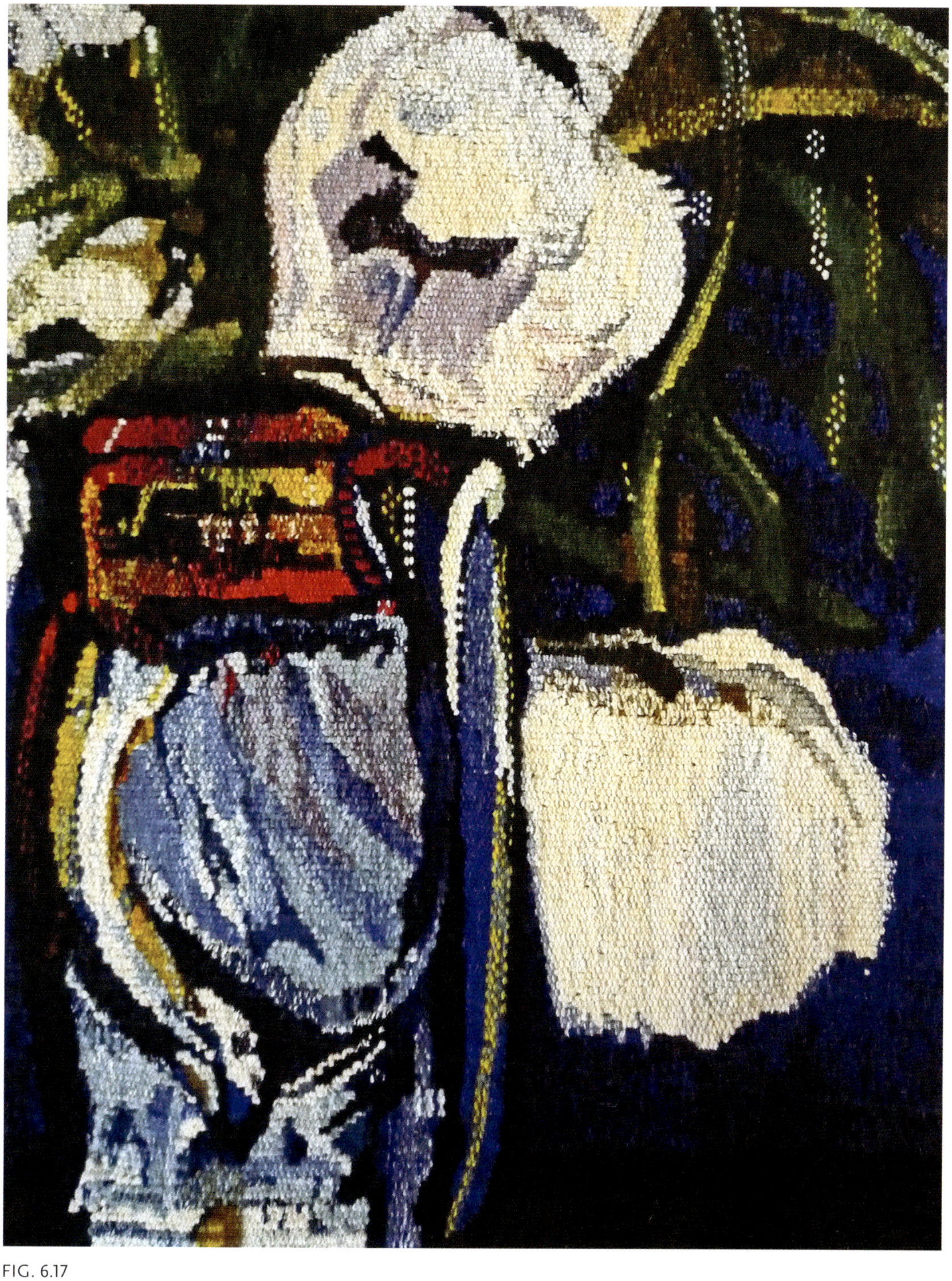

FIG. 6.17
Detail from *Poppies on a Blue Ground*
photo: the author

be seen. A smaller retrospective of seventy-four works was subsequently curated by Philip Long at the Scottish National Gallery of Modern Art exactly a decade later.

In the early 1990s, his painting was seen in one or two commercial exhibitions, including the new Bruton Gallery in Bath, where the show in November 1991 included a variety of media. It might be said that, like Matisse, towards the end of his life his art had tended towards the decorative and inventive more than the intellectual. But the Bath exhibition [fig. 6.18] drew praise for more than this. Richard Jacques, writing in the *Arts Review*, referred to its centrepiece, *Zigzag of Time*, as 'magnificent ... encapsulating Philipson's qualities at their painterly and philosophical best'. In the painting a curtain parted to reveal two tumbling waterfalls of mankind in 'a riot of colour'. Jacques deemed it would become seen as one of the great paintings of the twentieth century. In a sense the painting and its title summarised Robin's passion for life with its pleasures, trials and complexities. Like David McClure, Robin enjoyed painting domestic furniture, and his home was joyfully decorated: mantelpiece panels sported odalisques and horsemen, or a still life; kitchen benches, painted with Diana, featured red poppies.

This was a time of great activity, domestic peace and critical acclaim. But the cancer, first diagnosed in France in 1972, returned, and Robin died following further operations on 26 May 1992.[9] Today he is of course remembered primarily as a painter but also by some as a dedicated and strict teacher and by others as one of the hardest working and memorable presidents of the RSA. He had also been a printmaker, had contributed to the colour design of woven textiles, worked with tapestry weavers, and given time to charities and committee work. One of the last times Jack Firth had visited Robin in the Glenorchy Terrace studio, he saw a large, newly finished canvas of pale pink and purple poppies on the easel. The petals, as he recorded, were 'as big as dinner plates, pellucid and flouncing and breath-thin in texture'. In his long painting career – and this will remain the art for which he will always be most remembered – Robin had explored the condition of man and of beast, painting disturbing subjects but also some which were expressions of deep beauty. Among the many obituaries, writer and critic Judith Bumpus told movingly in her tribute of the solitary ebb and flow of emotion in the studio. She said that there was 'a vitality and immediacy about all his work that belied the long reflection that produced it'. Robin was as 'subtly contradictory as the themes he dealt with: beauty (not a term he was afraid to use) and ugliness, pleasure and suffering, the spirit and the flesh, tolerance and prejudice ... To all the world a gregarious and outgoing personality, he was, by his own admission, a loner and a dreamer'.[10]

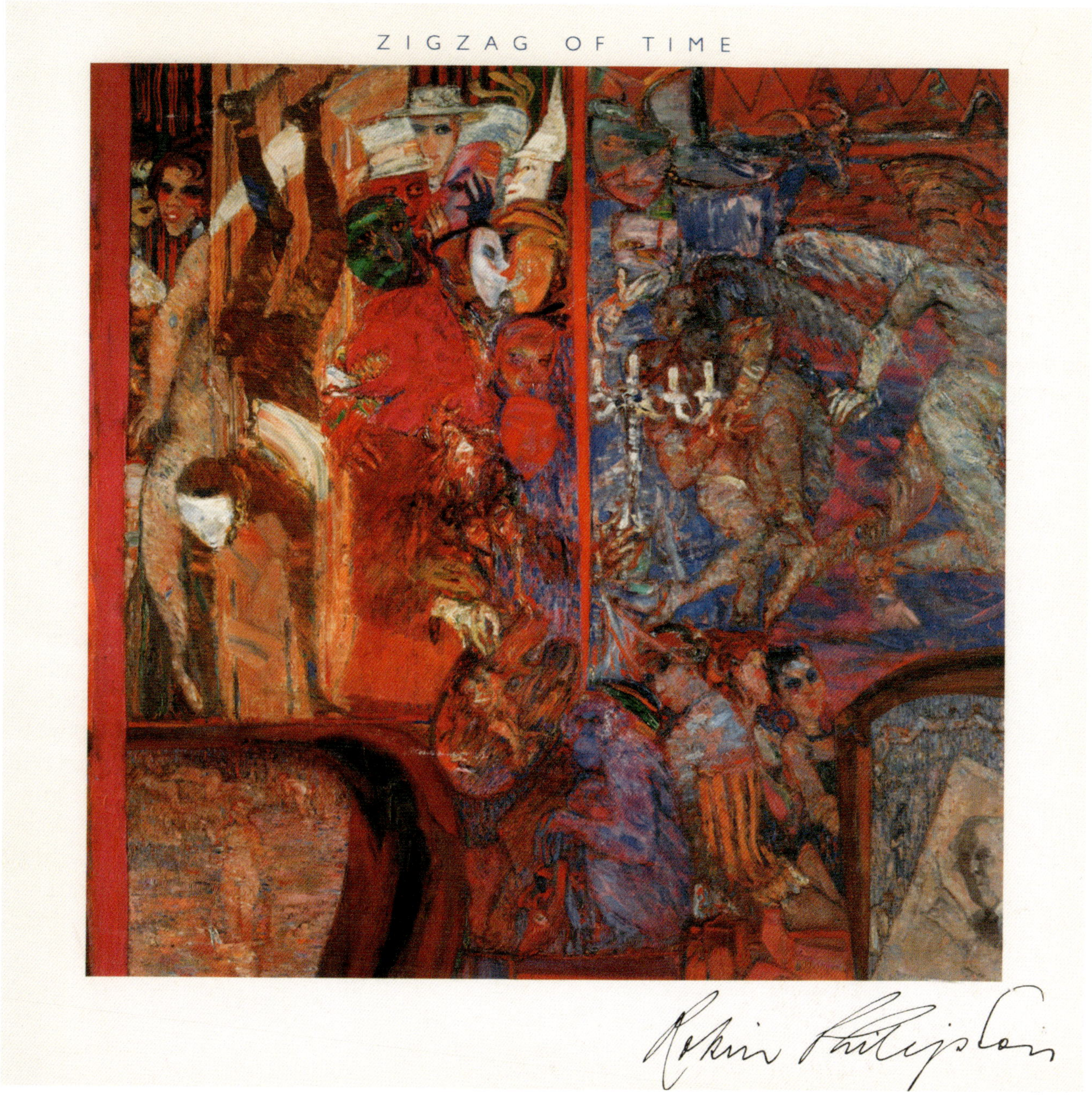

FIG. 6.18
Private view invitation for the 'Zigzag of Time' exhibition at the Bruton Gallery, Bath, November 1991
private collection

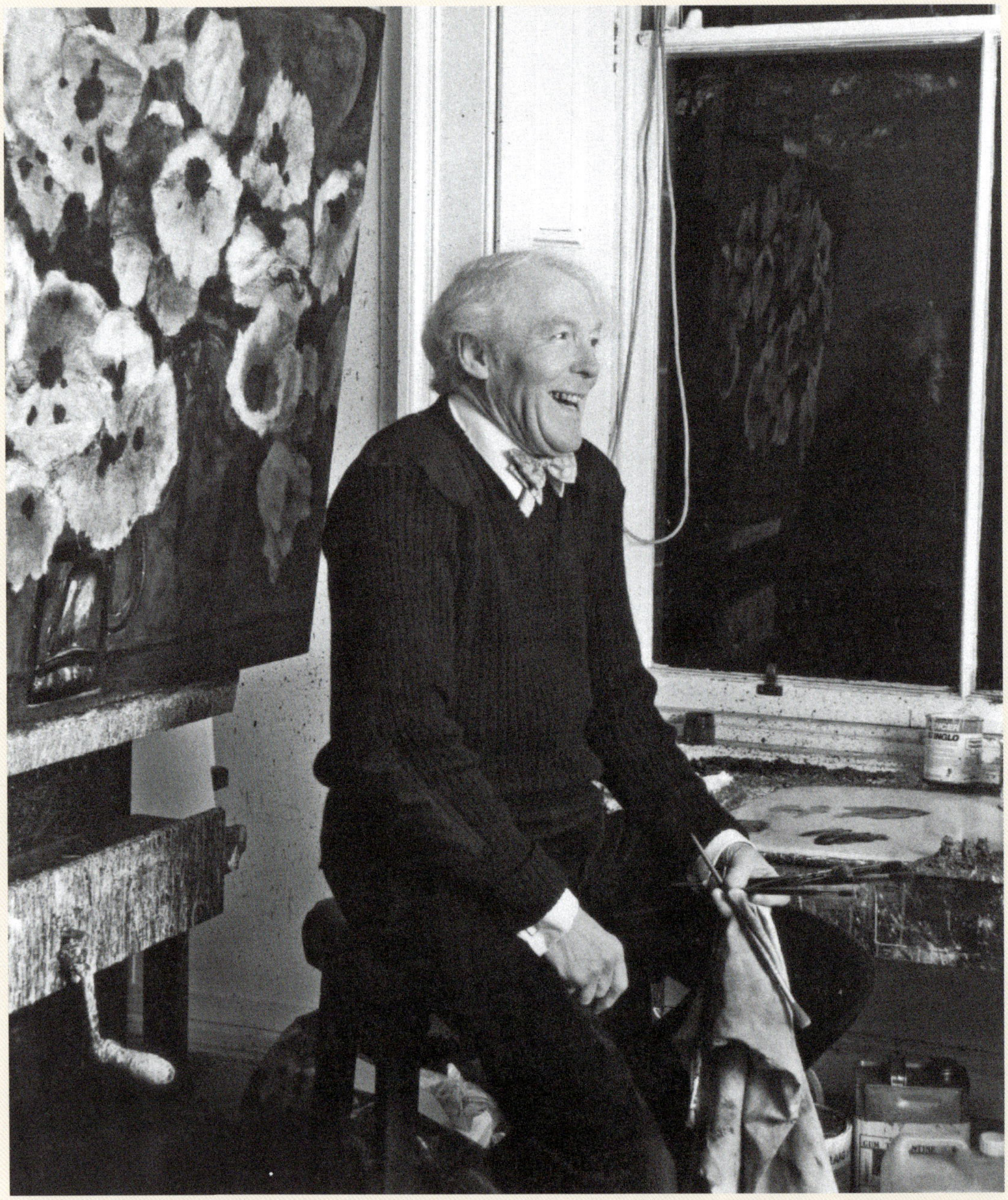

Robin in his studio, *c.*1985
private collection

CHRONOLOGY

1916 Born 17 December in Broughton-in-Furness
1933–36 Attends Dumfries Academy
1936–40 Studies at Edinburgh College of Art
1940–45 War service with the King's Own Scottish Borderers and the Royal Indian Army Service Corps
1946–47 Teacher training at Moray House College of Education, Edinburgh
1947 Joins staff of Edinburgh College of Art
1948 Professional member of the Society of Scottish Artists
1952 Associate member of the Royal Scottish Academy
1954 First of many solo exhibitions at the Scottish Gallery (Aitken Dott) in Edinburgh
1955 Member of the Royal Scottish Society of Painters in Watercolour
1957 Shows in the first John Moores Exhibition, Liverpool
1957–58 Works with Edinburgh printers Harley Brothers to develop artist prints
1958–59 Designs publicity material for the Edinburgh International Festival
1959 Work shown in mixed shows in Nottingham and again in Liverpool, first television broadcasts on art
1960 Appointed Head of the School of Drawing and Painting at Edinburgh College of Art; first solo London exhibition with Roland, Browse and Delbanco
1962 Member of the Royal Scottish Academy
1963 Professor of Advanced Painting at the University of Colorado at Boulder summer school; 'Four Scottish Painters' shown at the Edinburgh International Festival
1965 Visits European museums
1970 Solo exhibitions at Carnegie Festival of Music and the Arts, Dunfermline and with the Scottish Arts Council
1973–83 President of the Royal Scottish Academy
1974 One-man exhibitions in Elgin and Haddington
1976 Knighted; visits South Africa; major exhibition at the Scottish Gallery
1977 Retrospective at University of Stirling
1981 Royal Academician
1982 Retires from Edinburgh College of Art
1983 Major exhibition at the Scottish Gallery
1987 Joint exhibition with David Donaldson at the Fine Art Society
1988 First of several tapestries woven at Dovecot Studios
1992 Dies 26 May

NOTES

INTRODUCTION

1. Dr George Bruce OBE, 'Tributes to Sir Robin Philipson', *Robin Philipson*, Haddington, 1992.
2. Ibid.

THE MAKING OF AN ARTIST

1. The family was not particularly well off. Under Edward Barrow's will, on Agnes's remarriage she lost any income from his estate and the family relied on the railway income. My thanks to Chris Gwilliam, son of Phyllis, and Guyda Sharp, daughter of Betty, for supplying family information used here and elsewhere in the text.
2. Whitehaven County Secondary School Admission Register, ref. YDS69/1/6. Alison Hurst of Cumbria Archive and Local Studies Centre kindly provided information used here.
3. Colette Douglas-Home, 'Nonconformity as an Art Form', *The Scotsman*, 14 August 1989.
4. Dumfries Academy admissions register, Ewart Library, Dumfries. Previous books and exhibition catalogues have stated that Robin and Phyllis were up to two years younger when they enrolled at Dumfries Academy. My thanks here to Cathy Gibb at the Ewart Library for new information.
5. Maurice Lindsay, *Modern Scottish Painters No. 6: Robin Philipson*, Edinburgh, 1976, p. 2.
6. Ibid. Philipson mentioned to Roger Billcliffe for his catalogue introduction to 'Robin Philipson Retrospective' (Edinburgh, 1989) that he had been asked (or offered) to accompany an elderly lady to the capital.
7. Philipson's twin sister Phyllis, in an interview by Victoria Keller, quoting Robin as a child holding such a sweet to the light and saying 'I just love the colour.' Victoria Keller, *Robin Philipson 1916–1992*, Edinburgh [National Galleries of Scotland], 1999, p. 9.
8. W. Gordon Smith, *Philipson*, Edinburgh, 1995, p. 27.
9. Lindsay, p. 3.
10. John Maxwell painted the mural *Neighbourhood Scenes* in Craigmillar, 1934–35, and Westwater an *Alice in Wonderland* in Wardie in 1936, while Tom Whalen provided the sculpture *Mother and Child* for Prestonfield in 1935. Tom Pow, who taught College trade classes for housepainters and decorators, painted scenes depicting *King Arthur and His Knights* on the walls of Musselburgh Grammar School, and Denis Peploe illustrated *The Life and Times of Paracelsus* in the students' common room of Heriot-Watt College.
11. John Bellany, an early 1960s student, is quoted as saying he was 'dry as a stick, spouting Berenson way over our heads'. John McEwen, *John Bellany*, Edinburgh, 2013, pp. 38–39.
12. Lindsay, p. 7.
13. Leonard Rosoman addressing the first Decadents' Dinner, Edinburgh College of Art, 2005.
14. *Prospectus of the Edinburgh College of Art* for 1950–51.
15. The students decorated the Church of Scotland's Arts and Crafts Centre in Eyre Place in the session 1950–51. See *The Art Student: The Magazine of the Edinburgh College of Art* (1951), Edinburgh [College of Art], p. 25.
16. Maureen Hodge et al., *Master Weavers*, Edinburgh, 1980, p. 50.

PAINTER, PRINTMAKER, DESIGNER

1. 'My Weekend', *The Gleneagles Hotel Magazine*, 1983, p. 59.
2. Colette Douglas-Home, 'Nonconformity as an Art Form', *The Scotsman*, 14 August 1989.
3. 'At Home with the Philipsons, Artists', newspaper cutting in the Philipson family archive, 1955 (no publication or day/month).
4. Life drawing was also taught by Derek Clarke, portrait painting by David McClure in 1954–55 and

John Houston and John Busby in 1958–59.
5. The painting had been presented by the Czechoslovak Government in Exile to the National Gallery of Scotland in 1942.
6. Philipson recalling the painting in 1989 for the catalogue of his retrospective at the College of Art.
7. My thanks to David Black for helping to identify the commission.
8. Sax Shaw would become director of weaving at Dovecot Studios from 1954 to 1958.
9. My thanks to Kevan Shaw and to Thora Clyne for sharing information on Robin's French holidays.
10. Edward Gage, 'Philipson: Evolution of Compelling Style', *The Scotsman*, 6 April 1970.
11. *The Listener*, 14 May 1959.
12. T. Elder Dickson, 'Robin Philipson RSA', *The Studio*, vol. 164, no. 834, October 1962, p. 144.
13. W. Gordon Smith, *Philipson*, Edinburgh, 1995, p. 60.
14. This account of the history of the Harley Brothers print firm is indebted to the researches of Chris Allan. See Chris Allan, *Artists at Harley: Pioneering Printmaking in the 1950s*, Hunterian Art Gallery, University of Glasgow, 2000. The Harley Brothers archive is on deposit at the Hunterian Art Gallery.
15. The working arrangement between Harley's and the St George's Gallery is detailed in Allan's account.
16. McClure taught evening classes in portrait painting, as did Robin.
17. The Harley archive, as recorded by Chris Allan, lists Elizabeth Blackadder as making four prints in 1958, John Houston two prints and Willie Wilson two in the same year, and David Michie, Redpath's son, two in 1959.
18. Colin Thompson was assistant keeper of the National Gallery of Scotland, and from 1967 its keeper.

NEW WORLDS
1. All Robin's subsequent cars would be French, and from the Citroën factory.
2. Eric Newton, 'Cathedrals and Cockfights', *The Manchester Guardian*, 24 October 1960.
3. Katherine Whitehorn, *The Observer*, 16 October 1960.
4. From an advertisement placed in *The Tailor and Cutter*, 21 October 1960, by Lear, Browne and Dunsford of Exeter.
5. *The Wool Record*, Bradford, 6 April 1962.
6. *The Manchester Guardian*, 14 April 1962.
7. A tapestry of some 35 square feet woven at 8 warps per inch (wpi) or 28 square feet at 12 wpi was mentioned in a letter dated 10 November 1962 (Edinburgh College of Art archive). Robin's reply is dated 21 November.
8. Letter of 21 November 1962 to Harry Jefferson Barnes, Edinburgh University Library CRC Acc. 1996/7, box 3.
9. T. Elder Dickson, 'Robin Philipson RSA', *The Studio*, vol. 164, no. 834, October 1962, p. 144.
10. T. Elder Dickson, 'Robin Philipson', *The Scottish Art Review*, vol. VIII, no. 2, 1961, pp. 22–23.
11. Two of her brothers, Dan and Henry, had already studied at the College, Dan in D&P and Henry in sculpture. Henry Clyne (born 1930) had worked alongside Daphne Dyce Sharp with Leonard Rosoman on the sets of the College's 'Diaghilev' exhibition in 1954.
12. Robin's words quoted in *Robin Philipson Retrospective*, exhib. cat., Edinburgh, 1989, unpaginated.
13. See Roger Billcliffe (introduction), *Robin Philipson Retrospective*, exhib. cat.; also W. Gordon Smith, *Philipson*, Edinburgh, 1995, pp. 68–69.
14. In a statement recorded in the Annual Report for 1961–62, the governors referred to the 'current avant-garde view' being that 'traditional disciplines of the life rooms are out of touch with the modern spirit'.
15. *Edinburgh College of Art Prospectus* for 1969–70.
16. Philipson family archive.
17. Copy of typed reference, RSA Archives.
18. Edinburgh University Library ECA Collection Acc. 1996/7, box 3.
19. *Robin Philipson Retrospective*.
20. John Bellany as recorded in Smith, *Philipson*, p. 7.

THE ACADEMIC ARTIST
1. From a discussion between Robin and Colin Thompson published in *Robin Philipson Retrospective*, exhib. cat., Edinburgh, 1989, unpaginated.
2. Losey's film was on general release from September 1964. My thanks to Robin Rodger for this information.
3. Dore Ashton, 'Art: Avant-garde Pole', *The New York Times*, 12 April 1960.
4. W. Gordon Smith, *Philipson*, Edinburgh, 1995, p. 83.
5. Letter of 20 April 1965 to George Buchanan, curator at Glasgow Art Gallery and Museums (copy with the Philipson family archive).
6. Letter of 13 January 1969 to Michael Laird (copy with the Philipson family archive).

7. Leverhulme Research Award report sent to the Leverhulme Trust, October 1965, Edinburgh University Library ECA Collection Acc. 1996/7, box 3.
8. From a second copy of letter of 20 April 1965 to George Buchanan, curator at Glasgow Art Gallery and Museums, Edinburgh University Library ECA Collection Acc. 1996/7, box 7.
9. The earlier ideas of easel art influencing and infusing cloth colour resurfaced several times in Packer's time and remained part of Robin's legacy. In late 1967 a new collection of twist-worsted suitings for the following season would be announced, based on the paintings of Rembrandt, Velasquez and Hals, where 'the rich brilliance of the painted canvas' was 'transformed into woven cloth'. The early discussions on art would again resurface in a collection which drew most directly of all on painting: Reid & Taylor's autumn and winter 1988 'Scottish Colourists' collection was developed by Reid & Taylor designer Alan Morton to reflect directly the brushstroke colours of J.D. Fergusson, S.J. Peploe, F.C.B. Cadell and Leslie Hunter.
10. Dr Lakowski (known as Ronnie, 1926–2013) was originally from Poland. He had studied at Glasgow University and married a Scot. His doctoral thesis, awarded by Edinburgh University in 1965, was on 'Age and Colour Vision'. In 1970 the Lakowskis emigrated to Canada, where Ronnie taught in the departments of psychology and ophthalmology at the University of British Columbia. My thanks to Margaret Campbell for this information.
11. Womersley had a warm relationship with the College and in spring 1970 provided a decorative scheme for the principal communal spaces.
12. Sydney Goodsir Smith, referring specifically to Moffat and Bellany 'as very much of a "school"' in *The Scotsman* on 2 September 1963, mentioned the 'two by now traditional shows that are hung on the railings of Castle Terrace, open to wind and rain, and those hung on the Scotsman Steps'.
13. John McEwen, *John Bellany*, Edinburgh, 2013, p. 48.
14. Ibid, p. 47: 'The stationmaster asked who we were responsible to so we grudgingly said Robin Philipson, thinking this was definitely the end of our studio careers. Philipson soon appeared, all decked out for some posh dinner. But instead of going at us, he went for them. It was brilliant: "How dare you treat my students in this way? Don't you realise these are valuable works of art you've got on your train! I want the whole matter dealt with immediately."'
15. The line-up of artists was Alvermann, Becher, Beuys, Bohmler, Brecht, Brunning, Christiansen, Dohl, Filliou, Gerstner, Graubner, Heerich, Iannone, Kagel, Klapheck, Knoebel, Kohlhofer, Kriwet, Luther, Mack, Mommartz, Morgan, Palermo, Polke, Reusch, Richter, Rinke, Rot, Ruthenbeck, Spoerri, Thomkins, Uecker, Walther, Weseler and Wewerka.
16. Quoted from the *Edinburgh College of Art Prospectus* for 1978–79, Edinburgh University Library ECA Collection.
17. Copy of letter of 16 May 1978 to Kim Kempshall, Edinburgh University Library ECA Collection Acc. 1996/7, box 7.

'THE MAGICIAN OF THE BRUSH'

1. Tom Fleming, writing in the catalogue of the exhibition of paintings by Sir Robin Philipson to mark the jubilee of the Lamp of Lothian Trust in 1992.
2. The Scottish Arts Council, successor to the Arts Council Scottish Committee, had been established in 1967.
3. Terence Mullaly, *The Daily Telegraph*, 29 August 1970.
4. Quoted from *Robin Philipson Retrospective*, exhib. cat., Edinburgh, 1989, unpaginated.
5. Edgar J. Driscoll Jnr, 'Scots Shun Modern Trend', *The Boston Globe*, 9 May 1971.
6. Copy of letter of 26 January 1972 to Lord Polwarth, Edinburgh University Library ECA Collection Acc. 1996/7, box 8.
7. Copy of letter of 25 July 1972 to Lillian Browse, Edinburgh University Library ECA Collection Acc. 1996/7, box 9.
8. Robin Philipson, *Robin Philipson*, exhib. cat., The Scottish Gallery, Edinburgh, 1976.

GARDENS OF DELIGHT

1. Robin Philipson, 'My Weekend', *The Gleneagles Hotel Magazine*, 1983, p. 59.
2. Cutting from the Philipson family archive.
3. *Robin Philipson Retrospective*, exhib. cat., Edinburgh, 1989, unpaginated.
4. Sir Robin Philipson obituary written for *The Scottish Arts Club Newsletter*.
5. *Radio Times*, 13–19 August 1983, p. 58.
6. Felix McCullough, *Arts Review*, 11 October 1985.
7. *Tapestries: The Scottish Collection 1*, Dovecot Studios, Edinburgh, 1987.
8. *Modern Collections*, the Edinburgh Tapestry Co. Ltd, Dovecot Studios, Edinburgh, 1991.
9. W. Gordon Smith had interviewed him during these last months and in 1995 published his biography based on many interviews with him and others.
10. From the obituary published in *The Royal Academy Magazine*, No. 31, Autumn 1992.

BIBLIOGRAPHY

BOOKS, CATALOGUES, ARTICLES

- 'The Artist Speaks: Robin Philipson PRSA', *The Scottish Educational Journal*, vol. 59, no. 14, 9 April 1976, pp. 8–11
- Chris Allan, *Artists at Harley: Pioneering Printmaking in the 1950s*, Glasgow, 2000
- Roger Billcliffe (introduction), *Robin Philipson Retrospective*, exhib. cat., Edinburgh, 1989, unpaginated
- William Buchanan (introduction), *Cockfight Rosewindow*, Edinburgh, 1970
- T. Elder Dickson, 'Robin Philipson', *The Scottish Art Review*, vol. VIII, no. 2, 1961, pp. 20–23, 32
- T. Elder Dickson, 'Robin Philipson RSA', *The Studio*, vol. 164, no. 834, October 1962, pp. 142–5
- T. Elder Dickson (foreword), *Robin Philipson*, Elgin, 1974
- Colette Douglas-Home, 'Nonconformity as an Art Form', *The Scotsman*, 14 August 1989
- The Edinburgh Tapestry Co. Ltd (Dovecot Studios), *Modern Collections*, Edinburgh, 1991
- Edward Gage, 'Philipson: Evolution of Compelling Style', *The Scotsman*, 6 April 1970
- W. Gordon Smith, *Philipson*, Edinburgh, 1995
- Douglas Hall (foreword), *Robin Philipson*, Dunfermline, 1970
- Victoria Keller, *Robin Philipson 1916–1992*, Edinburgh, 1999
- Maurice Lindsay, *Modern Scottish Painters No. 6: Robin Philipson*, Edinburgh, 1976
- John McEwen, *John Bellany*, Edinburgh, 2013
- Eric Newton, 'Robin Philipson', *The Listener*, 14 May 1959
- Eric Newton, 'Cathedrals and Cockfights', *The Manchester Guardian*, 24 October 1960
- Robin Philipson, 'My Weekend', *The Gleneagles Hotel Magazine*, 1983, p. 59
- Obituaries published in: *The Scotsman*, 28 May 1992; *The Independent*, 1 June 1992; *The Guardian*, 3 June 1992; *The Daily Telegraph*, 6 June 1992; *The Times*, 5 June 1992

FILM

- 'Distortion', *Counterpoint* series, BBC, 1959
- 'Look at This', BBC, 1959
- 'The Maitland Collection', *Counterpoint* series, BBC, 1960
- *Three Scottish Painters: John Maxwell, Joan Eardley, Robin Philipson*, Templar Film Studios, 1963
- *A Feeling for Paint: Irwin, Philipson, Blackadder and Tindle*, BBC, 1982

ACKNOWLEDGEMENTS

This has been an enjoyable book both to research and write, and I wish to thank the many people who have made it so by offering encouragement and sharing their personal knowledge of Robin and his work. In particular, I should like to thank Diana Philipson, who first suggested the book, and her brother Nigel Pollock for their support in a variety of ways. Chris and Laramie Gwilliam, Guyda and Bob Sharp, and Thora Clyne could not have been more generous with their time in meeting with me, answering questions and in providing images. Guy Peploe introduced me to Sansom & Company, where Paul Deaton willingly took the book on; my thanks there also to Clara Hudson for seeing it through production, Ann Kay for her editing and Ian Parfitt for the design. I should especially like to thank the following for their interest and valuable support in different ways: Margaret Campbell, Fiona Clasen, Neil Curtis, Patrick Elliott, Rob Fairley, Dawn Henderby, Matthew Jarron, Eileen Lawrence, Liz Louis, Laura Feliu Llobera, Glen Onwin, Robin McClure, May Matthews, James Morrison, Lisa Muxworthy, Sue Palmer, Ronnie Ryan, Britt Scholnick, Helen Scott, Kevan Shaw, Carly Shearer, Kerry Watson, Tommy Zyw, and not least Murray Simpson, who read the final draft of the book.

I am particularly grateful to Sandy Wood and Robin Rodger at the Royal Scottish Academy, who gave me access to their archives, and to Rachel Hosker and Aline Brodin, who unlocked as yet uncatalogued Edinburgh College of Art archives. Kay Hodgson, head designer at Kinloch 1788, kindly allowed access to the Reid & Taylor archive. Ania Karwat at the Warsaw Academy of Fine Art Library helped with details of the life of Aleksander Kobzdej. Aaron Fleming at the Royal College of Surgeons of Edinburgh offered information on one of Robin's many honorary offices, while Alison Hurst at Whitehaven Archive Service, Angela Kearney at Dumfries Academy and Cathy Gibb at the Ewart Library, Dumfries, all provided new facts concerning Robin's schooling and early home life.

I thank especially the Binks Trust, who responded immediately and generously to a suggestion that they might support illustration costs.

Elizabeth Cumming

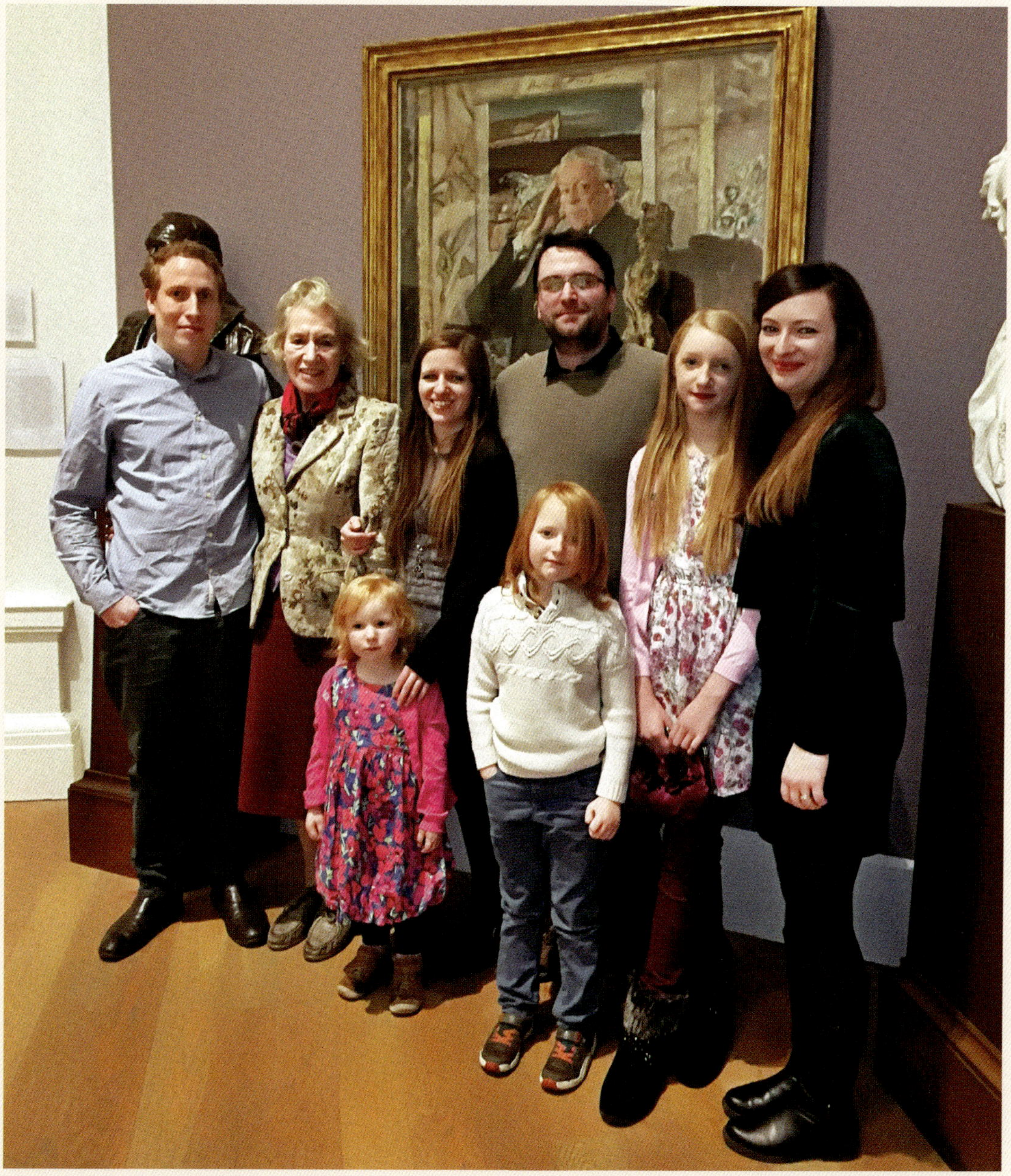

The Philipson family with David Donaldson's 1987 portrait of Robin in the Royal Scottish Academy's 'Ages of Wonder' exhibition, 24 December 2017
(left to right) Anthony, Diana, Thalia, Rebecca, Jasper, Jacob, Freya and Cheryl (married to Anthony)

INDEX

Works illustrated are in **bold**